THE GLOBAL MANAGEMENT SERIES

Marketing Communications:

An advertising, promotion and branding perspective

Geraldine Bell & Babak Taheri

(G) **Goodfellow Publishers Ltd**

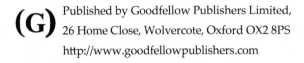 Published by Goodfellow Publishers Limited,
26 Home Close, Wolvercote, Oxford OX2 8PS
http://www.goodfellowpublishers.com

First published 2017

British Library Cataloguing in Publication Data: a catalogue record for this title is
available from the British Library.
Library of Congress Catalog Card Number: on file.

ISBN: 978-1-910158-94-4

This book is part of the Global Management series

ISSN: 2514-7862

 Design and typesetting by P.K. McBride, www.macbride.org.uk

Cover design by Cylinder

Printed by Baker & Taylor, www.baker-taylor.com

*"A brand is not so much about rational arguments, but
the way that the company resonates with people emotionally"*

Steve Jobs (1955-2011)

Contents

Acknowledgments

This book draws upon our own learning, practice, and in particular our teaching and research experiences in marketing communications. We have come to the conclusion that there is a genuine need for a guidance book to help students not only navigate through the challenges of developing their own interest in marketing communications, but also as they progress through both their undergraduate and postgraduate degrees, and also in preparing their future careers in business and maybe even in marketing communications! Our expert marketing colleagues in the Department of Business Management at Heriot-Watt University have very kindly contributed to this book, and we thank you for your contribution in making it a richer resource. To our colleagues at Goodfellow Publishers, we remain grateful. We also wish to express our sincere thanks to Professor Kevin O'Gorman and Professor Robert MacIntosh, for their constant support, encouragement and many pearls of wisdom.

GB & BT

Dedication

To Alice with all my love as you embark on your own exciting future.

GB

To my beautiful wife, and my parents and brother. Thank you!

BT

Biographies

Geraldine Bell BA (Hons) MBA ACIM is Assistant Professor, Marketing, with 25 years' industry experience in marketing management and marketing communications roles. With a degree in the History of Art, she started her career as a graduate trainee in a global advertising agency in London working on a variety of FMCG accounts including jeans, tights, toothpaste, whisky and leisure. After a short stint at Revlon International, she handled the advertising and PR for Scottish brands such as Harris Tweed and Shetland knitwear. She then moved to British Airways Holidays, working on the Sovereign and Enterprise brands – a brand portfolio that grew to include Falcon and Twenty's after acquisition by Owners Abroad – all of which is now consolidated in the First Choice brand and owned by TUI. The mid-nineties, and into the noughties were spent as UK Group Brand Manager at the Scottish Tourist Board/VisitScotland managing Scotland's Autumn Gold campaign, before moving into education. She currently teaches Leisure Marketing, Marketing Communications and International Marketing.

Elaine Collinson BA (Hons) MPhil is Associate Professor in the Department of Business Management in the School of Management and Languages at Heriot-Watt University. She is Director of Postgraduate Studies and Deputy Director of Corporate Executive Development. With over 25 years' experience in the Higher Education sector, she has held roles in an academic and research capacity but also in developing transnational education and industry links across the globe. She teaches on the International Marketing Management suite of programmes, specialising in Branding & Communications, Strategic Marketing Management and Entrepreneurship. Working closely with industry, involving her wide network of contacts on the programmes she ensures business relevance for students. Throughout her academic career she has published in the areas of Internal Communications, Small Business Marketing and Entrepreneurship.

Ross Curran is a final year PhD candidate at Heriot-Watt University, Edinburgh, where he is a member of the Intercultural Research Centre. His primary research interests focus on nonprofit marketing and volunteer management practices, as well as authenticity and heritage in tourists' experiential consumption. He has published research in leading journals including *Nonprofit and Voluntary Sector Quarterly*, *Tourism Management*, and the *International Journal of Tourism Research*, as well numerous conference papers and book chapters.

Chris Dodd PhD is a consumer psychologist with a particular interest in the social, psychological and experiential aspects of consumption. He has developed and delivered many courses within psychology, management, marketing and communications, catering for both academic and practitioner audiences. His research is particularly informed by a focus upon people and their relationships with social and physical environments. His work has been published in numerous international journals and he sits on the Editorial Advisory Board of the journal *Young Consumers*. He is a chartered psychologist and Associate Fellow of the British Psychological Society.

Martin Gannon is a Teaching Associate at the Hunter Centre for Entrepreneurship, Strathclyde Business School (University of Strathclyde). He holds a variety of research interests include entrepreneurial philanthropy, family business governance and marketing, heritage marketing management, tourism, and consumer behaviour.

Keith Gori is a PhD student in the School of Management and Languages at Heriot-Watt University. His doctoral research centres on understanding the social and cultural significance of consumption in historical context, with a specific interest in the British home front during the Second World War. He is involved in a range of marketing and consumer research projects utilising multiple theoretical and methodological approaches. He has published a number of journal articles and chapters in edited texts and has presented at conferences both in the UK and overseas. He teaches on management, marketing and methods courses in the Department of Business Management. He holds BA and MA degrees in history from the University of Sheffield.

Sean Lochrie PhD is an Assistant Professor in Management at Heriot-Watt University, Dubai. His primary research interest focuses on the creation of custodianship behaviours within World Heritage Site management. Recent publications have explored stewardship and local community engagement in World Heritage Site management. He has published research in journals including the *Journal of Marketing Management*, and the *International Journal of Contemporary Hospitality Management*.

Rodrigo Perez Vega PhD is a Lecturer in Marketing at Henley Business School. His research interests are in social media, digital marketing and social influence marketing. Prior to finishing his PhD, Rodrigo had marketing experience in several digital marketing and brand management roles within FMCG and service industries.

Graham Pogson MBA has been a lecturer for 25 years, first in the field of Textile Technology with the Scottish College of Textiles and for the last 14 years in Business Management subjects with the School of Management of Heriot Watt University. He is a generalist having taught subjects from introductory economics and finance to strategic management, with marketing and organisational behaviour in between. Recent areas of interest have been in the field of employment relations within human resource management.

Kitty Shaw is an experienced marketing practitioner with 22 years' experience in the financial services sector, working in a variety of research, communications and planning roles, most recently in a senior role responsible for strategic marketing planning in a FTSE 100 company. Having originally completed an undergraduate degree in Politics at the University of Edinburgh, she took an MSc in Marketing Management from the University of Glamorgan and also holds post-graduate Diplomas from both the Market Research Society and Chartered Institute of Marketing. Her current research interest include the marketing of pensions in the UK corporate pensions market.

Babak Taheri PhD is an Associate Professor in Marketing Management. He worked in industrial engineering and services marketing management areas in the UK and Middle East. Babak has a PhD in services marketing (Strathclyde), an MRes in management science (Strathclyde), a PgD in research methods (Strathclyde), an MSc in information systems analysis (Glasgow Caledonian) and a BSc in industrial engineering (Tehran), where he specialised in consumer behaviour and services marketing management, putting his industrial experience and academic knowledge into practice. As a result, he has published over 60 academic articles, book chapters and conference papers in these areas. Babak has been awarded a Horizon 2020 project involving a range of partners across Europe.

Geraldine McKay is an Associate Professor in Marketing and chartered marketer with a special interest in the impact of branding across stakeholder groups. Following a career in marketing, she became a university lecturer, developing and leading a number of postgraduate, undergraduate and professional programmes. She moved to New Zealand to manage an international education project and on returning to the UK she became the academic head for the globally delivered Heriot-Watt management programmes. She has previously contributed to the *Global Management* series and is currently registered for a PhD investigating transnational education and the teacher/student experience.

Kathryn Waite, BA (Hons), Dip CIM, MBA, MSc, PhD, is Assistant Professor of Marketing in the School of Management and Languages at Heriot-Watt University. Her research interests relate to information provision and use within the online environment. Kathryn is interested in trust, engagement and empowerment strategies used by organizations within the digital environment. She is a member of the editorial advisory boards of the *Journal of Financial Services Marketing*, *Journal of Research in Interactive Marketing* and the *International Journal of Bank Marketing.* Kathryn teaches undergraduate and postgraduate courses in digital marketing, which contain frequent references to Pokémon, 1970s science fiction, chocolate and cats.

Preface

Overview

The most important task faced by a marketer is to identify and select an optimum promotions mix to help achieve business objectives. And this design, development and implementation of promotional campaigns, takes place against a backdrop of considerable change. All of us, both marketers and consumers, live and work in an information-obsessed world. We live in a media-saturated world where there is such an incredible choice of brands available. These brands are revolving around us because of the exceptional impact that technology has had on the way we process (see and read) and think about (feel and believe) communication messages. To have a successful marketing communications campaign, your brand must be engaging and compelling, yet empowering and inclusive in such a way as to achieve stand-out amongst the plethora of activity. In this book, we have not managed to cover everything, but we have given coverage to what we think you need to progress through your studies. The following gives you the structure for our book on marketing communications, and some details of the contents.

Book contents and layout

Chapter 1: This attempts to tackle the existing *theory of communications* as it applies to consumer and marketing communications in particular. In outlining the topic of marketing communications, it details the marketing communication mix and makes an attempt to explain the processes of communications using the models which underpins of understanding of this topic. This is so that your thinking evolves in such a way as to give you the confidence and skillset needed to enable you to make the pre-requisite decisions relative to designing and planning for an integrated marketing communications mix.

Chapters 2 and 3: The cornerstone of these two chapters is to expand our worldview of the subject of marketing communications, embedding it in both a history timeline and giving advertising its position in social science. The *history of advertising* can be traced back to medieval times and beyond, and Chapter 2 gives us a timeline. There's no doubt that the internet has changed our daily lives. Arguably, the introduction of the printing press in the 15th Century did for renaissance Europe what the internet has done for modern communications in the 21st century. Newspapers and magazines were, and still are, an important feature of capitalist economies, just as today sees the prominence of emails, websites and tweets which sway us to attend to information and persuade us to do something.

Whereas history gives us a sense of perspective from the past, *advertising as a discourse* delves into the realm of languages as places, which helps us to further our understanding of the present. Discourses are places which are the means by which, according to Foucault, we 'reproduce ideologies and interpret cultural materials', and nowhere is this more so than in advertising. Depth is provided with a meaningful discussion on semiotics, which looks at the relationship between image and texts. The chapter also draws on the illustration of political marketing and PR as an exemplar of marketing communications discourse.

Chapter 4: The focus of this chapter is on consumer decisions when *consuming communications.* It explores why consumers are driven to make certain decisions, and how they manage their experiences before, during and after consuming marketing communications. It draws on consumer values, motivations and involvement as a means of framing our understanding around what consumers do in terms of behaviour, what they feel by way of emotion and what they think in terms of cognition.

Chapters 5 and 6: A judicious approach to marketing communications calls for an analysis of the tools available and *planning for marketing communications* looks at planning as a means to achieve the required outcome in terms of marketing communications strategy. Chapter 5 argues that whilst there is no particular distinction between the various parts of strategy, there is a need for a structure in evaluating strategy and the discussion concludes with a suggested framework for marketing communications planning. And whilst Chapter 5 provides an approach to planning for marketing communications, Chapter 6 outlines the key points to consider when not just planning for the short term with *brand communications,* but when building long term brands. This chapter draws on the science of semiotics outlined in Chapter 3 and makes the link to how brands use signs and symbols to leverage advantage. This chapter also draws on the concept of positioning, first posited in planning for marketing communications, taking the concept deeper in order to further develop our knowledge so that marketers can be more efficient in designing brand communication strategies.

Chapters 7, 8 and 9: Chapter 7 gives us a more detailed look at the impact a clear market positioning has on the promotions mix, and on *integrating* *marketing communications*. It examines the efficiency gained from market positioning as it is used to maximise the effect of using multiple media platforms which also allows managers to save on resources. And whilst Chapter 7 outlines the merits and limitations of the various degrees of integration, Chapter 8 explores the nature of *creativity* within an advertising context, making the case for the one 'big idea' which can be translated from the positioning concept into a creative platform of aesthetic values (content and appeals), which will further benefit and deepen integration. Whilst the creative platform provides a framework for understanding creativity in an advertising context, Chapter 9 explains the importance of digital media within the multiple platforms available, saying that d*igital marketing* is a new and exciting phase in the development of marketing communications. This section of our book looks at how to use digital media to best effect when developing marketing communications. It aims to provide you with core knowledge so that you can navigate this stimulating communications landscape.

Chapter 10: This chapter on *international advertising* presents you with a global view of marketing communications. It covers the challenges that the culture brings to the question of whether marketing communications should be standardised or localised. It explores the degree to which country of origin affects the perceptions and decisions consumers have about certain products and services, and how marketing communications can exploit this and leverage it to best effect.

Chapter 11: The profusion of new media opportunities has presented marketers with a challenge in terms of measuring the *effectiveness of marketing communications*. Added to this are the numerous stakeholders who have a vested interest and attempt to influence organisational goals. This chapter explains how marketers research and evaluate marketing communications activity both whilst they are implementing tactical campaigns and also whilst planning campaigns for the future.

Chapter 12. This chapter holds several *case studies* for you to develop and deepen your core knowledge, allowing you to gain insight by applying knowledge to practice. This also gives you an idea of how some firms tackle marketing communications in this modern communications environment.

We wish you all the best,
Geraldine and Babak. *Eds*

1 Introducing Marketing Communications

Geraldine Bell

One of the key features to managing marketing operations, and marketing communications in particular, is how best to select an optimum promotions mix to achieve your objectives. This implies that you know what your objectives are, (which you may not know at this stage) and how the elements of the promotions mix works best to deliver on your objectives (which you may have some knowledge of already from previous feedback or again, you may not know). Within the practice of promotion, a good starting point is to review the nature of the communications process, so that you have an understanding of the role it plays in shaping the thinking behind the choices you make (for example, media, appeals and timing). Therefore it is useful to examine the theory of communication as it relates to both how it is reviewed, and how it influences decision making. This introductory chapter attempts to do this.

Our journey starts with an outline of the topic of marketing communications and takes us through to understanding the nature of the process of communications, and reinforces the insights that marketers need to draw on to help them design and develop marketing communications. Finally, we acknowledge the new marketing topic of WOMM (word of mouth marketing) and we recognise that marketing communications cannot be accepted as separate from patterns of consumption, hence we feature likely consumer responses. First though, let us establish a baseline with this simple question: what exactly is marketing communications?

What is marketing communications?

The purpose and intention of marketing, according to Baker, is "the creation and maintenance of mutually satisfying exchange relationships" (2016: 5). The inference here is that both parties enter into an exchange on a voluntary basis. The value in the exchange is that both parties will be satisfied – so much so that they will want to repeat the exchange and further the experience should the need arise.

From a management perspective, marketing communications has a prominent role to play in a range of other managerial domains, for instance, in competitive strategy. Marketing communications is relevant when considering the three resource-based marketing strategies – undifferentiated, differentiated and concentrated. Take, for example, launching a new product or repositioning an existing product, which suits the undifferentiated approach and requires marketing communications effort. So does the differentiated approach whereby products and services are modified to suit subgroups. This segmented tactic requires a different approach to the marketing mix – pricing, distribution and in particular promotion. For a smaller enterprise, a more concentrated strategy may be appropriate because of resource allocation. In this case marketing communications plays a key role in the promotion of its products and services. Simply put, marketing communications is significant in terms of supporting the marketing mix underpinning marketing strategy, and therefore has a prominent role in generating value in achieving competitive advantage.

The job of marketing communications, as pointed out by marketing guru Kotler, is to inform, persuade and remind customers (both internal and external) either through direct (for example, TV or cinema advertising) or indirect means (for example, giving a product away for trialling and PR purposes) about the products, services and brands the enterprise seeks to exchange. Kotler et al. go on to say that, in a way, "marketing communications represents the *voice* of the company and its brands, and are the ways in which it can establish a dialogue and build relationships with customers." (Kotler et al., 2016: 630). Marketing communications also has several functions surrounding the market offering, which sends out a signal helping both the firm and customers to better understand and further the exchange as clarified below:

- How and why a market offering is used; what type of person is it for/is using it; where it can be used and also when it can be used
- Who is it that has designed, developed and produced the market offering
- What is the reward for me as the customer for usage

■ What are the opportunities for me as a business to get involved in partnership with your products and services

In short, marketing communications plays a key role in contributing to brand equity because its helps to:

■ Establish the brand in our long-term memory

■ Create a brand image

■ Drive sales

■ Affect shareholder value.

The marketing communications mix

Marketing communications works through a platform known as the marketing communications mix, which is made up of methods that offer either one-to-one communications, one-to-many or many-to-many forms of marketing communications activities.

Table 1.1: The marketing communications mix in general.

Marketing comms mix	Communications objective(s)	Marketing communications methods & activities
Advertising	Paid; non-personal; identified sponsor designed in the main for awareness.	Product & services, direct response advertising, corporate.
Direct marketing	Communicate directly; solicit a response, prompted information	Direct mail/email, telecon, mobile - information services (contact centres & websites & mobile technology).
Sales promotion	Short term incentives designed to stimulate trial and purchase, merits of personal experiences.	WOM, trialling, packaging, point of sale, promotions, exhibitions, merchandising.
Public relations	Project and protect image, reputation, and market offerings (products/services/ideas) – to gain positive editorial, to address crises, to correct information	WOM, sponsorship, publicity, stakeholder communications, corporate identity, lobbying, familiarisation trips/trialling for editorial gain, event management.
Personal selling	Company sponsored activities developed and produced to create product/service or brand exchange and interaction	Direct sales, over-the-counter, telemarketing, trade fairs, factory tours, event experiences, presentations.

Activity

List as many marketing communications methods and activities as you can. There are some illustrations in Table 1.1 but these are generalisations. For example, what about company museums, chatrooms, and annual reports?

The artistry in marketing communications is planning how best to use all the different methods and activities to optimise effectiveness and to manage resources in a competent manner. First we look at underpinning theory and then we take a more detailed look at the effects the different methods and the subsequent consumer response models. This provides us with a platform for going forward with this book.

Understanding marketing communications effects: how does it work?

To help us better understand how marketing communications works, it is beneficial to start with communications theory beacause it provides a rationale for how and why certain marketing communication activities happen like they do. The delivery of marketing communications involves processes and corresponding complexities that need to be understood, and getting to grips with the foundations of marketing communications means that you are more more likely to be able to develop and shape dialogue because you are working towards the key objectives of 'sharing meaning', as Baines et al. put it (2008: 433). If the purpose of marketing communications is to interact with an audience and facilitate exchange (both now and in the future) then knowing more about communications theory helps us to make sense of marketing communications and moreover be able to exploit the opportunities available to managers and marketers as the sender (the source).

■ Forms of marketing communications

Communications can be interpreted through three models – the one-step or linear model, the two-step or influencer model, and third the multi-step linear and non-linear, better known as the interactive model.

One-step or linear model of communications

Most marketing textbooks (see for example, Baines et al., 2008; Baker, 2016; Fill & Turnbull, 2016; Smith & Zook, 2016) will give you a detailed outline of Schramm's 1955 linear model of communication and will pinpoint his approach as being that of "the process of establishing a commonness or oneness of thought between a sender and receiver" (cited in Baker, 2016, p. 400) implying that communication has a unified aspect to it. The more basic model consists of only three elements:

Sender → Message→Receiver

This implies that both the source and the destination of the communication are tuned into each other but, with humans, this isn't the case. Schramm argued that this was too basic in that it did not allow for the transference of thoughts whereby ideas are translated into symbols for transmission – in other words the conveyance of ideas and the translation into decipherable and meaningful sense. He called this encoding and decoding and added to the basic model thus:

Sender (source)→ Encoder→Message (signal) → Decoder→Receiver (destination)

Whereas in telecommunications, the encoder is the transmitting device, in face-to-face both the source and encoder are the same person. Likewise, the decoder and the destination are the same with the message substituting the signal (which becomes the language used).

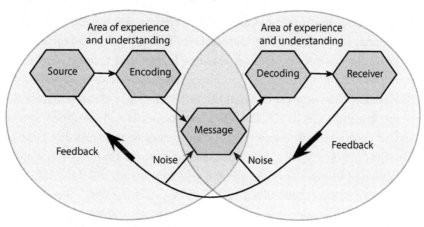

Figure 1.1: The one-step linear model of communication
Source: Adapted from Baker, 2016: 400, Dahlen et al, 2010: 38 and Fill & Turnbull, 2016: 41.

Note the feedback loop in the above model. This tells us that through feedback, the source can determine how its signals are being interpreted. In personal communications, feedback is prompt and based on the words we use in the message and the how we use them – signalling through the intonation of our voice and/or gesticulation (nod, shrug and wave), whereas in the impersonal communication through mass media, the effectiveness is indicated through circulation figures, in the case of newspapers and magazines and in audience size in the case of radio and TV. The UK programme, *The Great British*

Bake Off (#GBBO) had a domestic audience of 13 million (Sweney, 2015) and this figure would have been used in its contractual negotiations with the BBC over transmitting the show for the following years. As the model depicts, the more that both sides are atuned to each other, the more likely there is to be an overlap. And the bigger the overlap, the more likely there will be shared meaning (the more effective the message is likely to be). The final point in the model is the noise which surrounds the exchange of meaning or as Baker calls it, the fields of experience (2014: 401) between the source and destination, which is subject to not only the extent to which we are tuned in, but also environmental disturbance. This disruption is prevalent between encoding the message, message delivery (channel) and decoding the message. What's important to note is that there is no such thing as a perfect transmission – there is always noise and some form of potential disruption to contend with, whether it be "selective attention, distortion and retention" operating within the realms of experience and understanding (Kotler et al., 2016: 634). As Dahlen et al. concur, this area represents both the sender's and receiver's frames of reference (2010: 38)

Despite advances in marketing communications (see below), and along with the cries that mass media is dead, there is still a valid role for this more traditional form of mass communication. This is because advertisers can reach large audiences very quickly, at reasonable cost, and through a medium which provides a dynamic, filmic environment where the creative appeal is often more compelling than any other medium. For example, we can progress the narrative surrounding #GBBO! The BBC has announced (13.09.2016) that it can no longer compete with commercial broadcasters to transmit this popular show. The producers of #GBBO have decided to move to Channel 4, which is reportedly paying in excess of £25million a year to transmit the show. This follows on from ITV, another commercial broadcaster, poaching BBC's *The Voice*. And why are these popular entertainment programmes so highly prized by commercial broadcasters? Because they can command huge advertising airtime costs. From 2017, UK audiences will be viewing #GBBO with several advertising breaks. The format will also include the patronage of products and services related to baking, such as small and large electrical items, along with kitchenware. This proves that despite audience fragmentation, there is still a big role for mass communications, especially in television, where the programming provides an environment, where airtime can be commercialised through advertising to a mass audience.

The one-step linear model is the most basic of models in helping us to understand communications, but is a two-way process in that communication travels from the source to destination with feedback. The next model develops this into a two-step model to include personal influencers, of which there are two key types which filter communications.

Two step or influencer model of communications

The influencer model of communications assumes that there are two key filters in mass communication – opinion leaders (OL) and opinion formers (OF). Katz and Lazarsfeld's (1955) hypothesis argues that whilst the sender directs communication to a target as in the linear model, there are also personal influencers, in the form of opinion leaders and formers, who act as intermediaries and filter messages, altering the shared meaning between sender and target destination. (Smith & Zook, 2016: 151). In short **opinion formers** are formal experts whose opinion has influence through their authority, and **opinion leaders** may be amateurs, but who are connoisseurs who have profile and a status that gives them a view, which makes them in demand and results in them being given airtime. So on the one hand there are specialists (OF) such as governors, judges, MPs, journalists, analysts, critics and even some academics, and on the other hand there are other notables (OL) such as celebrities, bloggers, early adopters as triallists, reviewers, seniors, and other confidentes. Both formers and leaders are sanctioning the communications by endorsing it with either a positive or negative spin – the key point being that communications through these two filters are more persuasive and thus credible. For example, the *London Evening Standard* fashion critic may dislike Victoria Beckham's (VB) new fashion collection and write about it to say so, and meanwhile, Cameron Diaz in Hollywood has been leant a VB dress from the new collection by VB's fashion PR team and chooses to wear it to the Academy Awards ceremony on the night, hence being seen to support the new VB collection! In this case, the fashion critic is the OF whilst Cameron Diaz is the OL, both of whose opinions and views carry weight. Fashion firms regularly send shoes and handbags to both journalists, critics, and celebrities in the hope that they will either write or wear the article to give it editorial profile. This influencer model of communications can be visualised below in Figure 1.2.

The two-step model, which as mentioned above is more commonly known as the influencer model of communications, tells us that the power of communication is not just with mass media which gives us information, but is also subject to personal influences which tells us information in a more persuasive way, exerting influence over us, the target audience. (Fill & Turnbull, 2016: 48). The merit of this form of communication can be illustrated by the coffee brand Nespresso, whose George Clooney TV commercials are well known globally. A rival brand called the Espresso Club, has used a George Clooney look-a-like in their advertising, leaving the original creators and producers to sue the imposter firm for misleading its target audience. This indicates the power of persuasion that George Clooney has, as the face of Nespresso, as an opinion leader in communications. (Associated Press, 2016)

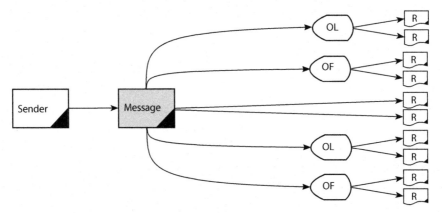

Figure 1.2: Two-step influencer model of communications.
Source: adapted from Smith and Zook (2016:152)

Multi-step or interactional model of communications

The next thought in the progression of our understanding about communications comes from the fact that interaction takes place amongst and between all parties in the communication process. This is refered to as the multi-step model and/or the interactional model of communications.

This model centres around a network of interactions suggesting that influence and persuasion is not just OFs and OLs, as in the influencer approach to communications. Whilst persuasion and inducement is exerted through these types of personal influences, the volume of interactions suggest that there are many more types of influences eliciting different responses. Fill and Turnbull suggest that the influence is not only coming from people but is also relative to machines, commenting that communications are increasingly "characterised by attributing meaning to messages that are **shared, updated and a response** to other messages". (2016: 49). These exchanges of dialogue, or 'chats' and reviews, are conversations that are interactional in nature, as depicted in Figure 1.3.

The internet brought with it a much more useful way of facilitating customer communities, where all customers and stakeholders can talk and chat away to each other. This has given more weight to relationship marketing, which is now the dominant approach to marketing along with 'recombined' and integrated marketing communications (Baker, 2016: 402).

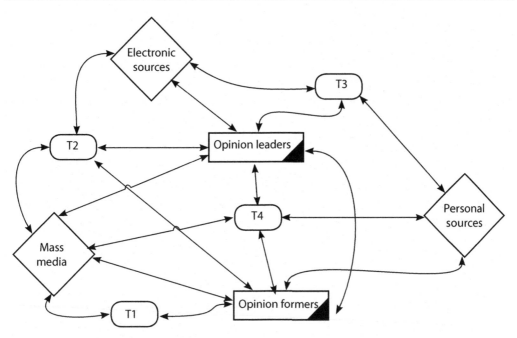

Figure 1.3: The multi-step or interactional model of communication.
Source: adapted from Fill & Turnbull (2016); Smith & Zook (2016) and Kotler et al (2016).

Firms now look to being a key participant in the conversations taking place – so much so that they like to steer the conversations so that the flow of chat is built around the brand and therefore deepens relations. They do this through newsgroups and discussion rooms sponsored by the brand, set up to discuss the brand, its applications, problems, issues, ideas, improvements and also include a broader aray of topics that can be linked either directly or in some cases indirectly to the brand (Smith & Zook, 2016).

Evian's babies make us 'Live Young'!

There can be nothing more emotional than being at one with our inner-child and #evianbabyandme does just that. "Rollerbabies" was Danone's first taste with its Evian 'Live Young' brand where it reached almost legendary status within the digital-marketing landscape in 2009. Rollerbabies featured computer generated imagery (CGI) babies doing some rather extreme stunts. The clip went viral and made history by being recorded in the Guinness World Records as being the most viewed online ad, with up to 25 million views over a two month period.

Danone's water brand, Evian, has continued with the CGI-aided baby concept where the infants continue to perform hair-raising stunts – as in "Baby Inside" in 2011. Then, in 2013, came Evian's "Baby & Me" which recorded 50 million YouTube views and 100 million total views over several weeks and was seen on 4oD and Videology, supported with a Facebook page as well as a raffle draw along with other traditional broadcasts such as TV (during Britain's Got Talent) and cinema (during The Great Gatsby run) across 15 countries including USA, UK, Germany, France, China and Russia. The advert, or viral clip, featured adults looking into baby-versions of themselves where the CGI-baby copied their grooves and moved in tandem with them. https://www.youtube.com/watch?v=pfxB5ut-KTs

The campaign was strengthened by more innovative online promotion, with the introduction of a mobile app which allowed users to upload their photos of themselves and get 'baby-fied' revealing their inner-child, and to share the results across Facebook, Instagram and Twitter through #evianbabyandme. Most viral campaigns are 'done' and gone but Evian's babies continue to hold good because they never seem to grow old!

Adapted from various sources including Ankeny (2014) and Ridley (2013).

As the example illustrates, there are different means of channeling messages which can lead to a a web of many and different conversations circling around the brand and not just at one time, but at many different times. The key characteristic here with the revolving conversations is that the chat is accelerated by customers themselves becoming advocates. This extends the interaction model to include customers as thought leaders, and they too are facilitating conversations – either being more positive, leaning more towards the brand values or to detract from them, creating a challenge for brands. Of note is that all marketers need to understand more than just the **feedback loop** in the two-step communications model. The modern communications environment now includes, with the multi-step interactional approach, **customer responses**, and it is up to the company to turn this into a positive form of communication.

■ Word of mouth marketing

There is a new topic within marketing communications which needs to be considered, due to the prominence of the interactive form of communications enabled by new technologies. This is **word-of-mouth marketing** (WOMM). Understandably, this topic has gained significance since the advent of the internet and the resultant usage by both marketers and customers alike, leading to conversations being accelerated by customers themselves, hence the notion of **amplification** where customers can accelerate the chat – the degree of acceleration depending on the level of relationship with the brand, with the most intensive amplification coming from the 'tribal fanatic'.

WOMM is where firms deliberately shape consumer-to-consumer communications with purpose and intent. On its own, word-of-mouth is seen to be an organic activity because there is no "prompting, influence or measurement" by marketers, and is thus considered to be a naturally occurring phenomenon (Kozinets et al, 2010: 72). However, with intent, comes an active attempt by marketers to affect and change WOMM through deliberate marketing communications strategies. This links directly to the previous discussion on the two-step influencer model of communications, whereby unwilling consumers are socially engineered into buying through OFs and OLs as a persuasive means of marketing practice. Following on from this is Kozinet et al's "network coproduction model" which draws on the multi-step model discussed previously (see Figure 1.3) but which has one key element of importance within the topic of WOMM, and that is 'seeding'.

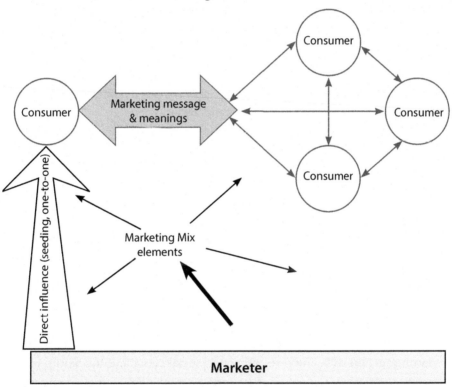

Figure 1.4: How WOMM communications are co-produced in consumer networks - the role of 'seeding'. *Source:* adapted from Kozinet et al., 2010:72.

A seeding strategy is where marketers initiate the communications through the various means available in the marketing mix, and in the marketing communications mix, in particular as depicted in Figure 1.4. In essence, WOMM is concerned with amplifying a message and content so that it penetrates the communications network – either naturally or judiciously (Fill & Turnbull, 2016: 60). There's no doubt that social media platforms have led to an exponential increase in the volume of conversations and chat as the multi-step or network communication model explains. But whilst most consumer communications occur spontaneously, many conversations are deliberate and are a direct result of a marketer's seeding strategy.

How we brought Trek America to the UK

I Trek Here was an innovative campaign designed to encourage social influencers and TrekAmerica customers to build excitement around their leisure product – adventure tours to the USA.

It was a tailor-made, content-led social campaign aimed at TrekAmerica's core target audience, where the leisure firm employed 10 high-profile, influential bloggers, sent them on a TrekAmerica trip and created social buzz around them experiencing their first trek in Southwest USA.

Source: The Drum Social Buzz Awards.

http://www.socialbuzzawards.com/social-buzz-awards-2015/best-travelleisuresports-social-media-strategy/how-we-brought-trekamerica-to-the-uk

Marketing practice suggests targeted one-to-one seeding within marketing communications programmes as illustrated by Trek America. This depicts the network approach to communications and reminds us that consumers are co-producers in creating value and meaning on the one hand, whilst marketers use innovative tactics and metrics to shape the communications put out by the opinion leaders on the other. What stands is the implication that marketing messages are traded amongst and between members within and around the network.

One further point put forward by Kozinets et al. (2010:74) is the fact that whilst co-produced narratives are shaped by character narrative (personal stories/expressions), communication forum (bogs, social networking sites), communal norms (age, lifestyle, interests, ethnicity, social class) and the nature of the marketing promotion (type of product/service, compelling nature of message/visual eg humour, hard sell or soft sell, aim/objectives), marketers need to be aware that marketing messages and meanings are also altered systematically when embedding them into the narrative. They are altered in a way that is 'attuned' to the consumer's own likes/dislikes when operating either as an individual or in a communally appropriate context. This is familiar in that in more traditional communications, such as PR, the control and shape of the message is with the journalist as intermediary. In the online world, the consumer now has control and is the intermediary, and the consumer's approach and context matters.

Lady Gaga and the one-percenters

Jackie Huba is a founding member of the Word of Mouth Marketing Association in the USA. Founded in 2004, it advocates "ethical WOM practices through education, professional development and knowledge sharing with top industry marketers" (www. WOMMA.org). It came into being at about the time of the rise of social media platforms. Today, Jackie is considered a leading expert in customer loyalty and WOMM. You can see her in action giving a keynote speech to the Marriot Hotels at https://www.youtube.com/watch?v=UMWw6V_Ztvl. What's interesting is her stance on customer acquisition vs retention. She cites Lady Gaga as a best practice exemplar. She says that the customer universe is made up of new, existing and advocate-type customers. Of note, is the fact that most companies fail to see the value in WOM relative to advocates. Advocates are those customers who are more loyal than just loyal – they are superengaged in your brand. They want to help you succeed and they will do anything for you. Take Lady Gaga. She has 57 million 'likes' on Facebook and yet her focus is on advocates, who make up a small proportion of her followers on social media. Jackie's research says that most brands have a population of advocates of about 1%. These 'one-percenters' have enourmous value because they are the ones that are going to spread the word on your behalf. Because they have an almost evangelical zeal about them, they are likely to shout loud and clear about products, benefits and value propositions. Lady Gaga, Jackie says, has identified one-percenters as the means of growing her business and giving her longevity in the music business. The focus, for Gaga, is to turn followers into fanatics as this will grow the Gaga brand. (See Huba, 2013 for more)

Amplification, accordingly (Fill & Turnbull, 2016) comprises both the behavioural and cognitive elements of the marketing-to-consumer, and the consumer-to-consumer concept. This involves searching, reading and writing of reviews about a brand as well as actions such as trialling (as in the TrekAmerica example where they take a familiarisation trip and follow this up with writing about it as a positive experience), other experiences and purchase, and subsequently sharing it with a number of networks. Trending content (popular topics) is amplified as a direct result of embedded tweets, sponsored stories and social advertisements. This has changed the way we view consumer behaviour as a topic – several texts specialising in this specific field of enquiry aim to enlighten us to the changes and highlight the considerations within this area of marketing. Meanwhile, it is still incumbent on us to have a baseline awareness of how consumers are likely to make a response to marketing effort and the next section explains this.

A composite model of consumer responses

The models that we have talked about so far are process driven. But how do consumers respond? What stages do they go through, or are likely to go through before actioning or making a commitment to your brand or service. Most marketers and practitioners subscribe to the view that consumers go through serveral sequential stages before coming to a decision to either buy or feel positive about something. Table 1.2 is a visualisation of a summary of customer's likely response to marketing communications. It highlights the stages that consumers go through prior to decision making. All of the models assume that the customer is either initially unaware of the product and service, or that there is a potential problem which they would like to resolve mutually.

Table 1.2: Summary of customers' likely response to communications – response hierarchy models.

Stages	AIDA	Purchase (Baker, 2016:201)	Hierarchy of effects	Innovation adoption	Communications (Kotler et al., 2016: 635)
Cognitive thought	Attention	Problem recognition	Awareness	Awareness	Exposure
			Knowledge		Reception
					Cognitive response
Affective (emotion)	Interest	Evaluation and research	Liking	Interest	Attitude
	Desire		Preference	Evalution	
			Conviction	Trial	Intention
Behaviour (conative/ motive	Action	Purchase	Purchase	Adoption	Behaviour

Source: Adapted from Baker, 2016: 201; Kotler et al., 2016: 635, and Fill & Turnbull, 2016: 120.

This presumes that consumers respond in a rational manner. There are times, however, when we respond in an irrational way – for example on impulse! For marketers, marketing communications can stimulate the desire to consume by tapping into our irrational behaviour. At best, this is done by feeding the desire to consume, but at worst, this can lead to an unreasonable and illogical form of consumption. Whilst it is not the key role of this book to understand consumer behaviour as a topic, that should not mean that you see marketing communications in isolation from patterns of consumption. Far from it. This is because, in the main, there are a myriad of consumer types, most of whom are operating in a world of continuous and endless consumer choices, who demand not just compelling types of marketing communications, but communications that is emotionally engaging. Consumers are becoming more and more discerning and demanding to know just how innovative you are being – and only then will they respond positively to your brand. This is why marketing communications has moved more and more towards a more 'integrated' approach.

Integrated marketing communications approach

In this introductory chapter, the focus has been on understanding the classic or more traditional approach to marketing communications, and introducing the changing nature of marketing communications as it moves to a more integrated marketing communications (IMC) approach – a summary of the key characteristics of which is outlined below in Table 1.3.

Table 1.3: Summary of change in characteristics between traditional and contemporary marketing communications

Traditional communications	Contemporary approach
Acquisition strategy	Retention strategy
Mass, volume communications	Targeted and more focussed communications
Monologue	Dialogue
Information is sent	Information is requested
Information provision	Information retrieval
Sender takes initiative	Receiver takes initiative
Offensive	Defensive
Repeated information	Relevant information
Hard sell	Soft sell
Brand salience	Brand confidence
Transaction	Relationship
Advertising management	Relationship management
Aim to change attitude	Aim to achieve satisfaction
Modern: linear, volume	Postmodern: cyclical, fragmented

Source: Adapted from De Pelsmacker et al, 2013: 9.

IMC is when there is a plan which evaluates the strategic roles of the different elements of the marketing communications mix (the toolbox as outlined in Table 1.1), so that the combination of the mix provides clarity and consistency, thus enabling the marketer to maximise the effect of communications (Baker, 2016). Understanding each of the different parts of the marketing communications mix (advertising, DM, PR, PS & SP) aids comprehension of, for example, the implications and impact each part has, so that these component parts (either singularly, with each other or collectively) can be "recombined and integrated" to best effect. Thus our understanding of how they work together, either with each other or collectively in practice is important (2016: 402). But managing IMC is a challenge in practice and assistance comes from the basic 4Cs framework.

The 4Cs framework (Picton & Broderick, 2005: 28) is useful as a basis for the evaluation of IMC. The 4 Cs are coherence, consistency, continuity and complementary and the framework explains the intended outcome of IMC as follows:

- **Coherence** – logically connected as opposed to disparate parts.
- **Consistency** – multiple messages support and reinforce the overall strategy as well as each other as opposed to being disjointed and unclear.
- **Continuity** – not just connected but consistently, rather than erratically so.
- **Complementary** – synergistic by way of working together and harmonising together, as opposed to being isolated and cut off from the purpose and intent of marketing communications.

The rationale behind looking at marketing communications in a more integrated way is acknowledgement of the customer approach to communications. Customers and other stakeholders may or may not be that aware of the subtleties between, for example, Nivea for Men's sponsorship of English football and a Boots on-pack promotion in-store. Customers just see the messages transmitted through various on- and off-line channels trying to persuade us to either attend to the message and content, to do something about it, or to entice us to talk and chat about it online. IMC adds value in that it offers a deeper and a more speedier means of comprehension of the communications. And integration is obligatory – it is planned carefully in order to optimise the objective of achieving the 4Cs as outlined above.

Moreover, the planning of an integrated approach to marketing communications takes into account the ability to control the method of marketing communications (for example, the level of control in advertising is limited should the context change, making it not that easy to adapt quickly and efficiently); the ability to manage the resource and costs (for example, cost per contact or the cost of the amount of wastage); the degree to which the audience is likely to perceive the credibility of the communications (for example, a narrative through an editorial intermediary in the *Financial Times* either online or offline is highly likely to be more believable and trustworthy than an advertisement); and also the role of the communications itself and the job it is trying to do (for example, the DRIP elements of aiming to Differentiate, Reinforce, Inform and Persuade).

Table 1.4 provides an overview of the criteria for consideration in relation to the means of communications available.

Table 1.4: Key selection criteria relative to the characteristics of the marketing communications mix

	Advertising	Sales Promotion	Public Relations	Personal Selling	Direct Marketing
Control:					
By manager and by audience, ability to target, to be flexible	Med Med	High High	Low	Medium Medium	High High
Costs:					
By investment, return, & cost per contact & wastage	High High waste	Med Med waste	Low High waste	High Low waste	Med Low waste
Credibility:					
Sincere, believable, reliable & trustworthy	Low	Med	High	Med	High
Communications:					
Level of dispersion, interaction & ability to forward	High Low Low	Low Med Med	Low Med Low	High Low High	High Medium High

Source: adapted from Fill 2013, p. 27.

Summary

This leads us finally to progressing forward to the rest of this book. This introduction has given us an outline of the theories of communication relative to understanding how marketers, and consumers in both one-to-one, one-to-many and many-to-many contexts attend to and use marketing communications. In addition, we are now aware of some of the issues surrounding the contemporary topic of word-of-mouth marketing, alongside the key criteria when selecting the different forms of consumer communications, as well as reminding ourselves of the sequential nature of likely consumer responses. This sets us up for a deeper analysis of the key concepts for consideration in marketing communications as a topic.

Further reading

Rosengren, S. and Dahlen, M. (2015) Exploring advertising equity: how a brand's past advertising may affect consumer willingness to approach its future ads. *Journal of Advertising*, **44** (1).

> This paper conceptualises 'advertising equity' relative to measurement in marketing communications. It focusses on past advertising being an influencing factor in building up a catalogue of perceptions about a brand. This gives brands a global value which has further merit in measuring brand equity. It also discusses advertising budgeting and forecasting, pretesting and evaluating advertising plus negotiating media as well as co-branding partnerships.

References

Ankeny, J. (2014) How these 10 marketing campaigns became viral hits. https://www.entrepreneur.com/article/233207 [accessed Sept 2016]

Associated Press. (2016) Nexpresso sues rival for using George Clooney lookalike. *Daily Telegraph*, 22 Jan http://www.telegraph.co.uk/finance/newsbysector/retailandconsumer/12113467/Nespresso-sues-coffee-rival-for-using-Geroge-Clooney-lookalike.html [accessed September, 2016]

Baines, P., Fill, C. & Page, K. (2008) *Marketing*. Oxford University Press.

Baker, M. (2016) *Marketing Strategy and Management*. 5/ed. Palgrave McMillan, London:UK.

BBC (2016) Great British Bake Off: BBC loses rights to Channel 4. http://www.bbc.co.uk/news/entertainment-arts-37344292 [accessed 13.09.2016]

Dahlen, M., Lange, F. & Smith, T. (2010) *Marketing Communications: a brand narrative approach*. John Wiley and Sons, West Sussex: UK

De Palsmacker, P., Geuens, M. & Van Den Begh, J. (2013) *Marketing Communications: a European perspective*. 5/ed. Pearson.

Fill, C. (2013) *Marketing Communications: Brands, experiences and participation*. 6/ed. Pearson.

Fill, C. & Turnbull, S. (2016) *Marketing Communications: Discovery, creation and conversations*. 7/ed. Pearson.

Huba, J. (2013) *Monster Loyalty: How Lady Gaga turns followers into funatics*. Penguin Group: New York.

Katz, E. & Lazarsfeld, P. (2006) *Personal Influence: the part played by people in the flow of communications*. Transaction Publishers, USA. Originally published by The Free Trade Press in 1955.

Kotler, P., Keller, K.L., Brady, M., Goodman, M. and Hansen, T. (2016) *Marketing Management*. 3/ed. Pearson.

Kozinets, R.V., de Valck, K., Wojnicki, A.C. & Wilner, S.J.S. (2010) Networked narratives: understanding world of mouth marketing in online communities, *Journal of Marketing*, **75** (March), 71-89.

Picton, D. & Broderick, A. (2005) *Integrated Marketing Communications*. 2/ed. FT Prentice Hall.

Ridley, L. (2013) Evian launches global baby and me campaign. www.campaignlive. co.uk/article/evian-launches-global-baby-campaign/1179271 [accessed Sept 2016]

Smith, P.R. & Zook, Z.E. (2016) *Marketing Communications: offline and online integration, engagement and analytics*. 6/ed. Kogan Page, London.

Sweney, M. (2015) The Great British Bake Off final gets biggest TV audience of the year. *The Guardian*, 8 Oct, https://www.theguardian.com/media/2015/oct/08/the-great-british-bake-off-final-nadiya-jamir-hussain-gbbo [accessed August, 2016]

2 | History of Advertising

Keith Gori

Advertising is a huge field with significant political, social and economic ramifications globally. To try and address all these concerns in global perspective is not possible in a chapter of this scope – here a chronological development of advertising broadly applicable to Western Europe and North America is provided, with more detailed examples from British advertising history used to illustrate the factors that drove change in the industry, and with a brief look at advertising history, written with a focus on 'non-Western' examples at the end of the chapter.

The chapter is largely structured chronologically, following an adapted version of MacRury's (2009) advertising history periodization:

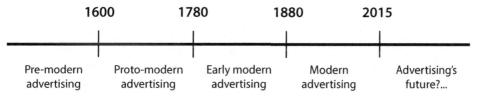

It should be borne in mind that such periodization can only give a loose indication as to the manner in which something like advertising develops. This do not suggest significant changes occurred exactly at the turning points where one period ends and another begins, but rather a loose application of the term (Hollander et al., 2005; Witkowski & Jones, 2006).

Earliest advertising

Though we do not know at which point the term advertising – derived from the Latin *advertere* meaning to turn towards – came in to usage, it has at its root the notion of getting a person's attention or a warning (MacRury, 2009). We can therefore examine early historical analyses for examples of attention-grabbing practices as predecessors of what is often termed 'modern advertising'. Many scholars suggest some practices now understood as advertising must have been in existence as long as trade has existed, in order to facilitate exchange between people; and examples of both oral and written efforts to increase the sale of goods or services can be traced back many centuries (Russell & Lane, 1996; Tungate, 2013). Babylonian tablets are often claimed as the earliest examples of lasting advertisements and were hung above sales locations, in addition to the use of oral advertising methods, to attract passers-by (Barker & Angelopulo, 2006; Presbrey, 1968). Though these early communications certainly played a role in facilitating change, they do not really represent anything like what we understand as advertising or marketing communications in this day and age. In order to try and trace that we need to consider the development of marketing and try to situate advertising amidst this.

Though the origins of marketing are equally difficult to place with an exact date, Shaw (1995, 2015) highlights that it was during antiquity that we can find the origins of features we now understand as the underpinnings of a marketing system, and in the work of Plato the first dialogue exploring the socio-economic foundations of marketing thought. He claims that during antiquity trade underwent its biggest transformation of any time from the Stone Age to the modern day due to the introduction on a large scale of three things: centralised marketplaces, sedentary retailing and coined money. Having started in Athens in the sixth century BCE, they were spread by merchants around the Mediterranean Sea and along ancient trading routes. As a result buyers and sellers were brought together efficiently, could ensure trade and production remained at their optimum and had a viable means through which to exchange and store value. Given the scale of this transformation, the increase in trade, and the increasing centralisation of retailers, we can assume that techniques for increasing sales by drawing people's attention to available products must have also increased. Fletcher (2008) claims that in Athens during this period town criers would interrupt announcements with paid-for oral advertisements such as that below from a cosmetic seller.

> For eyes that are shining, for cheeks like the dawn,
> For beauty that lasts until girlhood is gone,
> For prices in reason the women who know,
> Now buy their cosmetics from Aesclyptoe.

Sage (1916), using a four-point classification of advertising activities – Roman newspapers and magazines; shop signs and frontage; posters and billboards; and methods akin to modern direct mail advertising – found support for all but the last. Further, Beard (2008) quotes an example of promotional material for the leasing of property in Pompeii which offered "an elegant bath suite for prestige clients, *tabernae*, mezzanine lodgings [*pergulae*] and upper floor apartments [*cenacula*] on a five year contract", and others have suggested the Roman period was key in the intensification of promotional activities that evolved into modern advertising (Wharton, 2015). Vennarucci (2015) has argued that shopkeepers in the Roman period used shop design as one of their primary means of advertising, in an attempt to promote a respectable urban identity and build reputation in the face of a society that treated such traders with inherent suspicion. The use of shop signs and frontage is highlighted by other authors as a key method of promotion during the period (Holleran, 2012), and would further support Shaw's (2015) assertion that the development of marketing systems during this period is of importance. With retailers increasingly collected in centralised locations, methods such as these were necessary to make it clear to shoppers what was available and to distinguish between traders. Some example shop signs and shop frontage from the Imperial Roman period are shown in Figure 2.2, overleaf.

Given the evidence above we can see that both trade and the activities associated with modern marketing, particularly retailing and promotional activities, became increasingly embedded during antiquity. By the Middle Ages these activities had begun to be spread around the world along with trade, and we can presume they continued in the centuries that followed. Though this is likely the case, it is unlikely that there was much change in written advertising beyond the types discussed above which generally focussed on images to signify the types of trade. Given the continuation of, at best, semi-literate societies during the Middle Ages, written advertising would not have undergone any kind of radical transformation. Beyond this, the means for mass written advertising were not available: papyrus, parchment, inks and dyes were expensive and difficult to obtain for many traders. Paper, though invented in China during the Han dynasty around 200 BC and further developed under Cai Lun a century later, only arrived in Europe in the 11th century, having spread very slowly along the Silk Road and via Muslim settlers in modern-day Spain and Portugal (Carter, 1925). Paper mills spread through Europe in the twelfth and thirteenth centuries, and proved important in increasing the availability of writing materials across the continent, though literacy remained very poor and printing techniques were slow and limited (Basbanes, 2014). Given this, we can assume many of the methods which grew during antiquity remained centrally important in the promotion of trade.

Figure 2.2: Clockwise from top-left:

1. Shop sign for a wine shop depicting two porters carrying a wine amphora from a street corner in Pompeii (1st c CE)

2. Upper half: sign on façade of wine shop at Herculaneum. Lower half: sign promoting gladiatorial games in the town of Nola. (1st Century CE).

3. Tavern sign from close to the Castra Praetoria, Rome. The Latin lists the different food and drink available with the list arranged to resemble a gaming board in order to advertise gambling also takes place inside (Imperial period).

4. Sign, likely to be for a Roman textile shop (1st c CE). Present Location Uffizi Gallery, Florence. This is a photo of the cast of the original found at the Museo della Civiltà Romana, Rome.

Images reproduced with kind permission from original research collection of Dr. Rhodora G. Vennarucci, University of Arkansas.

A second technological innovation was central to the development of print advertising: the invention, in Germany, of the Gutenberg printing press in the mid-fifteenth century, which allowed for moveable type printing and vastly increased production (Tungate, 2013). As methods improved further, printing underpinned a slow revolution which increased literacy, the spread of ideas and an increasing democratization of knowledge (Cranfield, 1978). Just thirty years after the Gutenberg was introduced, the first printed advert, a poster for a bible posted on a church door, appeared in England. Over the following centuries the expansion of European colonialism saw many new trade routes opened and existing ones expanded, increasing the range of what needed to be promoted to people in order to generate sales (O'Barr, 2005).

Proto-modern advertising, 1600-1780

Both MacRury (2009) and Elliott (1962) highlight the essay *Of a Defect in our Policies*, written in 1595, by Michel de Montaigne, as a significant moment in the development of advertising, with Elliott referring to it as 'the germ of advertising'. In it, Montaigne highlights the need for a place in which buyers and sellers can both highlight their desire for or provision of goods. Over the course of the following century or so advertising in newspapers, on handbills, posters and other printed forms developed considerably, to the point that Samuel Johnson wrote in 1759 that any man would know a ready method of informing the public of all that he desired to buy or sell (quoted in MacRury, 2009, p.129).

Though forms of newspaper had existed for over a thousand years (for example, the Roman *acta* from 59 BC or the Chinese *tipao* from around 200 BC), it was in the centuries following the introduction of the Guttenberg that they became widely available, though this development took some time (Cranfield, 1978; Stephens, 2007). In the UK, newspapers were increasingly produced in the eighteenth century following legislation removing taxes and making this more profitable. Many newspapers quickly appeared, highlighting the presence of a ready and waiting reading public. Numerous newspapers came and went during the eighteenth century, with papers of various specialities and trades remaining popular, and the proliferation of 'quackery' medicinal advertisements. Circulation remained relatively low, with estimates for a daily paper in 1737 ranging from 1,000 to 2,000, though this number steadily increased over the course of the century. The eighteenth century was an important one for advertising; from an incidental position at the outset advertising grew to occupy more and more space in publications, more and more of which even adopted the word 'Advertiser' in their titles. By the end of the century, advertising was becoming increasingly important amidst the expansion of commerce and industry, and for newspapers in the UK was increasingly a major source of revenue (Cranfield, 1978, Elliott, 1962). Similar growth took place throughout Western Europe with coffee houses and salons influential in providing access to newspapers, spreading literacy and ideas (Ellis, 2011; Sawyer, 1990). Across the Atlantic, newspapers sales and the prevalence of advertising in their pages increased at a rapid pace also (O'Barr, 2005).

Advertising in this period typically made use only of text describing products or announcing events, with occasional grammatical and printing marks (!!, **, etc.) to grab attention. Early examples did not even include the name of the seller, but merely informed the reader that the publisher knew of a product available, with the readers presumably having to contact the publisher should they be interested. Over time publishers began to add the names of the producers, thus depersonalising the publishing intermediary and bringing producer and consumer closer together – something which remains evident in advertising to this day. MacRury (2009) argues that this adding of names represents the beginnings of the primary advertising relationship of advertiser, agent and audience, and to a crude form of early branding. By the end of this period, therefore, a system linking producers and consumers, rudimentary design features and persuasive writing, and the generation of revenue from placing advertisements in publications was developing (MacRury, 2009).

Early modern advertising, 1780-1880

Despite the increasing importance of advertising as a source of revenue for newspaper publishers, and the increasing circulation of newspapers by the start of the nineteenth century, the union of the two had produced a somewhat negative atmosphere, with critics attacking both the content and volume of advertising. For example, Samuel Johnson, in 1780, warned that its sheer quantity may lead to it being negligently perused by target audiences (quoted in Pearson, 2014: 54) and attacks from figures such as Thomas Babington Macaulay and Thomas Carlyle questioned the "taste and class" of the pursuit, rather than specific content. It should be noted that the majority of these attacks came from within the middle and upper-class elite, along with paternalistic claims to be looking out for the lower classes, who would be most at risk from exposure to advertising. In contrast there is nothing to suggest that the majority of the public shared any such view (Nevett, 1982).

Such examples have led to academic accounts which often paint this as a period in which advertising was able to operate in any way it wanted, making outlandish claims in socially unacceptable manners. In contrast to these perceptions as a century of little regulation (Fletcher, 2010), advertising in the UK was already subject to controls at the outset of the nineteenth century, both self-regulatory and legislative, which steadily increased in both volume and rigour.

Certain publications took a strong stance on advertising early in the century, particularly in relation to fanciful product claims, and prompted mounting debate within the industry, and over the course of the century advertising agencies rejected work for clients with questionable products (Nevett, 1982). Poster and postal advertising campaigns were also modified from within in response to complaints from local authorities and officials, and from the public at large (Cranfield, 1978; Nevett, 1982). For example, such was the outrage against the Bovril Company's proposal to adorn the outside of a company premises overlooking Edinburgh's Princes Street and the Mound that plans were first stalled to allow public consultation before being abandoned in light of the results (Nevett, 1982).

Legal controls were extended throughout the nineteenth century to tackle a number of problems within the UK advertising industry (Nevett, 1982). Obscene advertising in public places and in shop windows was outlawed by 1838. Other legislation attempted to curb the use of hoardings, pavement boards, sandwich-boards, billposters and wall-chalking, and though initially efficient enforcement proved troublesome, measures have been seen to have remedied many associated problems by the end of the century. The most important effect of a court ruling in the period has been seen as the ruling in favour of an aggrieved customer of an influenza prevention product, advertised with an accompanying compensation payment in the circumstance of failure. The customer, having used the product, contracted influenza, and was rejected in her request for compensation as promised. When heard in court the judge ruled that the advertisement formed a legally binding contract and the decision remained unchanged following appeal. The case gave clear precedent that the claims and offers made in advertising could be subsequently challenged and fired a warning to all within the advertising industry (Fletcher, 2010; Nevett, 1982).

The examples of controls above were in response to a minority of those in the advertising industry seen to act irresponsibly, something Nevett (1982) is quick to highlight as evidence that perceptions of the nineteenth century as one of uncontrolled, unscrupulous advertising are inaccurate. This view he believes is borne out of published accounts of advertising, too reliant on the use of bizarre, amusing and shocking advertisements from the period – those firmly in the minority. Beyond this, a tendency to apply more modern consumer standards to the adverts of this period, and a desire within the modern advertising industry to highlight progress, have contributed to the misconception. Rather the advertising industry in this period was one which had undergone a steady inclination towards control, both internally and externally. By the late nineteenth and early twentieth century the enhanced reputation of advertising allowed for wide utility, and the growth of a number of Victorian brands which remain popular two hundred years on, such as Bovril, Cadbury, Crosse & Blackwell, Lea & Perrins, Oxo, Rowntree, Schweppes and Pears Soap. Such companies have been seen as benefitting from strong early use of advertising to build brand strength, even if 'brand' was not part of the lexicon of the time, along with other modern principles of branding such as clear use of name, logo and product design.

The period was not only one in which advertising steadily became more controlled and regulated, beginning to achieve an acceptable professional standard, but one in which considerable developments were made in practice as well. Several authors have highlighted the innovative methods used by Josiah Wedgwood to establish his business as one of the foremost producers and retailers of ceramics (Koehn, 2001; McCracken, 1990; McKendrick, 1960). These promotional activities allowed Wedgwood to establish his goods with specific target audiences, in what Wernick (1991) argues is an early example of successful media planning. Though Wedgwood was a notable example, the use of advertising and other instruments common in modern marketing were central in fuelling the mass production of consumer goods, something further emphasised by other scholars (McKendrick et al., 1982; Wernick, 1991). Though the US is often viewed as the trailblazer of modern advertising, it was at this stage led by advances in Britain and Europe, with such activities as those highlighted above not in any common usage in the USA until the 1820s with P.T. Barnum highlighted as a trailblazing figure (Brown & Hackley, 2012; MacRury, 2009).

In tandem with the development of marketing and branding principles, the advertising industry developed significantly in the nineteenth century, laying the foundations for the flourishing of the modern advertising industry of the twentieth century, which remains recognisable today. This development lay in the interaction between producers needing to highlight the availability of their goods at a national level, the availability of a communicative means to do so through newspapers and magazines, a desire for income from the publishers of these, and an entrepreneurial will to bring these together on the part of advertising 'agents'. The key development that followed this period came in the function of the advertising agent; in MacRury's (2009) early modern advertising period these agents did not often produce adverts, though some early examples of this practice are highlighted below, they merely facilitated the bringing together of producers and publishers who placed adverts, whilst taking a commission for the service. Their role in the advertising industry developed considerably in the decades that followed.

The development of advertising agencies

Before considering the final period used in the periodization schematic, it is worth considering the development of advertising agencies in some detail, as this development is central to the changes in advertising that took place in the twentieth century. As highlighted above, the advertising agent of the nineteenth century was not reflective of the image of the twentieth century advertising agency recently popularised in the hit television show *Mad Men*. Advertising agencies first began to appear in London in the late seventeenth century, and in the mid-eighteenth century in the US. As newspaper publishing and circulation figures increased through the nineteenth century the amount of advertising space, and therefore the profits available to agents, did also. It was competition between agents to secure the business of producers and sellers that led to changes in the way advertising agents worked, and as highlighted above, it was in the US that most of the later innovations associated with modern advertising occurred. These innovations later spread to Europe, largely as a result the increasing presence of American agencies in Europe in to the twentieth century (Fox, 1990; Pouillard, 2005; Tungate, 2013).

Though Fox (1990) claims the nineteenth century as American advertising's 'prehistory', both Elliott (1962) and Nevett (1978) have highlighted the proliferation of advertising agents much earlier in Britain. The first advertising agent is credited as William Tayler, established in 1786, who described himself as 'Agent to the Country Printers, Booksellers & co.' Nevett (1982) claims that the largest part of his function was to pass advertisements from the proprietors to newspapers, for which he charged a handling fee, and his focus was on country papers with only one London evening paper amongst his contacts. Tayler also supplied newspapers with news items. The diversity of his operation is echoed by the variety of sources from which newspapers obtained advertisements; newsagents handled advertisements on behalf of the papers they stocked, tradesmen often handled advertising in addition to the normal running of their business, elsewhere there are records of advertising being handled by stock brokers, Clerks of the Roads in London, or in leading coffee-houses. Though not common, the early nineteenth century increasingly saw some examples of agents actually writing advertisements, an innovation credited to James White, whose work at the Christ's Hospital School and connection to London's literary and newspaper circles saw him stumble into a lucrative advertising career. A number of other agents operated in London at this time along similar lines – and their success induced the opening of an Edinburgh business in 1819 – to the extent that Nevett (1982) claims by the 1830s or 1840s agents were not agents of newspapers over advertisers. Similarly, agents by this time are seen to have not been involved with only a limited number of newspapers; rather, they offered the opportunity for advertisements to be placed with a number of publications at one time.

The number of UK advertising agents increased in the second half of the eighteenth century, along with the volume of advertising and the circulation of newspapers. From six registered advertising offices and ninety-two registered advertising agents in 1866, the numbers had risen to 126 and 339 respectively in 1906, and by the end of this period agencies were acting for most of the leading consumer-goods companies including Colman's Mustard, Cadbury's Cocoa, Fry's Cocoa and Pears Soap (Nevett, 1982). However there is difficulty in ascertaining how many of these functioned in the form outlined above due to 'all manner of people on the fringes of advertising' such as frame-makers, news-vendors and railway companies, in addition to the two types of agency outlined above; those who merely handled the booking of advertising space and acted as an intermediary, and those who offered creative and copywriting services. Larger advertising agencies in London had staffs of around 100 and six-figure turnovers by the end of eighteenth century, though this was not the norm and some of the smaller firms had less than ten (Field, 1959). In this period the geographic diversity of the advertising industry was widened and whilst London maintained its position as the hub of the industry, it did not hold a monopoly over it, though few of the provincial agents in this period offered the complete creative service that was beginning to take hold in London (Nevett, 1982.

Tungate (2013) and Fox (1990) have shown that American advertising agencies followed a similar pattern of development, though it seems that this occurred more slowly than in Britain, with agencies in the 1870s remaining small and focussed on the selling of advertising space rather than the production of advertising itself. In the decades that followed, and under the leadership of influential figures such as John E. Powers, Claude Hopkins, Albert Lasker and James Walter Thompson, the role of advertising agencies increased with more of the creative advertising production devolved to these organisations (Fox, 1990; Tungate, 2013). By the start of the twentieth century America is seen to be at the forefront of advertising and with the establishment of offices in London, large American agencies were able to start transporting their ideas over the Atlantic. J Walter Thompson was the first American agency to open a London office, in 1899, but closure during the First World War meant agency function only really applied from its reopening in 1919. Several other agencies followed suit in the 1920s but, led by Stanley Resor, JWT was able to forge a position for itself amongst the top agencies in Britain. Central to this was their use of market research, symbolised by JWT establishing the British Market Research Bureau in 1933 (Fox, 1990; Pouillard, 2005; Tungate, 2013; West, 1987). During the interwar period and the decades following the end of the Second World War advertising agencies expanded and were increasingly professionalized, establishing themselves amongst other aspirational 'city' careers in finance, law etc on both sides of the Atlantic. Though two world wars in the first half of the twentieth century slowed their development by the mid-1960s the advertising agency was a large organisation with research and art department, creatives and account managers, and the development of the advertising industry as understood by modern standards.

Modern advertising, 1880 onwards

The section above highlighted that from the late nineteenth century onwards there were significant changes in the organisation and function of advertising agencies. This section seeks to outline the impact some of these changes had. Though development towards the advertising industry outlined above was not complete by the end of the nineteenth century, it was beginning to have effect with adverts increasingly adopting visual styles, slogans to grab attention and as little as possible of the terse product information that had dominated advertising previously (Ohmann, 1996). The development of research and creativity helped to reinforce the professionalization of the advertising industry alluded to above, and to cement its position in the early part of the twentieth century. The actions of advertisers to support the war efforts in both global conflicts further aided this process, and during the interwar period a number of measures were taken in the UK to ensure that a set of professional standards were maintained by advertising agencies, with the establishment of the Institute of Incorporated Practitioners in Advertising.

This increased profile and respectable position, along with the increased trade brought about by onset of peace, saw the industry enter into a 'golden age' and advertising flourished amidst the socio-economic conditions of the latter half of the twentieth century. Though print advertising techniques evolved significantly over the twentieth century, with increasingly sophisticated use of images, humour, and evocative language, the primary forms of print advertising (in newspapers and magazines, on billboard posters, and via direct mail leaflets) have not changed. Rather these have been used to complement new forms of technology to further drive advertising into all aspects of media and social life amidst globalisation. Three of those technologies, and their impact on advertising are briefly reviewed here: radio, television and the internet.

■ Radio and advertising

Following the development of radio technology in the late-nineteenth and early-twentieth century, it was popularised in the interwar period on both sides of the Atlantic. As its popularity grew, and after considerable debates and suspicion towards its use in radio broadcasting, it became clear that advertising on radio was necessary as part of the funding model that accompanied the technology and the transmission of content. The first advert paid for by a third-party that was not a broadcaster or program maker was aired in 1922, and though debates about the role of advertising continued, most consumers accepted its necessity by the mid-1920s. In the decade that followed the practice evolved with the development of scripted commercials performed by actors, and singing commercial jingles becoming popular forms. As consumers increasingly sought to avoid radio commercials that were clearly delineated from programs, advertiser began to seek to merge content and advertising: advertising characters were created, product names found their way into programs, and programs were even made built around consumer products, as advertising became a dominant feature of radio broadcasting on commercial stations (Buchwitz, 2015).

■ Television and advertising

The development of television and associated advertising took longer than was the case with radio, due to the technology taking longer to become reliable and widely available to consumers, and its use not widespread until the 1960s. Its use as a medium for advertising was identified early, with proponents likely aided by the advance of radio advertising, and some examples broadcast on early sets and stations were subject to fines. The first authorised advert was aired in 1941 in the US, and commercial television launched in the UK in 1955. In addition to commercial breaks with delineated advertising the television industry has seen the merging of content and advertising through sponsored programming and other such techniques. In recent years the medium (along with cinema) has been the subject of significant debate surrounding the use of product placement within programming, particularly on non-commercial stations such as the British Broadcasting Corporation (NUJ, 2015). Electronics giant Apple has been at the forefront of exploiting this form of advertising, despite not paying for its products to be placed, instead they have been willing to provide large numbers of devices to programme makers in order to ensure visibility (Kaiser, 2012).

■   ## The internet and advertising

Buchwitz (2015) has argued that the development of internet advertising has followed a similar pattern to that of radio: first, a period of technology development (1990-1995); second, a period of establishing a consumer base through the development of content to meet their demands (1993-1998); third, once a consumer base is established, marketers become interested in using the medium and a vigorous debate about the role of advertising takes place, with acceptance of its need in order to generate revenue eventually accepted (1994-2001); and finally the merging of content and advertising once consumers seek to avoid adverts that can be clearly delineated from the content they seek out. The first online ad appeared in 1994 and software developers have been creating ways to avoid them ever since, though marketers increasingly find ways to embed their promotions inside content. With the spread of mobile technology allowing constant connection via portable devices and social media apps the development of online advertising is a continuing phenomenon.

In addition to changing the way advertising agencies functioned and cementing the place of the advertising industry as a respectable profession, and its adaptation to embrace new technologies, the industry embraced globalisation from within. Following this development in the modern period an industry that was treated suspiciously for much of the preceding centuries was firmly established as a "component part of the cultural and social establishment" and a "major component of the economic fabric of market-consumerist societies globally" (MacRury, 2009: 151).

Advertising elsewhere?

Thought the bulk of advertising history published in English has focussed on its development in Europe and North America, recent attempts have been made to increase the geographical scope of the subject (see Tungate, 2007). Though largely focussed on accounts of prominent individuals, Tungate explores advertising development in a number of settings not prominent elsewhere in the literature. For example, he highlights the development of Japanese advertising from the seventeenth century onwards, with adverts posted on important sites such as temples and shrines as well as more mundane structures such as fences and gateposts, along with a tendency to print early adverts in books as newspapers were not yet prevalent. Following increased foreign influence in the nineteenth century, newspapers and magazines became increasingly popular and advertising a way for the press to increase revenues. In the post-war period advertising underwent a huge expansion amidst the rise of a Japanese middle class and the emergence of mass consumption. In this period mergers between agencies saw non-Japanese advertisers develop a presence in the country and Japanese agencies expand their reach into new markets. Tungate (2007) also highlights significant difference in the style of broadcast advertisements with Japanese adverts much shorter and explosive – "like noisy, incandescent fireworks" – than the mini-movies seen in Europe and North America, which he believes is a result of cultural differences. He argues that cultural differences also affected the development of advertising style in Latin America, where an emphasis on "a certain warmth and sensuality" prevailed. It is not possible to look at further examples of differences in development and style globally here though the further reading can offer some insights. It should be expected that research in this area will continue to grow and offer exciting new comparative insights for advertising and marketing historians.

Conclusions and what about advertising's future?

This chapter has explored early examples of promotional activity which can be considered as predecessors to modern advertising, before looking at greater depth at the development of print advertising, and the modern technologies which changed advertising in the twentieth century. The review of advertising history above has, by the limits of scope, been necessarily superficial and covered only the broad turning points and developments in advertising. Further readings are suggested in order to better understand the complicated development of advertising and its relationship to developments in trade and business, and to media and culture.

There is no way to suggest what will come next in the history of advertising, but it is certainly safe to assume that it is something that will remain from many years to come. If this chapter has left you with one thing in mind, it should be that advertisers should never be underestimated in terms of their ability to adapt and move with the times. At various moments in its long history, advertising has been seen to be under threat as a result of societal concerns, polit ical regulation, or technological change rendering their preferred mediums of less value. At each juncture and against each threat the industry has proved itself able to meet challenges in such a way that not only allowed advertising to survive but often to grow. It is hard to anticipate where any of these environmental factors will lead the development of advertising next, but we can be almost certain that whatever it is, advertisers will find a way to remain relevant.

Who to read

A number of advertising text books and monographs explore, in varying detail the historical roots of advertising (see for example Leiss et al., 2005; MacRury, 2009; Richards et al., 2000; Wharton, 2015). Elsewhere texts devoted solely to the history of advertising explore the subject in greater detail and scope (see for example Tungate, 2013 for a 'global' history) though no single text can hope to nearly explore the full temporal and geographical history, or impact, of advertising. Studies more limited in their scope, but no less interesting or important in their contribution, can be found as part of the Conference for Historical Analysis and Research in Marketing with proceedings available via open access (http://charmassociation.org/).

References

Barker, R. & Angelopulo, G. (2006). *Integrated Organisational Communication*. Cape Town: Juta & Co. (Pty) Ltd.

Basbanes, N. A. (2014). *On Paper: The Everything of its Two Thousand Year History*. New York: Vintage Books.

Beard, M. (2008). *Pompeii: The Life of a Roman Town*. London: Profile Books Ltd.

Brown, S. & Hackley, C. (2012). The greatest showman on earth: Is Simon Cowell P.T. Barnum reborn? *Journal of Historical Research in Marketing, **4**(2)*, 290-308. doi: doi:10.1108/17557501211224467

Buchwitz, L. A. (2015). *A Model of Periodization of Radio and Internet Advertising History*. Paper presented at the Crossing Boundaries, Spanning Borders: Voyages Around Marketing's Past: Proceedings of the 17th Conference on Historical Analysis and Research in Marketing, Long Beach, CA.

Carter, T. (1925). *The Invention of Printing in China and its Spread Westward*. New York: Columbia University Press.

Cranfield, G. (1978). *The Press and Society: From Caxton to Northcliffe*. London: Longman Group Limited.

Elliott, B. B. (1962). *A History of English Advertising*. London: Business Publications Limited.

Ellis, M. (2011). *The Coffee-House: a cultural history*. London: Hachette UK.

Fletcher, W. (2008). *Powers of Persuasion. The Inside Story of British Advertising: 1951-2000*. Oxford: Oxford University Press.

Fox, S. (1990). *The Mirror Makers: A History of American Advertising*. London: Heinemann.

Hollander, S. C., Rassuli, K. M., Jones, D. G. B. & Dix, L. F. (2005). Periodization in marketing history. *Journal of Macromarketing,* **25**(1), 32-41.

Holleran, C. (2012). *Shopping in Ancient Rome: The Retail Trade in the Late Republic and the Principate.* Oxford Oxford University Press.

Kaiser, T. (2012). Apple Gets Free Product Placement in TV Shows, Movies. Retrieved July 2015, from http://www.dailytech.com/Apple+Gets+Free+Product+P lacement+in+TV+Shows+Movies/article24679.htm

Koehn, N. F. (2001). *Brand New: How entrepreneurs earned consumers' trust from Wedgwood to Dell.* Watertown, MA: Harvard Business Press.

Leiss, W., Kline, S., Jhally, S. & Botterill, J. (2005). *Social Communication in Advertising: Consumption in the Mediated Marketplace* 3rd ed. London: Routledge.

MacRury, I. (2009). *Advertising.* London: Routledge.

McCracken, G. (1990). *Culture and Consumption: New Approaches to the Symbolic Character of Consumer Goods and Activities.* Bloomington, IN: Indiana University Press.

McKendrick, N. (1960). Josiah Wedgwood: An eighteenth-century entrepreneur in salesmanship and marketing techniques. *The Economic History Review,* **12**(3), 408-433.

McKendrick, N., Brewer, J., & Plumb, J. (Eds.). (1982). *The Birth of a Consumer Society: The Commercialization of Eighteenth-Century England.* Bloomington, IN: Indiana University Press.

Nevett, T. R. (1982). *Advertising in Britain: A History.* London: History of Advertising Trust.

NUJ. (2015). Product placement on BBC World News is creeping commercialisation and must be stopped. Retrieved July 2015, from https://www.nuj.org.uk/news/ product-placement-on-bbc-world-news-is-creeping/

O'Barr, W. M. (2005). A brief history of advertising. *Advertising & Society Review,* **6**(3).

Ohmann, R. (1996). *Selling Culture: Magazines, Markets and Class at the turn of the Century.* London: Verso.

Pearson, D. (2014). *The 20 Ps of Marketing: A Complete Guide to Marketing Strategy.* London: KoganPage.

Pouillard, V. (2005). American advertising agencies in Europe: J. Walter Thompson's Belgian business in the inter-war years. *Business History,* **47**(1), 44-58.

Presbrey, F. (1968). *The History and Development of Advertising.* New York: Greenwood Press.

Richards, B., MacrRury, I. & Botterill, J. (2000). *The Dynamics of Advertising.* Amsterdam: Harwood Academic Publishers.

Russell, J. T. & Lane, W. R. (1996). *Kleppner's Advertising Procedure* 12th ed. New Jersey: Prentice-Hall.

Sage, E. T. (1916). Advertising among the Romans. *The Classical Weekly,* **9**(26), 202-208.

Sawyer, J. K. (1990). *Printed Poison: Pamphlet Propaganda, Faction Politics, and the Public Sphere in Early Seventeenth-Century France.* Berkeley, CA: University of California Press.

Shaw, E. H. (1995). The first dialogue on macromarketing. *Journal of Macromarketing,* **15**(1), 7-20.

Shaw, E. H. (2015). *On the Origins of Marketing Systems.* Paper presented at the Crossing Boundaries, Spanning Borders: Voyages Around Marketing's Past: Proceedings of the 17th Conference on Historical Analysis and Research in Marketing, Long Beach, CA.

Stephens, M. (2007). *A History of News.* New York: Oxford University Press.

Tungate, M. (2013). *Adland: A Global History of Advertising* 2nd ed. London: Kogan Page.

Vennarucci, R. G. (2015). *Marketing an Urban Identity: The Shops and Shopkeepers of Ancient Rome.* Paper presented at the Crossing Boundaries, Spanning Borders: Voyages Around Marketing's Past: Proceedings of the 17th Conference on Historical Analysis and Research in Marketing, Long Beach, CA.

Wernick, A. (1991). *Promotional Culture: Advertising, Ideology and Symbolic Expression.* London: Sage.

West, D. (1987). From T-Square to T-Plan: The London office of the J. Walter Thompson Advertising Agency. *Business History,* **29**(2), 199-217.

Wharton, C. (2015). *Advertising: Critical Approaches.* London: Routledge.

Witkowski, T. H. & Jones, D. G. B. (2006). Qualitative historical research in marketing. In R. W. Belk (Ed.), *Handbook of Qualitative Research in Marketing* (pp. 70-82). Northampton, MA: Edward Elgar.

2

3 Marketing Discourse and Semiotics

Babak Taheri and Martin Gannon

In everyday life we are regularly exposed to, and interact with, many different forms of advertising. For example, through television and radio commercials, billboards, direct (or junk) mail, and carefully staged large-scale public relations exercises, advertisers draw upon different narratives and discourses to communicate the benefits of their brands, products, and services to us as potential consumers. Within the context of marketing, discourses serve as the places where the advertiser and the consumer communicate, interact and engage in choreographed events within the position of a particular semantic context (Oswald, 2012). Such advertisements are often comprised of several interactive elements which may draw upon images, photographs, music, societal observations, paralanguage, language, scenarios and situations, and the existing preconceptions of consumers in order to spread an advertising message in an effective and entertaining way (Cook, 2001).

There are often extremely strong relationships between the images used and the language employed in advertisements. This study of signs is called *semiotics*. Here, signs, text, and symbols serve as crucial elements of the consumer experience and are vital tools employed throughout advertising and marketing. Language, gestures, art, heritage, television advertisements, films, and even sales pitches and conversations, all contain signs that are used to convey specific meanings or are used to share a precise communicative purpose in marketing a product or service (Cook, 2001). For example, phrases such as 'your flexible friend' (Access credit card), 'naughty but nice' (fresh cream cakes) or 'it's the real thing' (Coca-Cola) have passed into British vernacular from advertising copy. However, contemporary marketing communication is not only concerned with catchphrases and levity, nor is it solely focused on furthering the commercial interests of organisations. Politicians and their advisers also utilise discourse and marketing communication tools to appeal to their followers and voters. As such, this chapter aims to make sense of marketing discourse and semiotics within the context of advertising and promotion, and marketing management in general. It also explores political marketing discourse as a particularly revealing illustration of everyday marketing interactions.

■   Defining discourse

The use and importance of discourse and 'texts-as-statements' are well established within the field of marketing communications and advertising. Indeed, Said (1978: 167) notes the underlying power and ubiquity of text in discourse-building by stating that: "texts, in fact, are in the world ... as texts they place themselves – one of their functions as texts is to place themselves – and indeed are themselves, by soliciting the world's attention". Discourse is the primary way of reproducing and communicating ideas, and discourse provides a platform that allows individuals to interpret a range of cultural materials in an accessible and relatable fashion (Foucault, 2002). The way in which discourse is employed embodies the cultural importance of language and is linked to power relations and reality within any given social context (Fairclough, 1995). This is because actors perceive, and subsequently gain an understanding of, social phenomena by consulting and processing information in the form of texts, symbols, images and photographs (Berdychevsky et al., 2016; Gee, 2005). Some argue that 'language-in-use' exists everywhere and that typically "people construct situations through language by carrying out seven interrelated building tasks. These are: significance, activities, identities, relationships, politics, connections, sign systems and knowledge" (Berdychevsky et al., 2016: 111). Table 3.1 demonstrates the interoperation of these seven stages, which Gee (2005) argues can be understood from both a micro- and macro-structure perspective within the marketing and advertising context.

Table 3.1: The 'seven building tasks of discourse' (Berdychevsky et al., 2016; Gee, 2005)

Building task	Example question
Significance	What situated meanings are evoked by or linked to some of the words or objects used?
Activities	What activities, actions, or undertakings are linked with the particular term(s) used?
Identities	What type of identity is being invoked by, or is consistent with, a particular term(s)?
Relationships	Which relationships are taken for granted or ignored?
Politics	What social, societal, or political connotations are relevant or irrelevant with regards to the term(s) employed?
Connections	What relationships or linkages are established between the particular term(s) used and existing texts or discourses?
Sign systems & knowledge	What sign systems are relevant or irrelevant with regards to the term(s) employed?

Exercise

Think about an experiential marketing situation, such as going to your favourite night-club, and consider it in relation to the questions posed by the 'seven building tasks of discourse' model.

Emerging from social constructionist psychology (Potter & Wetherell, 1987), the utility of discourse has also been noted by scholars such as Elliott (1996), Thompson and Haytko (1997), Thompson (2004) and Fitchett and Caruana (2015) in marketing and consumer research. For example, Thompson and Haytko (1997:15) describe the way in which discourse is used in fashion marketing: "Fashion discourses provide consumers with a plurality of inter-pretive positions that, because of their diverse associations, can enable them to juxtapose opposing values and beliefs. Consumers use these countervailing meanings of fashion discourse to address a series of tensions and paradoxes existing between their sense of individual agency (autonomy issues) and their sensitivity to sources of social prescription in their everyday lives (conformity issues)". However, Thompson (2004:175) criticises advertisement-centric analy-sis of text and suggests: "critical consumer researchers should study how power relationships operate and shift through institutional discourses and practices". Fitchett and Caruana (2015) also argue that the use of discourse in marketing and consumer research has been saturated and paradoxically conceptualised. They suggest possible ways of adopting a discourse perspective in a more robust and consistent fashion within market-based relations, as outlined in Table 3.2.

Consumers typically engage with advertising discourse for different pur-poses. This engagement can occur in both every day, general consumption situations and when communicating (either directly or indirectly) purposefully with brands (de Waal Malefyt & McCabe, 2016; Hackley, 2012). For example, de Waal Malefyt and McCabe (2016) discuss the use of discourse analysis when exploring advertising relating to women's vulnerability (i.e., menstruation) and its role in the consumer identity formation process, and suggests that advertis-ing is influenced by gendered ideologies into producing different messages. Additionally, the source of cultural materials for evolving creative advertis-ing is problematic, as advertising agencies showing the whole at one view in material located in culture (de Waal Malefyt & McCabe, 2016). Questionably, the ready and craft consumption is more than just customisation, since "for consumption activity to warrant being described as a craft, then the consumer must be directly involved in both the design and the production of that which is to be consumed" (Campbell, 2005: 31).

Table 3.2: Applying discourse and market-based relations (Adapted from Fitchett & Caruana, 2015: 6)

Market-based relations	Example Questions
Consumer-product	How is the consumer's product knowledge constituted? How is consumer sovereignty constructed, maintained and subverted?
Consumer-market	How is consumption influenced by the institutional context of the market?
Consumer-consumer	How do consumer interactions construct product knowledge? How do some consumers influence others?
Consumer-producer	How do consumption practices co-opt the producers of products and services?
Marketer-consumer	How do consumers and marketers use power to influence each other?
Marketer-corporation	How are functional activities and/or marketing agents constrained by wider corporate discourse?
Consumer-citizen	How do market-based behaviours influence/transform consumer citizenship?
Consumer-society	How does marketing discourse penetrate other public domains such as health and education?
Consumer-environment	How do marketing texts shape consumer relations with the natural environment?

Activity

Identify an example and analyse it using the market-based relations example questions outlined in Table 3.2.

Another example of this stems from the use of discourse in Web 2.0 advertising, where rapidly improving digital technologies have shifted the balance of power between consumer and producer in recent years. Here, discourse challenges the established producer-consumer dichotomy and its dialogical relationship within the advertising environment. The opportunity brought about by technological change subverts Marx's distinction between 'use value' and 'exchange value' by removing the typical, well-defined barriers between production and consumption. Instead, many are now embracing this by turning consumption into a form of temporary employment (often termed 'prosumption') (Cova & Cova, 2012; Humphreys & Grayson, 2008). Beer and Burrows (2010: 4) argue: "the opportunities Web 2.0 has created for forms of consumption that require active participation are crucial in understanding contemporary consumption". Thus, cultural practices, as well as customer engagement, play important roles in shaping narratives and the interpretation of meaning in contemporaneous consumption, advertising and marketing (Jafari & Taheri, 2014; Taheri & Jafari, 2012). Fellesson (2011) expands upon this notion of consumer empowerment by arguing that, from a discourse perspective, customers can now influence organisational culture and practice in three distinct ways (see Table 3.3).

Table 3.3: Capturing the situated customer (Adapted from Fellesson, 2011: 235)

Element	Example questions
Organisational rhetoric	As an organisation, how do we describe and characterise our customers?
Operational procedures	As an organisation, what influence does the customer have on how we operate?
The physical customer environment	In what way is the customer reflected in the design and function of the physical service environment?

Activity

Apply the 'capturing the situated customer' framework to three well-known organisations of your choice.

Political marketing discourse: An example

As a discipline, political marketing was developed in response to the increasing professionalization of political actors and the political marketplace. Political consumption experiences take many forms, such as the act of voting, canvassing for politicians, or taking part in organised protests, and are stimulated by general feelings of democratic freedom (Dermody & Wring, 2001). An individual's political compass and their level of attachment to a political party are influenced by the political orientation of their family circle, their social class, and who they socialise with throughout their formative years. Nevertheless, political loyalty typically lessens over time as voters disengage with, and become more critical of, their political party (Lees-Marshment, 2001), and consumers subsequently use their sovereignty to pledge their support to those who campaign on issues that they consider important for the betterment of society (Moufahim & Lim, 2009; O'Cass, 1996).

Lees-Marshment (2001) defines political marketing as when political organisations adopt marketing concepts and strategies from the commercial world in order to help them achieve their political goals. Political marketing has existed under the guise of *propaganda* since for thousands of years. However, propaganda is concerned with convincing the electorate that a particular ideology is correct. It does not consider the mutual fulfilment of needs between politician and voter, nor is it focused on stimulating the electorate's understanding of the key issues required to encourage political dialogue and empowerment (O'Shaughnessy, 1996). Niffenegger (1989) provides a more contemporary political marketing framework underpinned by the simple marketing concept of the 'four Ps. This adapted framework includes the particular political 'product' on offer to the voter, the 'promotion' of information to the electorate through manifestos and party political broadcasts, the 'price' of the political product for the people (i.e., the potential economic, societal, and civil improvements they are likely to benefit from), and the 'place(s)' where information is communicated to the electorate.

Politicians make broad use of marketing tools (e.g., market research, media campaigns and segmentation) in attempting to achieve their political goals, and political parties spend more time and money on selecting political consultants based on their marketing expertise than their political leanings. This is why we often hear phrases such as exchange, stakeholders, market research and similar marketing jargon across the media during political campaigns (Dean & Croft, 2001). Thus, contemporary political marketing is "the study of the processes of exchanges between political entities and their environment and among themselves, with particular reference to the positioning of these entities and their communications…As an activity, it is concerned with strategies for positioning and communications, and the methods through which these strategies may be realized, including the search for information into attitudes, awareness and response of target audiences" (Lock & Harris, 1996: 22).

Marketing helps us to understand discourses and practices and can help to shape society and social relations (Hackley, 2012). Marketing discourse refers to how people view the world, their environment and the consumption of 'space'. Morgan (1992: 154) suggests that it is "part of the process whereby a particular form of society is constructed, one in which human beings are treated as things, where identity is reduced to ownership of commodities, and all social relations are conceived in market terms". It acts as a discourse which allows us to understand actors in relation to social processes, and thus fits well with the purpose of political marketing (Morgan, 1992). Here, discourse considers the dialectical relationship between the structure of sign systems and existing social codes. The next section explores the importance of semiotics in relation to this and associated concepts.

Activity

Identify examples of political marketing discourse. Are they effective in spreading the intended message?

Semiotics

The word 'semiology' has been used interchangeably with 'semiotics' to refer to the science of signs, where "[the semiotic perspective] interprets reality in terms of cultural codes that structure phenomena into signs and meanings" Oswald (2012: 8). Contemporary understanding of semiotics is based on the work of the American theorist Charles S. Peirce and the French philologist Ferdinand de Saussure. Peirce focuses on exploring the structure of meanings in the human experience. He defines semiotics as "…action, or influence, which is, or involves, a cooperation of three subjects, such as a sign, its object, and its interpretant, this tri-relative influence not being in any way resolvable into actions between pairs" (Peirce, 1934: 411).

de Saussaure views semiotics from a linguistic perspective and focuses predominantly on how words and language function as a system of signs. He describes the linkages between a signifier (which is a word) and the signified (which is an 'object expressed'). He highlights these two terms by emphasising that a 'signifier' is the physical manifestation of a sign and that 'signified' refers to the mental meaning linked with this physical object. He also defined three main binary concepts that provide insight into how signs are constructed, processed, and understood (Ellis et al., 2011):

1 **Synchronic vs. diachronic**: Many concepts recognise meaning as a result of their location within a series of signs (synchronic), rather than locating changes in meaning over time (diachronic).

2 **Syntagmatic vs. paradigmatic**: Paradigmatic concepts concentrate on the individual element of a sentence (e.g., the choice of verb or adjective) and evaluate the selection made by the writer. The syntagmatic view concentrates on the sequence of words in any sentence and the way in which these words are interrelated.

3 **Metaphor and metonymy**: Metaphors are typically used to explore the paradigmatic position of texts, whereas metonymy is used to explore syntagmatic relationships.

Metaphors and metonyms typically encompass a range of meanings. Ellis et al. (2011) provide an example of an FT advertisement using a paradigmatic metaphor with the image of dark, heavy and oppressive rain and the subheading: "Where would your money take shelter in turbulent times?" This arouses notions of 'economic turbulence caused by the financial crisis' to the reader (Ellis et al., 2011). A visual representation of de Saussaure's theory is presented in Figure 3.1.

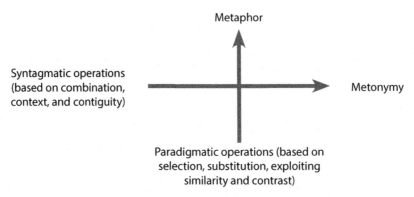

Figure 3.1: Metaphor and metonymy along the paradigmatic and syntagmatic axes (Ellis et al., 2011: 202)

Activity

Identify examples of recent television advertisements. Use Figure 3.1 and de Saussaure's three binary concepts to categorise your examples.

■ Denotative and connotative meanings

Barthes (1990) investigated the way in which *meaning* is derived from images in advertising. He suggested that all images have different meanings, and categorised these as existing on two distinct levels:

1 The **denotative** level is the basic and constant meaning that a sign or image bears. It allows us to identify the product or service a brand stands for or represents.

2 The **connotative** level refers to the more powerful, emotional level a brand signifies. On this level, a product or service can bes linked to culturally shaped symbolism and values. The higher the number of connotations a brand can generate, the greater its 'connotative index (CI) (Danesi, 2004).

Linguistic messages use denotative and connotative elements to carry out the two main functions of *anchorage* and *relay*. Relay has a narrative ability to carry a story forward, whereas anchorage fixes meaning in order to avoid multiple or undesirable meanings. The prevailing moral ideology of a society stems from those meanings that are fixed through *anchorage* (Barthes, 1990). He also explains that 'non-coded iconic' messages present objects that appear totally natural in an unconditionally analogical manner, whereas a series of signs are apparent in coded messages. It is important to note that semiotics offers an elegant, nuanced and powerful account of the plural and active nature of the process of meaning making.

Activity

Identify examples of denotative and connotative images and signs in recent television advertisements.

■ Semiotics and the simple marketing communication process

MacCannell (1989, p. 3) defines semiotics as "a technical perspective for close analysis of the forms and processes of communication. It is a meta-language for describing the hidden ideology of existing theories and methods. Semiotics is not owned by any field or discipline". In simpler terms, semiotics is the study of signs and their inherent and implied meanings – what they stand for or represent. Consider, for example, the letter 'X'. At a fundamental level its physical appearance, a letter of the alphabet constructed by two intersecting lines, can be considered a *signifier*. This signifier refers to the 24th letter of the English alphabet (the 'object expressed' – signified). Signs are read and their meaning is interpreted based on cultural codes, which we must learn in order to make sense of and process the signs around us (Hackley, 2012). This is how signification occurs. Meaning does not exist in an absolute sense, but in relation to other meanings. For example, the Macintosh (brand) is, to many, synonymous with the terms: 'user-friendly', 'highly functional' and 'well-designed', whereas the 'Apple' name and logo is used to evoke the biblical theme of 'forbidden knowledge' and 'temptation'.

A sign should be communicated through some form of discourse. This mediation is a vital component of the communication process and can be influenced by a range of factors, such as the context where the transmission of the message occurs and the way in which it is delivered. An idea, such as an advertising message, should be passed through a recognisable medium to someone who understands that message, as well as sorting through any noises or disturbance that might impact upon the interpretation of its intended meaning (Oswald, 2012). According to rhetorical theory, the sender's intention is to influence their audience based on creative delivery. The sender constructs the message using shared cultural knowledge of various conventions and connotative indexes (CIs). Thus, it is important for them to utilise visuals which are likely to influence consumers and which represent concepts, actions, metaphors, visual vocabulary or symbolic systems that they are familiar with (Scott, 1994). Based on this principle, Fill ((2009:41 and 2011)) describes Schramm's 1955 'linear model of communication' (outlined in Figure 3.2).

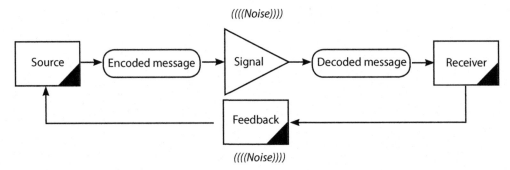

Figure 3.2: The communication process (Fill, 2011)

In this model:

- *Source* represents the individual or organisation sending the advertising message.

- *Encoding* refers to changing the message into a symbolic style that can be easily conveyed. The message that is communicated should come from a source that has authority and the trust of the customer. Using suitable staff members and training them appropriately with regards to how to devise this message is time-consuming and expensive, but it can create trust (Fill, 2011; Hackley, 2012; Percy & Rosenbaum-Elliott, 2012).

- *Signal* refers to the actual transmission of the message.

- *Decoding* describes the process whereby the receiver (or consumer) attempts to understand the message being conveyed. Differences in education, prior knowledge, attitudes and interests will influence the decoding process.

- The *Receiver* refers to the individual or organisation receiving the message.

- *Feedback* is the receiver's communication back to the source on receipt of the message. Feedback is very important as it helps to determine whether communication was successful or not and it can highlight problems with the consumer's interpretation of the message.

- Finally, *Noise* is distortion throughout the communication process, making it difficult for the receiver to interpret the message as intended by the source. Communication is typically considered successful if 'noise' is minimized or eradicated entirely, as there is a higher likelihood that the message will be understood by the receiver as intended by the source (Fill, 2011; Hackley, 2012; Oswald, 2012; Percy & Rosenbaum-Elliott, 2012).

Further, Williamson (1978) argues that for advertisements to be effective they *must* mean something. This typically involves connecting objects and people and making the two interchangeable. Williamson uses semiotic terminology to describe the transmission of meaning to products through *signs*. Goldman and Papson (1996) identify advertising as a key method of producing and reproducing material which can lead to ideological changes and commodity associations. They term this phenomena *'commodity hegemony'*. Advertisements contribute to commodity hegemony as they encourage a range of different people to consider products and services in the same way. Here, the 'mortise and frame' represents the main approach to advert and image interpretation. The mortise structures the creation of meaning within the advertisement via routing the connection between the image (as signified) and the products (as signifier). Regardless of the content of individual advertisements, this represents "an ideology and practice of commodity fetishism at a deep level of communicative competence" (Goldman, 1992: 65). Therefore, greater attention and significance is devoted to the rigidity of meaning within advertisements.

Activity

Drawing upon Fill's communication process (Figure 3.2), discuss and interpret a recent television advertisement of your choice.

■ The truth behind signs and polysemy

In order to understand and decode individual advertisements, we must consider the broader promotional system spanning production, marketing, and design (Wernick, 1991). Here, in order to appeal to consumers, the purpose of advertising is to further "the commodity they project, as the object of desire is simultaneously presented as a cultural symbol charged with social significance; and the ego they seek to engage as the subject of desire is induced to adopt the socio-cultural identity attributed to those who already use the product" (Wernick, 1991:31).

However, it can be difficult for consumers to understand the truth behind signs. The postmodernist French philosopher Baudrillard (1989) argues that it is not only signs that advertisers use to camouflage the 'truth', and he highlights that simulative signs do not always refer to something 'real'. Here he explores the distinction between 'true' and 'false': "It is no longer a question of imitation, nor of reduplication, nor even of parody. It is rather a question of substituting signs of the real for the real itself; that is, an operation to deter every real process by its operational double, a metastable, programmatic, perfect descriptive machine, which provides all the signs of the real and short-circuits its entire vicissitudes. Never again will the real have to be produced" (Baudrillard, 1989: 167).

With this in mind, an advertiser can take advantage of opportunities relating to what is 'true' and 'false', and may create a new spelling in order to engineer a pun in the hope that it appeals to consumers. For example, the maker of Corona Lemonade guaranteed consumers that 'every bubble has passed its fizzical'. Advertisers also utilise words that are 'polysemous' (a linguistic term employed to explore the semantic process whereby a single word has multiple related meanings). For example, 'foot' can refer to the anatomical structure found at the bottom of the leg, a unit of measurement, or to the base of a mountain. The use of such polysemous terms can result in lexical ambiguity, and advertisers and copywriters often use these multiple meanings strategically. Such lexical ambiguity can also emerge from use of 'homonyms', words with different meanings that are either pronounced the same, (homophones e.g., through and threw), or which are spelled the same (homographs e.g., lead, the metal, and lead, a dog's leash). Some homonyms have the same pronunciation and spelling, but unrelated meanings, for example, bear (the animal) and bear (the verb meaning to tolerate). Here through imaginative use of homonyms and polysemy, social context and interpretive space can play an important role in advertising, whereby the creative use of language and signs help to encourage consumers to engage with advertisements.

Activity

Identify examples of advertisements that utilise lexical ambiguity. Categorise these into those that use homonyms, and those that rely on polysemous terms to get their message across to consumers.

■   Semiotics and branding

A brand is a *sign* in the semiotic sense. Brands are laden with meaning, represent a range of things and can engender a multitude of feelings to different parties. The semiotic study of brands focuses the capacity that signs have in communicating and generating meaning. It attempts to reveal the codes through which humans draw meaning from signs in particular cultural contexts. Cultural context frames the interpretation of signs; different people utilise different interpretive strategies in deriving meaning from the same signs. Branding allows consumers not only to identify certain products and services, and to distinguish them from those made by others, but also to relate to them in cultural and emotional (connotative) terms. Therefore, such understanding of brands derives from symbolic consumption, which highlights the role of products and services in communicating the social and emotional benefits of consumption that can subsequently fulfil consumer needs such as love, satisfaction and the bolstering of self-image or self-identity (Oswald, 2012). For example, this can help in brand-naming strategies in a multitude of ways. Some well-known, global examples are outlined below:

1   The use of the manufacturer or founder's name (e.g., Gucci, Armani, Disney)

2   The use of an acronym e.g., (IKEA (Ingvar Kamprad Elmtaryd Agunnaryd), FCUK (French Connection UK), ESPN (Entertainment and Sports Programming Network)

3   Alluding to established (often religious or cultural) organisations (e.g. All Saints, True Religion, Quaker Oats)

4   Referring to a fictitious personality (e.g., Mr Clean, Red and Yellow (M&Ms), Churchill the Dog)

5   The use of descriptive words or phrases. Some of these link the brand to the manufacturer (e.g., Carnation Evaporated Milk, LEGO (a derivation of the Danish phrase 'Leg godt' which can be translated as 'play well', Vanish Stain Remover)

6   The use of place names to identify where a product, service or company is located or was founded (e.g., Hitachi, Bank of America, and Santander)

7   Cars named after animals (e.g., Mustang, Jaguar, and Cougar). This evokes a perception of the automobile as a replacement for animals as transporters of people, or imbues the automobile with some of the animal's desirable attributes.

Consumers generate meaning from brands, and brands can position themselves based on their ability to respond to and satisfy consumers' personal, social, and cultural needs. As such, many brands draw upon multidimensional sign systems in order to fulfil all elements of the consumer interpretation process, and to appeal to as wide a range of potential consumers as possible. Oswald (2012) suggests that there are four dimensions through which we can explore this perspective. These dimensions are: material, conventional, contextual, and performance (Table 3.4).

Activity

Drawing upon the "semiotic dimensions of brands" (Oswald, 2012), discuss and interpret a fashion brand from a material, conventional, contextual, and performance perspective.

Table 3.5: The semiotic dimensions of brands (Oswald, 2012)

Material	The intelligible dimension of marketing signs or subunits of meaning (e.g., words, images, spaces, brand names, jingles, trademarks, taglines, logos, packaging, etc.) **Example**: McDonald's 'Golden Arches' logo
Conventional	Different conventions or codes shared by consumers in a market. These include brand codes (linking material signifiers, such as a logo, to a set of connections in the consumer's mind), category codes (consumer expectations about products, retail categories and purchase decisions), cultural codes (consumer's interpretation of marketing communications), and counterfeit codes. **Example**: Products that claim to be healthy (e.g., Pepperidge Farm crackers)
Contextual	The meanings that consumers attach to signs can be changed from one market to the next. They can be observed through the filter of the sociocultural codes that shape meaning in the consumer's world (e.g., gender identity, social identity, religious identity). Here, the denotative and connotative interpretation of marketing signs plays an important role. **Example**: Nike's tagline: 'Just Do It!'
Performance	How the advertiser and consumer use semiotic codes to communicate. This is categorised into subject address (voice) and reference (linking a material signifier to an abstract concept). **Example**: the irony of statements such as 'what a great deal!' is only apparent if the agent recognises that the sale price was too high to begin with.

Summary

This chapter has provided an introduction to the core concepts of discourse and semiotics within the context of marketing communications and advertising. It highlights and explains the important discourse models underpinning contemporary marketing communications, including the seven building tasks of discourse, discourse and market-based relations, and capturing the situated customer. It also explains the crucial role that marketing discourse plays in today's political environment. Additionally, the chapter highlights the importance role of different types of visual messages within the communication process from sender (or advertiser) to receiver (or consumer).

Further reading

Cook, G. (2001). *The Discourse of Advertising*. London: Routledge.

Hackley, C. (2012). *Advertising and Promotion: An Integrated Marketing Communications Approach* (2nd ed.). London: Sage Publications.

Saussure, F. (1966). *Course on general linguistics*. New York: McGraw Hill.

Schroeder, J. (2002). *Visual consumption*. London: Routledge.

3

References

Barthes, R. (1990). *The Pleasure of the Text*. Oxford: Basil Blackwell.

Baudrillard, J. (1989). *The Consumer Society: Myths & Structures*. London: Sage Publications.

Beer, D., & Burrows, R. (2010). Consumption, prosumption and participatory web cultures: an introduction. *Journal of Consumer Culture*, **10**(1), 3-12.

Berdychevsky, L., Gibson, H. J. & Bell, H. L. (2016). "Girlfriend getaway" as a contested term: Discourse analysis. *Tourism Management*, **55**, 106-122.

Campbell, C. (2005). The craft consumer: Culture, craft and consumption in a postmodern society. *Journal of Consumer Culture*, **5**(1), 23–42.

Cook, G. (2001). *The Discourse of Advertising*, London: Roultledge.

Cova, B. & Cova, V. (2012). On the road to prosumption: marketing discourse and the development of consumer competencies. *Consumption Markets & Culture*, **15**(2), 149-168.

Danesi, M. (2004). *Messages, Signs, and Meanings: A basic textbook in semiotics and communication* (3rd ed.). Toronto: Canadian Scholars Press.

de Waal Malefyt, T. & McCabe, M. (2016). Women's bodies, menstruation and marketing "protection:" Interpreting a paradox of gendered discourses in consumer practices and advertising campaigns. *Consumption Markets & Culture*. **19**(6), 555-575.

Dean, D. & Croft, R. (2001). Friends and relations: long-tenn approaches to political campaigning. *European Journal of Marketing*, **35**(11/12), 1197-1216.

Dermody, J. & Wring, D. (2001). Message: New developments in political communication and marketing. *Journal of Public Affairs*, **I**(3), 198-201.

Elliott, R. (1996). Discourse analysis: exploring action, function and conflict in social texts. *Marketing Intelligence and Planning*, **14**(6).

Ellis, N., Fitchett, J., Higgins, M., Jack, G., Lim, M., Saren, M. & Tadajewski, M. (2011). *Marketing: A Critical Textbook*. London: Sage.

Fairclough, N. L. (1995). *Critical Discourse Analysis: The critical study of language.* Harlow, UK: Longman.

Fellesson, M. (2011). Enacting customers–Marketing discourse and organizational practice. *Scandinavian Journal of Management, 27,* 231-242.

Fill, C. (2009) *Marketing Communications: Interactivity, Communities and Content.* 5th ed. FT Prentice Hall.

Fill, C. (2011). *Essentials of Marketing Communications* Pearson.

Fitchett, J., & Caruana, R. (2015). Exploring the role of discourse in marketing and consumer research. *Journal of Consumer Behaviour, 14,* 1-12.

Foucault, M. (2002). *The Order of Things: an archaeology of the human sciences.* Abingdon: Routledge.

Gee, J. P. (2005). *An Introduction to Discourse Analysis: Theory and method,* New York, NY: Routledge.

Goldman, R. (1992). *Reading Ads Socially:* London, Routledge.

Goldman, R., & Papson, S. (1996). *Sign Wars: The Cluttered Landscape of Advertising.* New York: Guilford.

Hackley, C. (2012). *Advertising and Promotion: An Integrated Marketing Communications Approach* (2nd ed.). London.

Humphreys, A. & Grayson, K. (2008). The intersecting roles of consumer and producer: a critical perspective on co-production, co-creation and prosumption. *Sociology Compass, 2*(3), 963–980.

Jafari, A. & Taheri, B. (2014). Nostalgia, reflexivity, and the narratives of self: reflections on Devine's 'removing the rough edges?'. *Consumption Markets and Culture, 17*(2), 215-230.

Lees-Marshment, J. (2001). The marriage of politics and marketing. *Political Studies, 49*(4), 692-713.

Lock, A. & Harris, P. (1996). Political Marketing: Vive la difference. *European Journal of Marketing, 30*(10/11), 14-24.

MacCannell, D. (1989). *The Tourist: A New Theory of the Leisure Class.* London: Macmillan.

Morgan, G. (1992). Marketing discourse and practice: towards a critical analysis. In M. Alvesson & H. Willmott (Eds.), *Critical Management Studies* (pp. 136-158): London: Sage.

Moufahim, M. & Lim, M. (2009). Towards a critical political marketing agenda? *Journal of Maketing Management, 25*(7-8), 763-776.

Niffenegger, P. B. (1989). Strategies for success from the political marketers. *Journal of Consumer Marketing, 6*(1).

O'Cass, A. (1996). Political marketing and the marketing concept. *European Journal of Marketing,* **30**(10/11).

O'Shaughnessy, N. (1996). Social propaganda and social marketing: a critical difference? *European Journal of Marketing,* **30**(10/11), 62-75.

Oswald, L. R. (2012). *Marketing Semiotics: Signs, strategies, and brand value,* Oxford: Oxford University Press.

Peirce, C. S. (1934). *Collected Papers of Charles Sanders Peirce.* Cambridge: Harvard University

Percy, L., & Rosenbaum-Elliott, R. (2012). *Strategic Advertising Management* (4th ed.). London: Oxford University Press.

Potter, J. & Wetherell, M. (1987). *Discourse and Social Psychology,* London: Sage.

Said, E. W. (1978). *Orientalism.* London: Penguin.

Scott, L. M. (1994). Images in advertising: the need for a theory of visual rhetoric. *Journal of Consumer Research,* **21**(2), 252-273.

Taheri, B. & Jafari, A. (2012). Museums as playful venues in the leisure society. In R. Sharpley & P. Stone (Eds.), *The Contemporary Tourist Experience: Concepts and Consequences* (pp. 201-215). New York: Routledge.

Thompson, C. J. (2004). Marketplace mythology and discourses of power. *Journal of Consumer Research,* **31**(1), 162-180.

Thompson, C. J. & Haytko, D. L. (1997). Speaking of fashion: Consumers' uses of fashion discourses and the appropriation of countervailing cultural meanings. *Journal of Consumer Research,* **24**(1), 15-42.

Wernick, A. (1991). *Promotional Culture: Advertising, Ideology And Symbolic Expression*: London: Sage.

Williamson, J. (1978). *Decoding Advertisements.* London: Marion Boyars.

3

4 Consumer Decisions in Marketing Communications

Christopher Dodd and Geraldine Bell

Introduction

Quite simply, consumers are the primary reason for the existence of marketing communications. Without consumers, there is no commercial imperative for marketers to create even the simplest of messages. The remarkable developments experienced over the last century are testament not only to our creativity and mastery of technology but, more importantly, to the identification of myriad consumer types. Nowhere is this better illustrated than within marketing communications. These consumers are represented through complex and often overlapping needs and wants, and exist within a world of seemingly endless choice. Marketers are driven to define these audiences and to construct tailored communications that typically seek to move beyond simple informational value. Increasingly, the goal is the creation of emotionally and socially engaging marketing communications that serve to persuade consumers not only to purchase or visit but, further, to connect and to become part of a much bigger offering – a relationship.

Increasingly, this abstract sense of connectedness between consumers, marketers and brands is being translated into more tangible, financially relevant terms, namely through its inclusion as a component of brand and advertising equity (Rosengren and Dahlen, 2015). It is not surprising, therefore, that marketers are keen to develop brand relationships, with marketing communications offering an expedient, if not always perfect place within which to manage them.

The cost to marketers of this approach is the need to understand consumers in ways not previously required. It is no longer enough to identify target groups and fire-off marketing communications in their general direction. Now, consumers exist as an integral part of the communications production process. They are not simply the audience, they are co-creators – designers, developers and users. Quite simply, they are 'one of us' and so it has never been so necessary for marketers to understand 'why' and 'how' consumers behave as they do.

By focussing upon consumer decisions, this chapter seeks to support and further our understanding, explaining why consumers are driven to make decisions and how they manage their experiences. First, we consider who consumers are, exploring definitions relevant to marketing communications that seek to explain their nature, location and value to marketing communications. Second, we present a modelled conceptualisation of this understanding, focusing upon the consumer's decision-making process. Here, we will explore representations of the consumer's journey through their decisions; identify the benefits and costs to consumers and marketers within this process and consider how the contexts of consumption moderate these experiences. Third, we consider some of the over-arching theories that seek to explain consumer behaviour. By exploring consumer values, motivations and involvement, we frame this understanding around what consumers do (behaviour), what consumers feel (emotion) and what consumers think (cognition).

Understanding consumers in marketing communications

In Chapter 1, we noted a prevailing conceptualisation of marketing communications, through Kotler et al.'s (2016: 630) definition:

> "Marketing communications are the means by which firms attempt to inform, persuade and remind customers directly or indirectly about the brands they market. In a sense, marketing communications represent the 'voice' of the company and its brands, and are the ways in which it can establish a dialogue and build relationship with customers."

The first part of this definition offers a fairly traditional interpretation of the role and function of marketing communications. This unidirectional (marketer to audience) approach is symptomatic of earlier attempts to conceptualise consumers and their behaviour, which emphasised the well-established, classical economic formula of production versus consumption. Within such approaches, the marketing environment is seen as a place where products and services are produced and subsequently offered to consumers as part of a wider system of (typically commercial) exchange. Marketing communications naturally fill the void between these ideas, providing information (via numerous forms) that enables these parties to move closer together and achieve satisfying exchange.

This view has served marketing well for many years, allowing the creation of a readily understandable system of (transactional) exchange for both the marketer and the consumer (see Bagozzi, 1978). The marketing environment has changed, however, with an associated re-conceptualisation of the consumer, the marketer and marketing communications. Whilst some may argue that the traditional view always represented a misconception of this marketing exchange relationship (e.g. Galbraith, 1958; Baudrillard, 1988), the tangible changes in the fabric of the marketing environment (not least through advances in technology) push forward the notion of a radically altered set of parameters/priorities. The second part of Kotler et al.'s definition gives a nod to this changing dynamic, acknowledging that marketers may see value in nurturing collaborative relationships with customers, around the desired values of their brands (see Dwyer, et al., 1987; Gronroos, 2004). Of course, by labelling consumers as 'customers', this definition significantly limits the scope of understanding available to marketers to commercial and transactional value.

Perhaps most challenging in the re-conceptualisation of consumers is the notion that consumers exist not only to consume but also to produce. Similarly, to consider marketers as merely producers of communications is to underplay their own consumption of that process and experience. For example, consider how consumers are involved more than ever before in the design process of products and marketing communications, with some markets' existence dependent upon the activity of participant consumers – so called *'prosumers'* (see Cova & Cova, 2012; Martin & Schouten, 2014).

It is likely that you will have contributed to and/or read online reviews, such as those on Tripadvisor. Your review sits alongside other existing reviews and/or elicits more responses regarding the experience. The provider of that experience may also contribute to that discussion, managing interpretations and expectations for the reviewers and readers. The validity of these reviews is bound up with an array of visible evidence to establish the credibility of authors (e.g. contribution ratings and rankings). Ultimately, the marketer may modify their offering and consumers may modify their understanding of the experience. Clearly, in that case, both consumers and marketers have qualitatively changed their position. The consumers (reviewers) have contributed to this offering production and the marketer has actively consumed this development process (at least at an individual level).

Of course, allowing consumers to contribute to marketing does not guarantee that consumers' and marketers' interests are synonymous. It does, however, demonstrate a shared process of marketing that challenges existing adversarial conceptualisations of this relationship. For some, this represents a move from *marketerspace* (where markets control the space) to *consumerspace* (where consumers direct offerings) (Solomon, 2003) although, more realistically, this remains a shared, co-created space!

Thus, consumers occupy various forms. They may be singular or collective; separate or interactive. They are potential customers; clients and users. They may be advocates or opponents. They may be the target audience and they may also have audiences of their own. They may be passive recipients of marketing communications or they may actively construct marketing communications. They are both consumers and they are marketers. Online or offline, they are ubiquitous. Faced with such varied and complex identities, it may seem an insurmountable task to create meaningful communications. Consumers are, however, bound by one ever present type of behaviour – the need to make choices. We will now turn our attention to explaining the process of decision-making and marketing communication's relationship with this process.

Consumers and choice

Being able to model consumers' decision-making behaviour offers considerable advantage to marketers. At a general level, communications may be assembled to target general approaches to understanding. Consider how bigger brands will focus upon consolidation of brand values within their campaigns. Chanel will routinely offer glimpses of exotic and exclusive worlds wrapped within a sublimely retro feel. Guinness would routinely release big budget, symbolism rich advertisements built around the two-toned colour of its products and brand. Here, the belief is that consumers are aware of the brand and the requirement is to maintain this brand presence as a pre-curser to decisions.

More specifically, decision making may be seen as a staged process, within which the different stages represent different actions on the part of the consumer. This allows marketers the opportunity to tailor communications to the specific behaviours evidenced within each stage (see Figure 4.1).

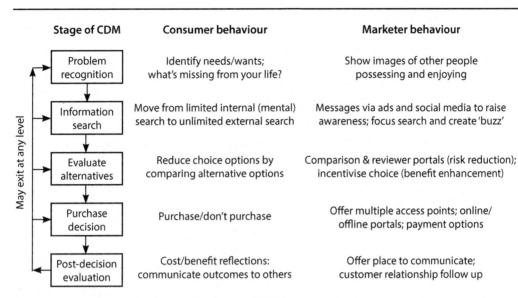

Stage of CDM	Consumer behaviour	Marketer behaviour
Problem recognition	Identify needs/wants; what's missing from your life?	Show images of other people possessing and enjoying
Information search	Move from limited internal (mental) search to unlimited external search	Messages via ads and social media to raise awareness; focus search and create 'buzz'
Evaluate alternatives	Reduce choice options by comparing alternative options	Comparison & reviewer portals (risk reduction); incentivise choice (benefit enhancement)
Purchase decision	Purchase/don't purchase	Offer multiple access points; online/offline portals; payment options
Post-decision evaluation	Cost/benefit reflections: communicate outcomes to others	Offer place to communicate; customer relationship follow up

May exit at any level

Figure 4.1: Consumer decision making model (CDM) and marketing communications tactics

The value of the CDM model is evident from its use to focus marketing communications activities. The main problem with such an approach however is its reliance on a rational approach to decision making. Clearly, some behaviours are not rational and do not proceed sequentially through stages. Irrational decision-making may be seen within compulsive and addictive behaviours, where consumers act on impulse and/or are less able to control the urge to consume. Marketing communication has been identified as a driver of this irrational consumption, offering unrealistic promises to vulnerable audiences and fuelling a desire to consume (Packard, 1957 and see Desmond, 2003). For effective marketing, there is a need to establish not only how consumers make decisions but, also, why they make decisions.

■ Drivers of consumer choice

Choice is a fundamental, permanent feature of our lives. We begin our days with a choice (to wake up properly) and fight our way through a seemingly constant process of decision-making until we close our eyes and sleep. (Some would argue that we are still making choices in our sleep!). Some choices are easier than others and some choices seem unachievable. Some choices are forced upon us; others we actively search for. Ultimately, our experience of choice shapes who we are and reveals this identity to others. This presents a fantastic opportunity for marketers to understand you and to influence your decision-making.

For marketers looking to satisfy consumers, identifying needs and wants and explaining why those drives exist offers the opportunity to create more satisfying exchanges. Most people will seek out positive experiences and avoid negative ones. Of course, what people consider to be positive may well differ but most people will be able to offer an explanation for their choices (even if they are not always completely certain why!). Nonetheless, this tendency to pursue outcomes helps us to understand consumers' engagement with marketing communications from a motivational perspective.

Consumer motives

By understanding motivation, we are able to understand why consumers behave the way they do. Much research on motivation takes a psychological perspective and this underpinned most marketing communications insights from the 1950s onwards (see Dichter, 1947). In essence, motivation exists because we recognise the existence of a need or want. This awareness is accompanied by a state of tension that we are driven to satisfy or remove. This is a common perspective in psychology, as cognitive (rational) and affective (emotional) processes are inextricably connected to physiological reactions (behaviours). The strength of your reaction to this tension dictates your drive to resolve it. Consider how you shop for food when you are hungry. Perhaps you make quicker choices, buy more food and eat the food sooner after purchase. The drive to resolve your negative state of tension is much stronger than if you are not so hungry.

Even psychologists are mindful, however, that these psychological processes do not exist in isolation. We are, at least in part, shaped by our experiences and our environments. When explaining hunger, sociologists and anthropologists may point to our fixation with set eating times (e.g. breakfast, lunch and dinner) and suggest that we are conditioned to feel hungry at certain times. Consider how we may sometimes 'forget' to be hungry if we are sufficiently distracted (for example, through work, fun and so on). Anyone who has adopted a nutritional diet will be aware of how many of these seek to subvert our normal embedded expectations of food and satiation of appetite (for example, the 5:2 diet effectively changes your consumption habit on 2 days out of every 7) (www.thefastdiet.co.uk). Clearly, our adoption of certain lifestyles and associated behaviours becomes a significant moderator of our behaviours.

Whilst earlier motivational theories (such as drive theory) emphasise a less controllable biological drive, other theories recognise the cognitive basis of behaviour. For instance, cognitive dissonance theory (Festinger, 1954) suggests that people are motivated to seek balance and harmony in their lives and any choice context will trigger a raised level of tension. Similarly, expectancy theory suggests that people use their learned experience to set the criteria required to achieve outcomes through, for instance, the setting of goals. Goals may be positive or negative (they have what we call 'valence') and many of us will be aware of setting positive goals that we strive to attain – consider how we may want a new job and will buy new clothes as part of our attempts to achieve this. Not all goals are positive, of course, and you will no doubt have experience of being motivated to avoid negative outcomes – consider how our use of personal hygiene products is driven by a belief that these will help us to avoid rejection and humiliation. The existence of differential valence inevitably causes conflict for consumers and offers marketers the opportunity to resolve this conflict. By grouping conflicts according to a consumer's desire to avoid or approach goals, marketers are able to offer solutions as part of the set of benefits derived from brands and products.

This is typically operationalised by three 'motivational conflict' dualisms: approach-approach; approach-avoid and avoid-avoid.

- Whilst **approach-approach** scenarios would seem to offer a win-win for consumers, the reality is that this represents a choice and choices create tension (remember cognitive dissonance!). Marketers may help to make this choice easier by bundling benefits together to create persuasive benefit bundles (e.g. who wouldn't want something that was tasty, filling and nutritious?) but the choice remains.

- **Approach-avoid** scenarios are perhaps more familiar to most of us. Here we want to achieve a goal but recognise that it is perhaps not in our best interests – consider how you feel when you add a large chocolate bar to your lunch or 'go large' at McDonalds. Marketers seek to offset these worries by taking a variety of approaches. Some may embrace over-consumption and incentivise the purchase. Saving money usually makes us feel better, as does believing that we are receiving multiple benefits within one purchase. Others may try to persuade you that you 'deserve' or 'have earned the right' to indulge yourself (https://www.youtube.com/watch?v=LRTq5BImIWg).

- Finally, **avoid-avoid** scenarios see the consumer with a choice few of us want, a choice between two undesirable alternatives. Consider how we often resent having to pay for repairs to products but don't want to accept the cost of replacements. For the marketer, the aim is typically to de-stress this decision. New products may be supported by favourable finance deals; payment plans may offer warranty and service options; all at manageable regular amounts. Of course, reminding consumers of the reliability and trustworthiness of a brand is a regular tactic within marketing communications to offset such concerns.

■ Consumer values

Your behaviour will, in no short measure, be shaped by your values. Yet this clear link to influencing consumers is not the panacea marketers may hope for. The problem is that values tend to be broad-based beliefs about life in general and your place within it. They may guide people towards certain behaviours but they may not always be so relevant to specific contexts. Further, whilst individuals may exhibit similar behaviours (e.g. food and clothing choices), the belief systems that underpin these behaviours may be different (e.g. religion, health, environmentalism). This makes them seemingly less controllable and less targeted for the specific briefs of brand managers and marketing communications practitioners.

Yet values offer real insights into the beliefs and desires of consumers. Further, our belief systems drive us to relate to others with similar beliefs. This tends to facilitate social network formation that fosters a positively determined consensus (we like to seek out people who agree with us and exclude those who do not) (see Turner et al., 1987). At its broadest level, our core values frame our essential relationship with our world. You may value your freedom, sense of belonging, connectedness and so on. You may also value less abstract ideas, such as cleanliness, privacy, manners or animal welfare.

For marketers, the usefulness of values may lie in identifying relative differences across groups. For instance, where value systems are contained within cultural groupings, we often see striking differences that set those cultures apart. This may be at a general, stereotypical (and often unsubstantiated) level (such as the belief that Germans are organised, Australians are rude and Spanish are passionate). It may also be at a specific, product attribute level (such as the belief that breakfast cereal should contain a particular set of vitamins, cosmetics should be formulated for specific skin types, and the towels in a 4 star hotel should be softer and fluffier than a 3 star hotel).

Schwartz (1992) preferred to create a motivation-based understanding of values. The **Schwartz value survey** accommodates 56 different values and positions them within ten 'motivational domains'. The domains are further contained within two core dimensions. The first dimension concerns our desire to look outwards to others, so at one extreme there is 'openness to change' and at the other 'conservatism'. The second dimension concerns our desire to develop our sense of who we are, identified by Schwartz as 'self-transcendence' or 'self-enhancement'.

For Holbrook (1999), the variations may be more usefully tied to the consumption experience, with consumers actively evaluating the benefits available to them from engaging with the object/offering. Holbrook (and his co-authors) note eight distinct types of consumer value:

1 **Efficiency** – potential for convenience (e.g. how easy is it to obtain/use).

2 **Excellence** – evaluations of quality (e.g. is it well constructed).

3 **Status** – potential for social movement (e.g. will it signal my status; can I manage impressions).

4 **(Self)-esteem** – potential to enhance self-esteem (e.g. does it make me feel better about myself).

5 **Play** – potential for enjoyment (e.g. is it fun to consume).

6 **Aesthetics** – potential to enhance beauty of self and others (e.g. is it beautiful).

7 **Ethics** – potential to support moral/ethical positions (e.g. will it help/harm others).

8 **Spirituality** – potential to transform (e.g. will it enhance experience beyond the norm).

Activity

Assume you have just returned from one of the following: i) a spiritual retreat in Thailand; ii) a spa break in Malaysia; and/or iii) a romantic break in the Maldives. Apply Holbrook's values to your holiday break and make a note of your comments. Can you identify any values which are more dominant than others. What are your reflections on the points you have made?

Rokeach (1973) rather sought to link *terminal* values (a person's desired end-state) with *instrumental* values (the action-based values needed to achieve the end-state). Hence, he suggested for instance that instrumental values such as courage, ambition, politeness or honesty may form the basis to achieve terminal values, such as happiness, friendship, or equality, amongst many others. This link between behaviour and values is further developed through the means-end chain model (Gutman, 1981; 1982), which assumes that people link product attributes to potential end-states. The value of this approach to marketers is fairly transparent. If attributes can be linked to end-states, creating and communicating value may become more transparent.

Example

"Find out what a Boot Camp Fitness Holiday in Spain can do for you" said the headline in the advertisement. The ad went on to ask me whether I was "interested in getting fit, losing weight, and feeling good" about myself. Yes, the voice in my head screamed out to me. "If so", the advert went on to read, "what better environment is there to make the changes to your life than in beautiful Almeria (Spain)". It finished by urging me to "make that change now and find out" what they can do for me!

Source: adapted from www.bootcampspain.net

Of course, life is not that simple. The reality is that whilst attributes may be linked to values, they will exist with varying degrees of importance and abstraction. Establishing exactly which attributes should be prioritised and to what degree of magnitude is enough of a problem to leave means-end analysis to those with enough time and resources to pursue useful answers.

One attempt to operationalise this model, however, has allowed advertisers to generate useful bases for the construction of messages. The Means-End Conceptualisation of the Components of Advertising Strategy (MECCAs) enables a mapping of product/service attributes relative to terminal values (see Reynolds and Craddock, 1988 for an advertising example). By asking consumers to identify and rank attributes of products/services, 'ladders' of expectations are developed for specific products/services. This mapping allows a conceptualisation of the strategy required to communicate effectively with the consumer. For instance, knowing which benefits consumers prioritise allows advertisers to select from those attributes the most appropriate (and so persuasive) features to use as elements within the message. If you believe a car enhances your status if it is fast and loud, then it is a short hop for the advertiser to create advertisements that prioritise speed and noise within the message.

Hence, values help us to understand how consumers prioritise elements of their world, and motivations demonstrate consumers' strength of desire to achieve their goals. Whilst these ideas are clearly useful in understanding consumer behaviour, they struggle to account for the inherent difference between consumers. For instance, whilst you may desperately want the latest version of your favourite tech, your friend may prefer a different brand, may be perfectly content with their older model or even prefer to have no tech at all! Involvement is a concept that allows marketers to explore these differences in preference by building understanding of motives around specific choice contexts.

■ Consumer involvement

Involvement has been defined as a person's perceived relevance of the object based on their inherent needs, values and interests (Zaichowsky, 1985). When considering *consumer* involvement particularly, 'object' typically relates to one of several contexts: product, purchase decision, advertisements and/ or consumption more generally (see O'Cass, 2000). Consumer involvement prioritises, therefore, the consumer's motivation to engage with and manage offering-related information. Consumers do not enter into decisions, however, bereft of psychological baggage. Consumer involvement conceptualises these decisions as part of a process, with antecedents moderating engagement with the context and outcomes offering evidence of decision effectiveness.

They are four types of consumer involvement including:

- **Cognitive** (i.e. heightened thinking and processing information about a goal object e.g., Amazon),

- **Affective** (i.e. heightened feelings and emotional energy e.g., a consumer responds positively to an ad for tissues featuring a fluffy white kitten),

- **Enduring** (i.e. interest in an offering or an activity over a long period of time i.e., long-term involvement with a target object e.g., a housewife with kids would consider children's toys important and self-relevant in general),

- **Situational** (i.e. a temporary interest in the goal object i.e., short-term or temporary involvement with a target object e.g., a single unmarried man would see children's toys relevant to him when he needs to buy a birthday gift for a nephew).

Prior research recognises the involvement concept as complicated with various operational and theoretical problems (Laaksonen, 1994). According to Taheri et al. (2017), arguably the discussion on the conceptualisation of involvement concentrates on three categories: the origin of involvement (occurring as a result of practical or role-related needs), the nature of involvement (continuous or dichotomous variable), and the object of involvement (product, person, particular message stimuli or situations). Moreover, there is an overlap between engagement and involvement concepts. Taheri et al. (2014: 322) highlight that "engagement goes beyond involvement to embrace a proactive consumer relationship with specific objects of engagement". They also argue that engagement is broader than involvement and it is a two-way interaction between consumers and brands.

Antecedents of involvement include several broad, overlapping factors:

- **Person** factors, such as needs, values and inherent interest in the object;
- **Situational** factors, such as whether it is a special occasion and/or require for a particular purpose;
- **Object** factors, such as the nature of the communication and/or how the object is differentiated from other objects.

Outcomes could represent anything, from brand preference to how much information the consumer searches for; from how much time is spent considering alternatives to the likelihood of the consumer generating a counter position to an advertisement's message.

We have already seen how values may drive motives to engage with decisions. Consumer involvement suggests that these values are part of a wider set of beliefs that are taken into every decision and moderated by other factors such as the environment within which the choice is being made and evaluations of potential outcomes from the decision. This underpins perhaps the main value of the involvement concept, the notion of levels of involvement.

We will all recognise that some decisions are more difficult than others. For the majority of consumers' decisions, we would expect to see high levels of involvement for high price offerings (such as houses) and low involvement for everyday purchases (such as milk). The value of involvement, however, is that it allows marketers to move beyond these simplistic understandings. Some consumers will find it more difficult to choose a new dress than they will a new car. This may, for instance, be due to their high disposable wealth or because clothes interest them more than cars. Similarly, consumers will buy into brands to the exclusion of other brands. This fierce brand loyalty is a holy grail for marketers, with loyal consumers usually willing to spend more and buy more frequently than for other brands. Of course, some 'brand loyals' may never spend anything on the brand, with their high involvement not translating to purchase (consider the football fan who never goes to a match, never buys merchandise but watches all the games on free-to-air television). They will, however, communicate their affiliation and preference to others and so perpetuate brand values.

If we consider that consumer involvement represents a continuum of a person's engagement with marketing offerings, we see that there may be differences in the way that information is processed depending upon their level of engagement. We may reasonably expect that those less engaged with an offering will engage in more simplistic processing, whilst those at the opposite extreme engage in more elaborate processing. A particular feature of much of our low involvement shopping is inertia. Inertia represents an absence of engagement, thought and deliberation in choices. We buy something because we always buy it. Of course, this does not mean that at some point previously, we have not pursued far more elaborate processing of information. Figure 4.2 represents involvement as an interest continuum.

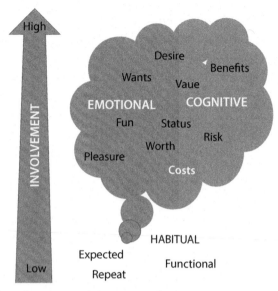

Figure 4.2: Levels of involvement and decision-making

At the higher end of involvement, we begin to notice different types of processing built around cognition (thoughts) and affect (emotion). This differentiation enables advertisers to use different communication tactics. We will often hear marketing communications practitioners talking about selling the 'sausage or the sizzle'. In this analogy, the sausage represents a cognitive approach, where messages will focus on content, ingredients, rationalised inputs and outputs. The sizzle is the affective approach, representing abstract emotional ideas such as fun, fantasy, anticipation, desire, and so on. Would you want to read about the significant features available on a new car or would you like to see it move and hear it roar? Of course, cognitive theorists would argue that emotion does not live in the heart but, rather, in the mind and so everything is cognitive – that is, everything is information that we understand in different ways.

Supporting consumer choice

Whilst marketing communications fundamentally inform consumer decisions, it is clear that they perform many other supporting functions. They assist in evaluations, offering alternatives and suggesting values that may or may not be hidden to consumers. They allow interaction with other people and other environments which, in turn, may allow confirmation of decisions and validate behaviour. They help to position individuals relative to others within their worlds, validating status and identity. Hence, consumers are enabled and empowered by marketing communications in a real and practical way.

Additionally, marketing communications are typically engaging, interesting and enjoyable. By offering consumers the opportunity to have fun; to experience worlds outside of their day-to-day existence and to indulge in fantasies, marketing communications allow separation from consumers' real lives (see Holbrook and Hirschmann, 1982). At both of these levels, marketing communications practitioners employ a variety of tactics to increase consumers' involvement and engagement to support decision-making.

You may recognise some techniques used by advertisers to increase audience involvement with messages. Product placement, for example, is now quite sophisticated. Branded products are not just 'plonked' into content anymore but are intricately woven into the entertainment narrative making a stronger and much more emotional connection with the consumer. Conceptualised by the advertising industry as 'branded entertainment' this concept sees the convergence of advertising and entertainment. (Hudson & Hudson, 2006: 489). Novelty is, of course, still a favourite (see Chapter 8 for further details of novelty within the context of creative advertising). New messages; new ways of constructing the message; unexpected content and delivery will always increase involvement. This perhaps explains the contemporary predilection with unusual approaches to marketing communications. We have seen an incredible rise in the use of interactive media and user-generated content. How many times do you respond to television, radio or mobile phone messages asking you to participate in competitions? Flash mobs take the advertising message to new contexts and audiences.

Who wouldn't stop to watch a choir welcome travellers home from their flights (https://www.youtube.com/watch?v=NB3NPNM4xgo, courtesy of T-Mobile); or unlock their inner James Bond for a few minutes (https://www.youtube.com/watch?v=5T6BCHCk6QY, courtesy of Coca-Cola). Of course, creating entertainment out of the messages is not new. Many early television programmes embedded the brand and message so completely into programming that the programmes were effectively an extended advertisement. What has changed is the accessibility of programming. Audiences are now able to control when and where they view their programmes. The rise of social media has enabled variable, consumer-led access to this content. Yet within the vlogs and channels of Youtube, we see a return to the branded entertainment tactics of the 1950s, with the latest generation of YouTubers regularly embedding advertisements within their offerings (see, for example, www.youtube.com/user/BrooklynAndBailey). So, should we see digital consumers as different to other consumers or consider them on similar terms?

Contexts of consumption – digital consumers

For some, so-called 'digital consumers' (i.e. consumers who use digital technologies and access the internet) are seen as being as mysterious as an undiscovered tribe, existing as a separate entity to 'normal' consumers (Ryan, 2014). The reality, of course, is that these consumers are still consumers – still people. The main difference is the environment within which they make decisions. As we have noted previously, consumers are faced with choices and construct these within an environment of complex information. The digital consumer has the greater potential of broader access to stimuli that may affect this process. For many, this is a simplification process, allowing algorithms to make decisions for them. For others, it is an elaboration, flooding their decision-making with excess information.

■ Social media

Many digital consumers will have a presence within social media (an umbrella term for technologies that allow users to create and share content). These include social network sites (SNS), such as Facebook, YouTube, Wikipedia, whatsapp, amongst many others. (Whiting and Williams, 2013) note that, amongst other factors, self-presentation drives users' satisfaction with social media. That is, the ability to present themselves and self-disclose as they wish is vital for these environments to be wanted and valued. Hence, an added complexity for marketers is that a consumer's adoption of, and engagement with brands and communications is visible to their friends, followers and others. The consumer is not simply a recipient of marketing communications but, rather they are also marketers, repackaging meaning within brand messages before release to their own target audiences. They are also, therefore, subsequently constrained by the pervading social pressures of their own audiences, as these develop to become populous and multifarious (Marder et al., 2012).

Summary

Consumers are considered fundamental drivers of marketing activity and this chapter has considered the value to marketing communications of understanding and explaining consumer choice. The nature of the consumer has been explored and subsequently located within the variety of contexts that form the marketing communications landscape. Key theoretical ideas including consumer values, motivations and involvement are presented and used as a basis to explain both the consumer's decision management and, also, their relationships with marketing communications. Figure 4.3 seeks to represent this process by placing these interconnected concepts as hierarchical foundations underpinning consumer choice.

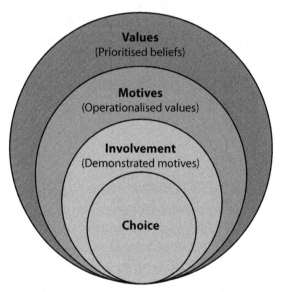

Figure 4.3: Relationship between values, motives, involvement and choice

The figure highlights the fundamental space occupied by values, which represent the core truths of individual identity – the reasons we are who we are. These values may be operationalised by our motives. That is, motives reveal our values to ourselves and others by signalling our liking and affiliation with certain goals and objectives. These motives shape our engagement with the marketing world in more tangible ways, by moderating our involvement with marketing offerings such as products and communications.

Consumers exist in various forms and occupy numerous spaces, places and times. For the marketer, the trick is perhaps to worry less about who consumers are but, rather, consider who they want to be. By embedding consumer values and motives within contextualised evaluations of involvement, marketing communications become usefully informed by the consumers. This allows for the co-creation of meaningful messages that will naturally occur within the spaces, places and times expected by those consumers.

For many, there may be an implicit assumption that all marketing communications are created for the purposes of persuading people to purchase products or to engage with services. Whilst this objective will undoubtedly drive much of the content of communications, there is an increasing realisation that communications are about more than persuasion. Whereas traditional methods of communication emphasise unidirectional approaches or, at best, cyclical approaches to understanding consumers' relationship with marketing communications, contemporary approaches (as outlined in Chapter 1) emphasise shared values and interactivity. Key questions, as noted previously, include whether we see consumers as different or similar and, if there are emergent patterns, how do marketers usefully manage these within mutually beneficial relationships?

Further reading

O'Cass, A. (2000) An assessment of consumers product, purchase decision, advertising and consumption involvement in fashion clothing, *Journal of Economic Psychology*, **21** (5), 545–576.

Whiting, A. & Williams, D. (2013) Why people use social media: a uses and gratifications approach, *Qualitative Market Research: An International Journal*, **16** (4), 362-369.

These scholars' papers are useful for further insight. The first paper by O'Cass (2000) gives good context for decision making and the second paper, by Whiting and Williams (2013) is more current and reflects the modern communications environment.

References

Bagozzi, R. (1978) Marketing as exchange: a theory of transactions in the market place. *American Behavioral Science*, **21** (4), 257-261.

Baudrillard, J. (1988) The system of objects, in Mark Poster (Ed.) *Jean Baudrillard: Selected Writings*, Cambridge: Polity Press, pp 10-28.

Cova, B. & Cova, V. (2012) On the road to prosumption: marketing discourse and the development of consumer competencies, *Consumption, Markets and Culture*, **15**, 2, 149-168.

Desmond, J. (2003) *Consuming Behaviour*, Basingstoke: Palgrave-MacMillan.

Dichter, E. (1947) Psychology in market research, *Harvard Business Review*, 25 (4) 432-443.

Dwyer, R., Schurr, P. & Oh, S. (1987) Developing buyer-seller relationships, *Journal of Marketing*, **51** (April), 11-27.

Festinger, L. (1954) A theory of social comparison, processes, *Human Relations*, **7** (2), 117-140.

Galbraith, J.K. (1958) *The Affluent Society*, London: Pelican.

Gronroos, C. (2004) The relationship marketing process: communication, interaction, dialogue, value, *Journal of Business and Industrial Marketing*, **19** (2), 99-113.

Gutman, J. (1981) A means-end model for facilitating analysis of product markets based on consumer judgement. *Advances in Consumer Research*, **8**, 116-21.

Gutman, J. (1982) A means-end chain model based on consumer categorization processes. *Journal of Marketing*, **46**(2), 60-72.

Holbrook, M.B. and Hirschmann, E.C. (1992) The experiential aspects of consumption: Consumer fantasies, feelings, and fun, *Journal of Consumer Research*, **9** (2), 132-140.

Holbrook, M.B. (1999) *Consumer Value: A framework for analysis and research*, London: Routledge.

Hudson, S. & Hudson, D. (2006) Branded entertainment: a new advertising technique or product placement in disguise. *Journal of Marketing Management*. **22**(5-6), 489-504.

Kotler, P., Keller, K.L., Brady, M., Goodman, M. & Hansen, T. (2016) *Marketing Management*. 3rd ed. Pearson.

Laaksonen, P. (1994). *Consumer Involvement: Concepts and research*. London: Routledge.

Marder, B., Joinson, A., Shankar, A. & Archer-Brown, C. (2012) Any user can be any self that they want so long as it is what they 'ought' to be: Exploring self-presentation in the presence of multiple audiences on social network sites. In Robinson, L. (Ed.) *Marketing Dynamism and Sustainability: Things change; things stay the same...*, Proceedings of the 2012 Academy of Marketing Science (AMS) Annual Conference, New Orleans, 621-626, Springer International Publishing.

Martin, D. & Schouten, J. (2014) Consumption-driven market emergence, *Journal of Consumer Research*, **40** (5), 855-870.

O'Cass, A. (2000) An assessment of consumers' product, purchase decision, advertising and consumption involvement in fashion clothing, *Journal of Economic Psychology*, **21** (5), 545–576.

Packard, V. (1957) *The Hidden Persuaders*, London; Penguin.

Reynolds, T.J. & Craddock, A.B. (1988) The application of the MECCAS model to the development and assessment of advertising strategy: A case study, *Journal of Advertising Research*, April/May, 43-54.

Rokeach, M. (1973) *The Nature of Human Values,* New York; Free Press

Rosengren, S. & Dahlen, M. (2015) Exploring advertising equity: how a brand's past advertising may affect consumer willingness to approach its future ads. *Journal of Advertising*, **44** (1).

Ryan, D. (2014) *Understanding Digital Marketing: Marketing strategies for engaging the digital generation*, London; Kogan Page.

Schwartz, S.H. (1992) Universals in the content and structure of values: theoretical advances and empirical tests in 20 countries, in M. Zanna (Ed.) *Advances in Experimental Social Psychology*, **25**, 1–65.

Solomon, M. R. (2003) *Conquering Consumerspace: Marketing strategies for a branded world*, New York, Amacom.

Taheri, B., Jafari, A. & O'Gorman, K. (2014). Keeping your audience: Presenting a visitor engagement scale, *Tourism Management*, **42**, 321-329.

Taheri, B., Farrington, T., Gori, K., Hogg, G. & O'Gorman, K. (2017). Escape, entitlement, and experience: Liminoid motivators within commercial hospitality, *International Journal of Contemporary Hospitality Management*. **29** (4), 1148-1166.

Turner, J. C., Hogg, M. A., Oakes, P. J., Reicher, S. D. & Wetherell, M. S. (1987). *Rediscovering the Social Group: A self-categorization theory*. Oxford: Blackwell.

Whiting, A. and Williams, D. (2013) Why people use social media: a uses and gratifications approach, *Qualitative Market Research: An International Journal*, **16** (4), 362-369.

Zaichowsky, J.L. (1985) Measuring the involvement construct in marketing, *Journal of Consumer Research*, **12** (December), 341-352.

4

5 Marketing Communications Strategy

Geraldine Bell

Like Alice in Wonderland, if you do not know where you want to get to, then you're likely to meander and have an adventure – fun perhaps but from a business perspective this would be a digression with a cost attached. Most enterprises operate in a world of the unknown and thus need explicit guidance to help reduce uncertainty as well as risk. Enterprises aim to promote innovation, facilitate decision making, and establish standards of quality to aid completion of work. In other words, enterprises want direction and help to focus towards a particular outcome. Along with controlling resources, strategy and planning do this.

Marketing strategy is broad in scope and looks at all the influencing factors, and considers both that which is known and that which is unforeseen – it asks the question 'why?' and seeks to understand competitive markets relative to "recognising and achieving an economic advantage that endures" (Wensley, 2008: 55). It therefore shapes and drives the plan towards the goal. The plan is the logical sequence of steps, or stages, towards a particular end. It asks the question: 'how?'. Together, marketing strategy and planning are the formalisation of an approach to marketing which provides the direction and says that goals and objectives form the basis of the marketing plan. As mentioned above, like Alice, the alternative is to digress and have a costly adventure! Therefore, where you are going needs to be articulated and communicated clearly to all to achieve success.

This chapter discusses how marketing communications strategy fits within marketing strategy. It also positions marketing strategy within the context of the firm's purpose and intent – its corporate strategy – and argues that there is no particular distinction between the parts of strategy as they are all interrelated and mutually dependent on each other. A structure for evaluating marketing communications strategy is given, and the chapter concludes with a suggested framework for marketing communications planning.

What is strategy?

Planning *or preparation* plus creating something "new and emerging which in effect becomes a reality" *or development* equates to strategy. Thus strategy, according to MacIntosh and Maclean (2015: 3) is:

> "…the craft of collectively rising to a significant challenge and accomplishing more than might be reasonably expected as a result of self-knowledge, resolve, foresight, creativity and genuine capabilities cultivated over the medium to long term."

What they are saying in effect, is that strategy is not just predetermined by means of crafting or preparing a plan to be acted upon by all, but that planning is only a part of what constitutes a successful outcome. Strategy also includes developing a platform which acts as a conduit for ideas, skills, creativity and fortitude, and that strategy acknowledges people's experience as well as key traits such as tenaciousness and willpower. One key point to capture from MacIntosh and Maclean (2015) is their focus on strategy being a process over time and that most importantly strategy includes people as *strategists*, and that this human element can make or break strategic direction, and consequently build value or destroy a firm's ability to make more value over time.

Take the case of the marketing director in the professional services sector – for example, in an accountancy firm where he has become 'frozen' in time. He is unmoving in his stance because he is convinced that his consumers would not use online search tools for information search (Frederiksen, 2013) so there is no reason to invest monies in this medium for marketing communication. That might be the case now but contexts change. And the environment for consumers searching for information on professional service firms can change too, so this manager needs to move with the times. This marketing director is frozen in time and is of the view that only at conferences and public speaking engagements will his consultancy business capture referrals which can be converted into business. Meanwhile, other more competitive professional service firms are innovating. They are using current marketing research data and more contemporary mediated communication platforms along with knowledgeable experts (agents) in order to capture new business. A marketing director as a strategist would take a more innovative approach. He would release monies and make decisions relative to trialling new means and methods of communication. And he would want to interpret and reflect in order to remain as innovative and competitive as possible. He is 'cultivating capabilities' in the sense that MacIntosh and MacLean describe above.

If strategy is a function of planning and creativity, and is a process which has the strategist at its core, then the heart of strategic planning has to be research – both marketing research and consumer insight, and this is captured for input at both corporate and marketing level – that is prior to any planning for marketing communications. As such it does shape marketing communications and this is illustrated as a chart in Figure 5.1. This illustration depicts the different levels of strategy and shows the context and strategic contribution made by marketing communications, and as such forms the structure for this chapter.

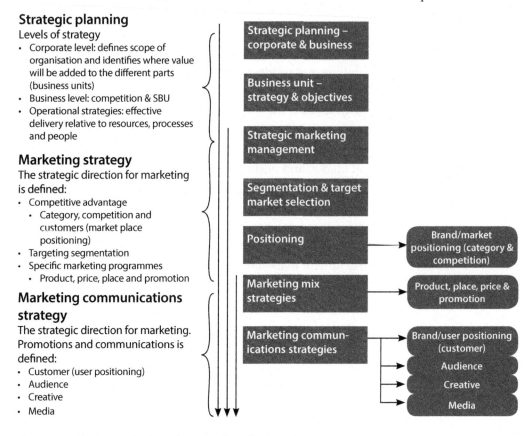

Figure 5.1: The strategic contribution of marketing communications.

Source: adapted from Baker (2014), Crawford et al. (1983), and Johnson et al. (2008).

Strategic marketing management

Whilst corporate level strategy is concerned with the broad picture of the overall purpose and intent of the firm, strategic marketing management takes the view that you are much more likely to see the marketing function as having both a firm-based position and an operational one, because it attends to market places as well as marketing behaviour (Baker, 2014). In other words, marketing strategy integrates at all levels and refers to the key choices made on "…products, markets, marketing activities, and marketing resources in the creation, communication and delivery of products that offer value to customers in exchanges with the organisation and thereby enable the organisation to achieve specific objectives" (Varadarajan, 2010: 128). Acknowledging that marketing strategy in a firm is inter-linked at various levels (for example, business and marketing management) leads us to surmise that the firm deals, at its business level, with issues around what, where and how it will compete and with what. Therefore marketing planning involves the marketing mix – promotion, product, price, place plus process, physical evidence and people.

Marketing strategy, as outlined by Varadarajan above, is, therefore, an explanation of capabilities and results in the process of developing a 'road map' which is modern business parlance for a route to deliver outcomes or planning. Figure 5.1 illustrates how the components of strategy interlink with each other. Note that there are two levels of positioning – one which is the major thrust of positioning within marketing strategy and that is the framework of segmentation, target market and positioning (STP). Positioning within marketing strategy concerns (i) the market place and (ii) the image in our minds (Baker, 2014: 284/5). The second positioning concept (image) underpins marketing communications and is about positioning an 'image' in the mind of consumers which is achieved through communication tactics in the main. This is explained more fully in the structure for marketing communications below, which sets out the strategic contribution of marketing communications.

A structure for understanding marketing communications strategy

Strategy within the context of marketing communications relates to how a brand is 'positioned', and how this positioning of the brand has a preferred way of communicating with consumers, customers and stakeholders. *Tactics* relate to the communications mix which is designed to deliver the positioning strategy.

Marketing communications *plans* relate to the promotional campaigns whose explicit intent is to convey and express the brand's marketing communication tactics and strategy (Fill, 2013). Therefore, marketing communications strategy is about the overarching theme and direction that the communications programme is going to take. How does the communications fit in with the rest of the company's strategic purpose and intent, and also its values, for instance? Also, for example, how will the communications flow in its delivery? Will it be a heavy burst of TV in August? It is also about identifying the target audience – who, what and how does this audience watch TV, for example – or are they on their holidays in August and less likely to watch TV? And what are we going to say? What are the key messages and themes if the target audience is young – how will they attend to the messages, and will it appeal to them in a compelling and memorable way? Underlining these questions are the key points of positioning an image (Baker, 2014) and the triad of audience, message and media (Dahlen et al., 2010). Taken together, a structure which Fill (2013) calls 'the four approaches', and which latterly he refers to as the '4 interpretations' (Fill & Turnbull, 2016:154), for planning a marketing communications strategy looks like this:

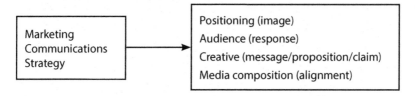

Figure 5.2: Four approaches to planning a marketing communications strategy.
Source: Adapted from Baker (2014), Dahlen et al. (2010) & Fill (2013)

Strategic planning for marketing communications

The strategic considerations for marketing communications, as outlined above in Figure 5.2, are therefore centred on how the target audience (TA) responds, the positioning both in the market place and in people's minds, the creative element by way of engagement with the audience, and in selecting and aligning media channels to suit. Each of these four modes of approach to planning for marketing communications is explained in turn.

■   The act of positioning and the position achieved

Positioning is a strategic activity which has two primary objectives according to Crawford et al. (1983):

1   To create a position for a product/service in the mind of the consumer. This position is made up of a bundle of consumer perceptions about the product/service relative to its competitors and many involve similarities and/or differences.

2   To set the tone for the marketing mix strategies that will communicate these perceptions and provide a common, unifying theme that is consistent across all marketing tools

A useful taxonomy for the positioning concept is put forward by Aaker and Shansby (1982) to explain and add clarity.

- ■ Competition (differentiation)
- ■ Segmentation (identifying features and associations which cause an overall impression)
- ■ Image (creating relative perceptions and images).

Marketing communications draws on positioning at marketing strategy level (the positioning in the market place) on the one hand, and within marketing communications itself (Baker, 2014), positioning is about developing an image relative to perceptions and other images. Reis and Trout (2001) call it a "battle for your mind" urging all business managers to create a position in the prospect's mind. They emphasize advertising as the vehicle to gain relative image positioning, but arguably (Crawford et al, 1983) there are other marketing elements to consider, such as price and distribution, that can assist in forming perceptions.

Thus, prior to marketing communications, the 'battle' for the consumer's mind is done by segmentation. Target market selection is the identification of distinct group(s) who display common characteristics and who recall and respond to messages in a similar way. This suggests a fixed view of the target segments but it shouldn't be thought so. Targeting must also recognise that a consumer's congruity (resemblance or similarity to …) judgement about a marketing communications image can be formed with both actual (who I think I am) and ideal self-images (who I'd like to be) and thus affect consumer evaluation (the closer the segment group resembles the communication, the more positive is the message evaluation). This is more of an emotional take on segmentation and draws on a manager's knowledge captured from consumer behavioural science, so that communications are shaped around how consumers perceive themselves, leading to a greater likelihood of engagement. Positioning in the mind needs to be relatively strong so that your brand is top-of-mind and recall is more than good and better than the competition.

Therefore, within the context of marketing communications strategy, positioning is centred on how you want to be positioned in the minds of your consumers, customers and stakeholders. It's about visibility and recognition (Fill, 2013) from a people or consumer perspective, and that segmenting the market and identifying target segments are the "prerequisites to successful positioning" (2013: 150). It is important at this point in this discussion to link to Chapter 6, *Brands and Brand Communications*, and make a connection between positioning and its relation to the triangulation of the three brand Ps of promise, positioning and performance, all of which shape and drive marketing communications. The promise in marketing communications is the propositional claim which is based on marketing research and the creative 'big idea' (often translated into a strapline) whereby the core positioning and creative idea for advertising, and the look and appeal of the message can be translated across all platforms. (See Chapter 8 *Creativity in Advertising and Promotion* for more discussion on this topic.)

How different audiences respond

Marketing is an outside-in approach to business, and the consumer audience is the 'outside'. Within the organisation, in marketing communications terms, there may be many different types of audience, both on the outside and the inside, and those related to the organisation through investment, community, policy, family and agents/consultants, as well as suppliers, buyers, and co-creators of production – especially employees. The following exercise give insight into communicating with employees at British Airways. Three distinct groupings become clear: consumers, trade associates and stakeholders – all of whom require different types of communications especially in terms of "what, where, when and how". According to Hughes & Fill (2008) they are:

- **Pull strategies** – to reach customers where the focus is on communicating directly with end-users (consumers and b2b)
- **Push strategies** – to reach members of the marketing channel where the aim is to move goods through these channels (trade and other intermediaries)
- **Profile strategies** – to reach all relevant stakeholders where the aim is to develop by building and growing long term relationships and to maintain a positive reputation

Pull and push marketing communications approaches to strategy are well known in the fundamentals of marketing knowledgem but not so the approach for profile where the core intention is to build reputation. This profile or stakeholder audience can influence the organisation and as such is more of an organisation-orientated activity and constitutes corporate communications. Corporate communications is the process that transforms corporate identity into corporate image and where public relations is the key element of the communications mix.

British Airways wants to rebuild its brand from the inside-out

BA has been dogged with problems over the last few years. It has suffered staff cuts, cabin crew strikes and other internal issues along with external factors beyond its control such as the global recession. As a result, staff morale is at an all-time low. In 2005, the then CEO Willie Walsh even 'culled' the internal communications department so BA had no chance of communicating with its 32,000 staff! Stories appeared in the British press highlighting negative accounts about staff seeing marketing campaigns for the first time on TV – no wonder they felt bruised! In 2011, BA reached a point where they had to do something, as they were a key sponsor of the London Olympics, and so they hired an agency whose brief was to communicate BA's commitment to the discipline of internal communications in the long-term and that this current effort was not a one-off project. BA said that they 'wanted to reignite the passion and belief in the brand starting with our internal colleagues' almost one year before the rebranding communications campaign began in earnest.

BA through trial and error now believes that having such a strong internal 'buy-in' from staff has allowed it to develop a consistent tone of voice throughout its marketing and communications. This has been important for the brand as London gets ready for the Olympics and with its 'My2012' campaign BA has managed to co-ordinate both its external sponsorship and mobilise its internal engagement at key moments in order to motivate colleagues to get ready to 'welcome the world to Britain'.

Source: Bashford (2011)

Review questions:

1. Identify and explain whether external sponsorship is a push, pull or profile strategy when communicating with an audience?

2. Identify and explain whether internal engagement is a push, pull or profile strategy when communicating with an audience.

■   Message – developing a creative platform

The 'creative' interpretation of marketing communications strategy involves a creative idea which acts as a conduit for orchestrating communications across different types of platforms such as advertising, brand-led communications or participatory interactions (Cox et al/IPA, 2011). This can be seen in more detail in Figure 5.3:

Type of creative platform	Form	Expression
No level of integration:	Unorganised. May use one media channel and/or only one piece of marketing activity, e.g. website.	Unconnected.
Advertising-led integration: Getting your publics to attend to your product/service/idea either through paid or non-paid media using one idea.	Recognisable as 'matching luggage', i.e. look and tone is the same but message may be different.	Creative expression can vary over time and by message but share a strong executional idea, e.g. a celebrity.
Brand idea-led orchestration: Staged development from being advertising-led as above to fulfilling brand resonance – loyalty, attachment, community, engagement. (Keller, 2001a)	Conceptual and centred around brand characteristics. Tangible – functional attributes; intangible more emotional ideas, abstract	Deeper engagement, consistent and based loosely around a shared brand-idea.
Participation–led orchestration: Interactive	Centred around participation and experience.	Narrative, conversations including all forms of chat.

Figure 5.3: New models of marketing effectiveness by integration and orchestration.
Source: Adapted from Cox et al./IPA, (2011:45-69) and Keller, (2001). See also Fill & Turnbull (2016: 344).

As Figure 5.3 points out, the four types of creative platform are expressed in different ways with differing levels of integration depending on communication and objectives as well as timeframes. What you do need is a core idea which can be transformed and explained across different types of media channels. Advertising is oftentimes referred to as the 'last remaining unfair competitive advantage' (IPA, 2007) and that is because it is one of the key variables that can make 'all other things unequal' through its influence in conveying a good idea. In the case of Honda's 'Power of Dreams' campaign which won a key industry award, the marketing director observed that the brand was gaining share in spite of not spending nearly the equivalent of other big brands (£20 million less than major competitors). The brand attributes this to the advertising campaign which delivered on brief – it reached those "three important parts of the human being: the heart, the head and the wallet" (2007: 2).

The creative idea is expressed through a promise which is more than a tag-line – it is a proposition which holds all the values associated with the brand and as pointed out above, the claim which makes it different. This customer-focused value proposition provides the rationale for the branding being efficient and effective (Kotler et al., 2016; Keller, 2013). And take note that the claim made by this proposition is underpinned with marketing research and has to be proven to the industry advertising ombudsman, known in the UK as The Advertising Standards Authority. This gives the advertising and brand legitimacy to orches-trate its promise either implicitly or explicitly. For example, L'Oreal's 'Because you're worth it' is implicitly stated and expresses the essence of the brand elicit-ing a response of 'yes, maybe I am worth it' or 'damn right I am' depending on your self-esteem on the day. This is because an advertising promise translated in whatever type, size and weight of campaign, sets customers' expectations about the kinds of interactions they are going to have with you. An explicit message of "You should've gone to Specsavers" has an underlying promise of you'll be in 'safe hands' because of our experts so you can trust us for spectacles! In summary, a promise is a single-minded proposition which 'hooks' in the consumer by commanding attention and if, as a proposition it is value-laden, expressed and positioned correctly, it will springboard your advertising and therefore garner success. More on creative appeals is discussed and explained in Chapter 8, *Creativity in Advertising and Promotion*, when we can ask this ques-tion: how does a simple proposition for Sony Television "Delivers colour like no other", lead to half-a-million rubber balls being let loose on the hills of San Francisco?

■ Media –composition and alignment

How media is composed by way of planning and selection involves an under-standing the following:

- *Frequency* of messages (how often do I need to talk to my audience to be effective);
- *Reach* (to whom am I going to talk and what is the likelihood of a response;
- The *media* channels identified for selection (the intermediate means and methods of enabling communications to flow either singularly or two-way)
- *Message* or the creative appeal which will compel the audience to do something such as respond (or just be aware of the brand and communication).

Taking all these factors into account enables a composition strategy where all the chosen media, loadings and timings are combined in such a way as to maximise effectiveness.

Scheduling

Scheduling includes planning for media selection. For example, a frequency strategy would be where the schedule may appear to be either intermittent or continuous. An *intermittent* decision looks like there are periods of intense activity (for example seasonal products like garden products and also travel) whereas a *continuous* stance (for example utility type products) is where there is a continuous pattern of messaging, thus gaining increased exposure. Exposure to the communications is key because it is likely that the consumer will move along the brand recognition continuum where the ultimate objective is for consumers to have a strong resonance with the brand so that the relationship is intense and so developed that it is a full relationship of loyalty, attachment, engagement and community.

It is also possible to plan a schedule which is both continuous and intermittent. For example, *pulsing* is where there is advertising which is continuous but also where there are moments of increased activity such as the holiday industry. In the UK, Thomas Cook advertisements appear regularly in the media under the guise of brand-led communications where 'awareness' of the brand is the key communications objective, but during January to April, there is intense activity in all media, but especially on TV and in digital media, sending out a message which is more advertising-led, with special offers for families for instance. The actual holiday bookings are for July and August but with all UK schools taking their annual holidays in the peak summer months, it therefore means that the company can advertise early for the holiday hotspots and increase revenue through deposits in the earlier part of the year which is unseasonal. This in turn leads to better planning for airline routes, airline seats and hotel beds along with resources to manage the service during the peak months.

Reach

Reach is important because it tells you the number of exposures your marketing communications is likely to reach given the size of the population that is likely to see your efforts during a given time period. Having identified the target audience, maximum coverage of that segment is the key objective of media and an important consideration is not to duplicate, which is an ineffective use of resource – that is, perhaps your money and effort are better used elsewhere on something more productive! Managers also need to be aware of the way media agents and consultants measure exposure. For example, the standard measure used by agencies is OTS (the number of people who have the opportunity to see) and not an absolute figure of those that do see it. And in digital media, the complexity of analysis and schedule design means there is a different way of looking at metrics (See Chapter 9, *Digital Marketing*, for more information on metrics).

Thus the media manager aims not to overload the audience so as to be ineffective but to load the audience enough to take effect. To achieve a balance in composition, credibility needs to be given to the content of the creative piece – the way the message is put together, how it will be conveyed and to whom will it appeal to most. And whilst it is important to understand that communications flow can be unidirectional or bidirectional, it is equally important to acknowledge the role of speed, for example in digital media, and the social interactions consumers make and enjoy, so that the brand may develop a lasting relationship which is more collaborative and thus deeper and more long term, in contrast to exchanges which are short and more likely to be forgotten sooner.

Planning marketing communications

Having understood the structured four ways or approaches – in other words the strategic means to designing a plan for marketing communications strategy (Positioning, Audience, the Creative, and Media composition), and where marketing communications fits into the role of marketing management within the context of the corporate firm, it leaves the practitioner to develop and design a plan for marketing communications. This aims to convey the context in which communications takes place, and the drivers that shape the design of the development process, for example the four approaches to planning for marketing communications, along with how the communications will be conveyed, and further explain the intention regarding interpretation of the marketing communications. This expression of a proposal or plan therefore provides cohesion amongst management and stakeholders in order to minimise errors and maximise efficiency and effectiveness.

A suggested illustration adapted from Fill's (2013:161) Marketing Communications Planning Framework (MCPF), and Smith's 1993 SOSTAC Planning System - Situation, Objectives, Strategies, Tactics, Action and Control (Smith & Zook, 2012:226) is visualised in Figure 5.4.

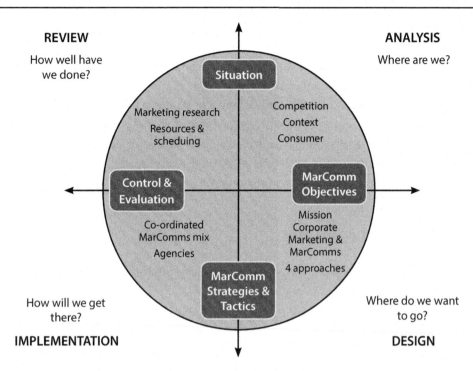

Figure 5.4: A marketing communications plan.

The illustration outlines the component parts of a marketing communications plan. The four corners of the diagram highlight the development phases so that the first phase is analysis, followed by design, implementation and finally control. The text outside of the ring tells us what the different phases are trying to achieve and the points of the circle depict the four structures of the marketing communications plan: the situation, marketing communication objectives, marketing communication strategies and tactics and, lastly, control and evaluation. The reference texts inside the ring list the sub-texts of the marketing communications plan. For example, you can clearly see where the four approaches of Positioning (image), Audience (response), Creative (message & appeals) and Media composition (alignment) are placed following Objectives and before Tactics Key points to note are that the marketing communications plan does not have any discrete parts as such. Most of the parts are inter-linked – some more so than others, but most are interdependent. For example, consumer insight and marketing research highlight the circular nature of marketing communications planning.

Summary

The marketing communications plan provides a framework for the direction of marketing communications and is a critical component of the communication process. If it is too abstract and deemed to be unclear, then it is highly likely that the subsequent activity will also be ineffective. Marketing communications also needs to be considered relative to other strategies because most levels of strategy are integrated and emerge through learning and experience, so that due reflection and review can feed into future planning cycles.

Recommended reading

American Marketing Association (AMA) see glossary of terms at https://www.ama.org/resources/Pages/Dictionary.aspx?dLetter=M

Caemmerer, B. (2009) The planning and implementation of integrated marketing communications. *Marketing Intelligence and Planning*, **27** (4), 524-538.

This journal article is an exemplar of application in the design, development and delivery of a real product launch by French car firm Renault as it redesigns its marketing communications programme in order to engage and communicate with the German market.

http://www.creativebloq.com/advertising/power-dreams-1113530,2
for more information and videos of Honda's Power of Dreams campaign.

References

Aaker, D. & Shansby, J.G. (1982) Positioning your product. *Business Horizons*. May/June

Baker, M.J. (2014) *Marketing Strategy and Management* (5ed). Palgrave McMillan.

Bashford, S. (2011) British Airways buildingbrand inside. *Marketing*. Haymarket Publications Ltd., http://www.marketingmagazine.co.uk/article/1081775/british-airways-building-brand-inside [accessed 20.06.2015]

Cohen, W. (2005) *The Marketing Plan*. John Wiley and Sons. NJ. USA.

Crawford, D.M., Urban, D.J. & Buzas, T.E. (1983) *Positioning: a conceptual review and taxonomy of alternatives*. Working Paper No 354. The University of Michigan.

Cox, K., Crowther, J., Hubbard, T. & Turner, D./IPA (2011) *New Models of Marketing Effectiveness: from integration to orchestration*. IPA/WARC, London. With thanks to Brian Coane, Chair IPA Scotland for access and usage.

Dahlen, M., Lange, F. & Smith, T. (2010) *Marketing Communications: a brand narrative approach*. John Wiley & Sons Ltd.

Fill, C. (2013) Marketing Communications: Brands, Experiences and Participation. Pearson.

Frederiksen, L. (2013) Online marketing for professional services: how to use online marketing to drive growth and profits. http://www.hingemarketing.com/blog/story/online-marketing-strategy-gone-wrong [accessed 16.6.2015]

Hughes, G. and Fill, C. (2008) *The Official CIM Coursebook : Marketing Communications*. The Chartered Institute of Marketing. Elsevier Ltd., Oxford. UK.

IPA (2007) *Judging Creative Ideas*. Institute of Practitioners in Advertising. http://www.ipa.co.uk/Document/judging-creative-ideas-best-practice-guide.

Johnson, G., Scholes, K. & Whittington, R. (2008) *Exploring Corporate Strategy*. 8/ed. Pearson Education.

Keller, K.L. (2001). Building customer-based brand equity: A blueprint for creating strong brands. *Marketing Management*. July/August: 15–19.

Keller, K.L. (2013). *Strategic Brand Management: Building, measuring and managing brand equity*. 4th ed. Pearson.

Kotler, P., Keller, K.L., Brady, M., Goodman, M. & Hansen, T. (2016) *Marketing Management*. 3rd ed. Pearson.

MacIntosh, R. & Maclean, D. (2015) *Strategic Management: Strategists at work*. Palgrave Macmillan.

Reis, A. and Trout, J. (2001) *The Battle for your mind – how to be seen and heard in the overcrowded marketplace*. McGraw-Hill. USA.

Smith, P.R. and Zook, Ze (2012) *Marketing Communications: integrating offline and online social media*. 5/ed. Kogan Page.

Varadarajan, R. (2010) Strategic marketing and marketing strategy: domain, definition, fundamental issues and foundational premises. *Journal of the Academy of Marketing Sciences* **38**, 119-140.

Wensley, R. (2008) The basics of marketing strategy, in Baker, M.J. and Hart, S.J. (eds) *The Marketing Handbook*. Elsevier Ltd., pp 55-80.

5

6 Branding and Brand Communications

Ross Curran and Babak Taheri

Brands

Brands have been used as an effective method of marking craftsmen's output from at least the Middle Ages. Brands are defined by the American Marketing Association (AMA) (1960) in their widely used definition as:

> "...a name, term, sign, symbol or design, or a combination of them, intended to identify the goods or services of one seller or group of sellers and to differentiate them from those of competitors."

Following the AMA definition, a brand consists of various elements, which could include combinations of names, signs, terms, symbols, URLs, and even employees (DuBois et al., 2014). In more recent times, developing technology and increasingly competitive markets have ensured that brands have evolved from basic marks of quality, to conduits of values, ideas, and sophisticated personalities (Aaker, 1997) allowing marketers new ways to connect with their customers, and stand out from the competition. It should be noted that products and brands are not necessarily the same thing. While products can refer to anything that may satisfy needs or wants, and can include things such as laptops, banking services, or charitable assistance; a brand is the addition to the product of elements that make it stand out from competition, or differentiate it. For example, an Apple or Dell logo conjure up very different perceptions of the laptop product, its typical users, and the tasks it can be used for. Likewise, although one type of car manufacturer (e.g., Volvo) is functionally very similar to another (e.g., Ford), the brand, or logo adorning it. influences the perceptions consumers subsequently hold (often Volvo is strongly associated with safety).

Consequently, branding affects consumers' perceptions of a product or service and allows them to associate products with certain attributes (e.g., trust, reliability, safety and fun).

Fill (2013) suggests successful brands incorporate three elements: promises, positioning and performance. Brands can therefore be seen as promises, underpinning their perceived positioning by stakeholders and resulting expectations. Where these promises and expectations converge, brand performances are the result. Figure 6.1 below illustrates this process.

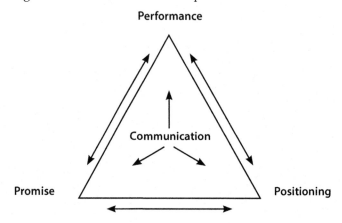

Figure 6.1: 3 Brand Ps

As Figure 6.1 shows, communication is critical as it is shaped and driven by the interaction of the three brand Ps. Communication variously conveys the brand promise, and accurately positions the brand, whilst encouraging its successful performance.

Brands can be manufacturer, or own-label brands. *Manufacturer brands* are developed and controlled by the producer of the product or provider of the service, whereas *own-label brands* (also called distributer/retailer brands) are developed and controlled by distributors. For example, Coca-Cola is a manufacturer brand, where the manufacturer retains responsibility and control over marketing. Large supermarkets may wish to enhance their retail revenue by developing an own-label cola drink, or in other words, an own-label brand. While generally these brands are priced as a cheaper alternative for consumers, they can be positioned as high quality, luxuries, or indeed healthier alternatives (such as Marks & Spencer's *Count on Us* range). To combat the rise of own-label brands, so called *fighter brands* are emerging. Fighter brands are additional manufacturer brands developed specifically to compete with own-label or competing brands, often in the form of a lower price alternative to the primary manufacturer brand, but also as a defensive competitive strategy. In the airline industry for example, to combat increasing competition from low-cost airlines such as Ryanair, British Airways ultimately unsuccessfully, launched its own low-cost airline under the 'Go' brand. Traditionally branding has focused on external stakeholders (Aurand et al., 2005), but growing evidence suggests brands have significant internal influence, and affect employees of their host organisation (Schlager et al., 2011). There are also *licensed brands* (i.e., a brand produced by a company under authorisation from the owner for a fee) and *pure play* brands (i.e., a brand which can offer manufacturer and own-label brands).

Table 6.1: Benefits attributable to brands

Benefit	Description	Example
Brand extensions	Strong core brand allows for subsequent brand extensions to retain positive associations towards the core offering.	Coca-Cola (core brand) and Diet Coke, Cherry Coke, Coke Lemon as brand extensions.
Trust	Products or services functionally on an equal footing, with high economic cost to the consumer, render trust important to the purchase decision. Trust is particularly important in online transactions (Grabner-Kraeuter 2002).	Coca-Cola's Dasani bottled water betrayed consumer trust when questions were raised about its source.
Quality guarantee	Aids consumer purchase decisions by indicating the level of quality the consumer should expect.	BMW cars are generally expected by consumers to be better quality than Ford, or Vauxhall, however this assertion is often solely based upon the brand.
Consumer perceptions	Successful brands can yield a positive influence on consumer perceptions through the perceptions the consumer gains from the brand.	Sports Direct owns several previously independent brand names such as Slazenger, Dunlop and Donnay. Despite changes in ownership, the brands continue to generate strong sales.
Barrier to competition	Although newly entering brands may be functionally superior to established brands, a strong brand with positive perceptions render it difficult for new brands to compete.	Virgin's attempts to take on Coca-Cola and Pepsi and launch its own Virgin Cola product failed due to the prevailing strength of the established brands.
Higher profits	Market-leading brands can command a higher price than weaker ones. Furthermore, they often benefit from established supply and sales networks, thus accruing economies of scale.	Kellogg's can command a price premium, due to the perceived added-value it offers consumers.
Increased company value	Strong brands can become valuable assets, and can add significantly to the value of a company.	Apple and Google's brands add significant financial value to such companies.

Developing and maintaining strong brands is time-consuming, costly, and requires high levels of commitment from organisations (Aaker, 2000). However, if cultivated properly, the benefits to an organisation can be enormous and not just limited to increased financial return. Table 6.1 illustrates the potential benefits brands can bring organisations.

As Table 6.1 shows, the benefits of strong brands are vast (Keller, 2002). Ultimately, as well as illustrating the primary offering of an organisation, they influence purchase decisions, reduce perceptions of risk, elicit trust, and promise a certain level of quality (De-Chernatony and Dall'Olmo Riley, 1998).

Brand strategies used by organisations and the planning process involved are now considered.

Exercise

Examine the packaging of your favourite branded product. What messages do you think the marketers are trying to convey? Are there several? Is there one? Who do you think the messages are intended for? In your opinion, are they effective? Do you think you are the type of person who is 'meant' to buy that brand?

Branding strategies and planning

Developing successful brands requires careful planning and consideration, resulting in the implementation of brand strategies. To be successful, organisations must be fully committed to investing in their brands over the long-term. The initial decision concerning brand strategy is in regard to whether to develop a brand at all. Some specialist, and industrial, products remain unbranded, although this is uncommon, as it can avoid burdening organisations with costly branding processes, nevertheless, this is increasingly rare and most products are branded to some extent. Second, an organisation must decide on the most suitable overarching brand strategy. The choice of brand strategy will be guided by the current situation, and aims, of an organisation. Several brand strategy options applicable to organisations marketing a *single brand* are described in Table 6.2.

Brand strategy	Use	Example
Line extension	One brand name is used for all new product introductions.	Ben & Jerry's use this strategy across their range of ice-cream flavours.
Brand extension	Where current brands are applied to products in different categories.	Ferrari, famous for manufacturing cars, uses this strategy in its clothing range.
Multi-brands	When various brands are used for various products and ranges.	Consumer goods company Unilever deploy this strategy amongst their diverse brand catalogue which includes male shower-gel Lynx, and Hellman's Mayonnaise.

Table 6.*2:* Basic brand strategies for single brand cases

Line extensions, as described in Table 6.2, are frequently used by marketers, and can aid an organisation's competitive position in several ways; through occupation of shelf-space that would otherwise be used by competitors, targeting a niche subgroup of consumers more effectively, and encouraging a dyadic flow of positive feeling between the new brand extension and its parent brand, potentially boosting sales across the brand portfolio (Reddy et al., 1994). Line extensions can also have negative impacts such as dilution of meaning in the minds of consumers regarding the attributes of a brand. Furthermore, there is the possibility that a brand extension, rather than winning market share from competition, takes sales away from the parent brand, negatively affecting an organisation's bottom line. Finally, unsuccessful brand extensions can have negative impacts upon the parent brand, for example, if a new brand extension become embroiled in controversy or was deemed to be of unacceptable quality, negative perceptions could adversely impact the parent brand's sales.

Brand extensions as described in Table 6.2 allow organisations to introduce new products or services at reduced risk, as they can 'piggy-back' upon the positive attitudes towards the original brand. Another advantage is the reduced cost associated with this approach as opposed to launching an entirely new and untested brand. Conversely, there are significant risks to the parent brand of brand extensions. First, if unsuccessful, the extended brand may damage the standing of its parent. Second, where brand extension is confusingly applied to products or services entirely unconnected to the parent brand, the meaning and essence conveyed by the parent brand can be diluted. Organisations using this strategy have to ensure the same core values of the brand are received by consumers across the portfolio, consequently, *corporate branding* is increasingly deployed (Knox & Bickerton, 2003). Here, one company brand pervades the range of products/services it offers. Corporate branding also allows for savings in advertising and branding costs, while mitigating the risk of new product/

service launches. However, when damaged, it can be difficult to change. Furthermore, corporate branding is less useful at tapping niche sub-groups of the market and tends to be constrained to holding only a broad appeal (Knox & Bickerton 2003). For example, Sony used corporate branding across both its range of televisions and its range of MP3 players.

Multi-branding, as noted in Table 6.2, allows organisations to have several distinct, strong, branded product ranges in various markets. Multi-branding is often used in conjunction with brand extensions and can reduce overall risk to an organisation should one of its brands gain a negative reputation, and allow for more complex targeting of market segments. However, it can be very costly and prevents products from accruing cross-brand benefits.

Dual branding strategies involve organisations incorporating more than one brand into their product/service. Typically, one of three dual branding strategies are deployed, these are described in Figure 6.2.

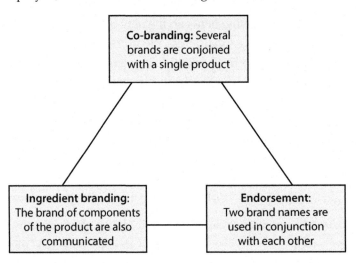

Figure 6.2: Multiple-brand strategies

Figure 6.2 describes co-branding, ingredient, and endorsement brand strategies. *Co-branding* pertains to the incorporation of two or more brands together in the marketing of a product, for mutual benefit. For example, All Nippon Airways (ANA) has announced plans incorporating the Star Wars brand into the livery of one of its aircraft (ANA, 2015). This benefits both parties, providing publicity for an upcoming Star Wars film while also supplementing the image of ANA as a modern, dynamic, quirky airline. Like most branding strategies, co-branding can result in negative as well as positive perceptions of one brand affecting the other, however prevailing research suggests stronger support of a net beneficial effect (Washburn et al., 2000).

With *ingredient* branding, airlines also provide a good example. By maintaining, and often explicating strongly their aircraft manufacturer brands, (e.g. through the Dreamliner moniker) ANA benefits from the notions of modernity and comfort the brand exudes. Similarly British Airways and Air France benefitted from the notions of style and sophistication inherent in the Concord brand. Consider boarding an aircraft for a respected airline that was embellished with Ilyushin Il-62 (a Soviet-made passenger jetliner still used by many airlines today), perhaps this would elicit feelings of apprehension, hence, ingredient branding can yield either positive or negative effects (Desai and Keller 2002).

Finally *endorsement* branding, whereby an organisation applies two brands to a product, straddles the area between the concepts of multi-branding and brand extensions (Saunders & Guoqun, 1997). For example, car manufacturers such as Volkswagen use endorsement branding when marketing their Golf range. The Golf brand conveys particular values and attitudes that appeal to certain market segments. The Golf brand benefits from the perceptions of quality and style traditionally associated with Volkswagen, while allowing Volkswagen to target various markets via other models and brands. For example, Volkswagen's coupe, the Scirocco, conveys different messages towards a different market segment than Volkswagen's MPV, the Touran. Nevertheless, both of these brands benefit from the overall Volkswagen brand suggestive of quality and style.

The brand strategies presented above are not intended to be exhaustive, but instead broadly representative of the most common brand strategies being applied. What is important to understand, is the frequency with which brand strategies are variously combined and tailored by organisations to best suit their needs. Ultimately, implementing the perfect brand strategy is a balancing act, there will always be benefits and drawbacks and the need to continually adapt a strategy to an increasingly cynical marketplace.

Exercise

Consider a car manufacturer, a sports clothing brand, and your local supermarket. What brand strategies do companies in these different sectors apply? Are different strategies appropriate for different sectors?

Brand image

Evolving from the field of psychology, and predicated upon a growing acceptance that products hold important existential as well as physical value to consumers (Gardner & Levy, 1955), brand image has emerged as an essential marketing concept, and an important contributor to brand equity. Brand image can be viewed as a multi-dimensional concept, a summation of consumer perceptions towards a brand derived from their personally held associations (Hsieh et al., 2004). In other words, brand image is about consumers not only buying a physical product, but also purchasing the brand image associated with it. These associations can be formed in numerous ways, both through traditional marketer-controlled techniques (e.g., advertising, promotions, price, product design) as well as via less conventional methods including:

- Direct experience and interaction with the brand
- Information conveyed by media sources
- Personal inferences made by individuals
- Associations between brands and particular people, places or events.

To generate a successful brand image, marketers have to be aware of the influence of these information sources, and control them where possible. Consider the brand image of the oil giant BP. BP invest large sums into marketing activity, which has generally allowed BP to avoid having a negative brand image. However, the Deepwater Horizon accident of 2010 caused significant harm to the brand image of BP; this incident was generally out of their control and unforeseen. Marketers must try and plan in advance for the worst, to devise strategies for dealing with brand image damaging events. Similarly, many companies have taken to court and sued individuals or media organisations for making public aspersions regarding a company, consequently acting as an effective deterrent to subsequent action.

■ Benefits of brand image

Successful brand image should be distinctive, positive in nature, and immediately recognisable. Brand image has been shown to positively affect consumer purchase decisions (Dolich, 1969), and to capitalise upon the growing value of the symbolic, rather than functional value of products (Levy, 1959). Ultimately, creating and projecting a successful brand image increases the likelihood of consumers buying into a brand (Hsieh, 2002; O'Cass & Grace, 2004). Brand image can manifest through three types of benefit: functional, emotional, and rational.

- *Functional* benefits communicate to the consumer the benefits of using one brand over another, for example, whether one brand of washing powder cleans clothes more effectively, at lower temperatures, and makes them smell fresher for longer.

- *Emotional* benefits reflect how the brand image makes the consumer feel when consuming a product, for example purchasing Body Shop products may, on an emotional level allow consumers to identify with environmental and ethical causes, consequently satisfying them.

- Finally, *rational* benefits of brand image concern the consumer's assessment of the difference between one brand and its competition.

Brand attributes are a holistic, all-encompassing evaluation consumers have of a brand. Ultimately, brand image is becoming increasingly important, an idea reinforced by Levy (1959) who has previously stated:

"If the manufacturer understands that he is selling symbols as well as goods, he can view his product more completely." (p. 124)

Levy's foretelling of the importance of brand image, and the symbolic rather than the functional elements of products has become increasingly relevant.

Exercise

Consider the low-cost airline Ryanair. Explore the company's adverts on YouTube; examine its website; and use the internet to understand the flying experience its passengers receive. Now describe the brand image of Ryanair. Is it consistent? Is it clear? Is it distinctive? Also consider how the airline can use non-traditional marketing methods to protect and project its brand image further.

Brand equity

The proliferation of the brand equity concept has developed in tandem with an increasing appreciation of the power brands hold (Keller, 2002). Nevertheless, despite general acceptance of the benefits, e.g. increased stock prices (Simon & Sullivan, 1993), improved long term cash flow (Srivastava & Shocker, 1991), and the ability to command premium prices (Keller, 1993), there is debate as to what brand equity is, and crucially, how best to measure it.

Understanding brand equity's interaction with different stages of the marketing process emphasises both the concept's importance, as well as the cyclical nature of marketing. Figure 6.3 below conveys the influence brand equity holds. Initial marketing activity (product development, pricing, distribution decisions, and promotional activity) along with the implementation of appropriate brand strategies contribute towards brand equity (Yoo et al., 2000). The development of brand equity consequently increases value for both the organisation and the customer, value that then feeds back to the marketing activity stage and influences the process all over again, while generating sustainable competitive advantage (Bharadwaj et al., 1993). The process can be described as cyclical, as marketing managers should constantly be seeking to elevate, and subsequently benefit from enhancing the value of brand equity.

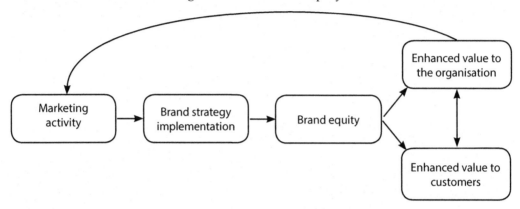

Figure 6.3: Marketing process. Adapted from Yoo et al. (2000)

Brand equity has been generally defined as "…the marketing effects uniquely attributable to the brand" (Keller, 1993: 1). Farquhar (1989) suggested the financial added-value to a product constituted brand equity, whereas Swait et al. (1993) consider brand equity to be the internal valuation consumers hold of a brand competing against other brands, compared to a non-competitive market. Feldwick (1996) offers an attempt at a universal definition of brand equity whereby it is a construct of brand value (evaluated through accounts and financial monitoring), brand strength (evaluated through consumer-brand attachment), and brand description (attitudes held by customers towards a brand). Subsequently, other researchers have variously suggested further elements, and definitional debates continue. Nevertheless, there is a general consensus of the benefits amid continuing attempts to develop it. Farquhar (1989) identified three approaches to generating, and increasing brand equity; to build, buy, or borrow it. These are explained in Table 6.3.

As Table 6.3 shows, there are several different approaches to acquiring brand equity. The most appropriate depends on the competitive environment, the strengths and abilities of the organisation, and the target customer base. Different markets will be more receptive to different techniques. Once organisations have established brand equity, to realise its value and derive the financial benefits it brings requires some form of measurement.

Strategy	Description	Example
Building brand equity	Building a strong brand through developing positive brand evaluations and well-received brand attitudes, whilst ensuring the projection of a strong brand image.	Apple have steadily enhanced their brand equity over a long period of time, honing and adjusting their brand to enhance reception, furthermore, they have been consistent in the image they project.
Buying brand equity	Acquiring a company, and gaining ownership of its products and brands can also develop brand equity. Obtaining licenses to incorporate other brands into a product is a variation of this approach.	Sports Direct purchased several brands such as Donnay and Karrimor, acquiring their brand equity. Walt Disney license many of their characters to external companies to produce products.
Borrowing brand equity	Brand extensions can allow products to 'borrow' the positive attributes consumers hold towards a brand when applied to a new product.	Mars use this approach across their range, for example, applying the Mars logo to their ice-cream range, as well as the core Mars bar product.

Table 6.3: Obtaining brand equity: Adapted from Farquhar (1989).

6

■ Measuring brand equity

The need to accurately measure brand equity has become increasingly impor-tant with growing awareness of the added-value derived through its posses-sion. Academia has lagged behind industry in this area, driven by desire to attain the benefits of brand equity, industry has focused on placing a monetary value on brands, often calculated from a financially biased perspective, leading to brands commonly being assessed on financial, rather than overall marketing value (Pappu et al., 2005). One example of this can be seen through the compila-tion of lists conveying brand value. Forbes compile their own brand value list; at the time of writing the top ten valuable brands are described as.

Global rank	Brand	Brand Value ($bil)
1	Apple	124.2
2	Microsoft	63.0
3	Google	56.6
4	Coca-Cola	56.1
5	IBM	47.9
6	McDonald's	39.9
7	General Electric	37.1
8	Samsung	35.0
9	Toyota	31.3
10	Louis Vuitton	29.9

Table 6.4: Valuable brands top ten. Source: (Forbes, 2015)

Table 6.4 presents the ten highest valued brands according to Forbes. Such lists can be influential to prospective shareholders, owners, and competitors, however, they represent the product of industry, where the emphasis invariably rests on the bottom line. Academic attempts have been advanced through the introduction of the five brand equity areas requiring measurement. These are described by Aaker (1996) as measures of loyalty, quality and leadership, brand associations, and measures of differentiation, brand awareness, and market behaviour measures. Aaker (1996) suggests that to be effective, brand equity measures should meet several criteria. They first should represent an accurate conceptualisation of the concept, evaluating it in its entirety. Additionally, measures of brand equity should be credible in the eyes of practitioners, ultimately resulting in valuable, actionable information. Furthermore, effective measurement of brand equity should be responsive, non-static, and thus a true reflection of changes in the marketplace. Finally, effective measures should have general applicability across an organisation's brand portfolio, consequently generating scope for useful comparisons between brands, thus allowing for strategic decisions to be made. Ultimately, owing to the multi-dimensionality of the concept, and influence of context upon it, the development of very complex, universal measures of brand equity is a Sisyphean cause (Barwise, 1993). Nevertheless, attempts continue with arguable rates of success.

Finally, Keller (2014) identifies four implications of marketing programs to build, measure, and manage brand equity, including:

- Identifying and developing brand plans (i.e., a clear understanding of what the brand is to represent and how it would be positioned with respect to competitors);
- Designing and implementing brand marketing programs (i.e., the marketing activities and supporting marketing programs and the way the brand is integrated into them e.g., pricing strategy and product strategy); also other associations indirectly transferred to the brand as a result of linking it to some other entity (e.g., country of origin);
- Measuring and interpreting brand performance (i.e., to manage brands profitably, managers should successfully design and implement a brand equity measurement system); and finally
- Growing and sustaining brand equity (i.e., understanding how branding strategies should reflect corporate concerns and be adjusted, if at all, over time or over geographical boundaries or multiple market segments).

Exercise

Consider the Forbes list of global brands. Are you surprised by any of the brands' position? Use examples to describe the benefits those organisations can accrue through their strong brand equity.

Brand positioning and repositioning

Having developed an effective, attractive brand, implemented it effectively with an appropriate strategy and brand image to derive the benefits of brand equity, organisations will, in order to maximise the likelihood of success, position their brands. Furthermore, in response to competition, organisations successful over the long-term will be required to engage in repositioning activities on an ongoing basis.

■ Brand positioning

Brand positioning is concerned with the transmission of information to consumers and stakeholders, influencing how they perceive a brand in relation to other competitors, and the resulting position they believe the brand holds in the market. In essence, brand positioning has little to do with the physical attributes of the product, but rather the perceptions held within the mind of the consumer regarding that product (Hassan & Craft, 2012). The challenge for marketers then, is to ensure consumers position the brand favourably. The brand positioning concept is not restricted to branded products, but can equally apply to services, organisations as a whole (private, public and third sector), as well as destinations. However, it should be noted that the added complexity of managing multiple stakeholders renders organisational and destination positioning more complicated. For example, consider the stakeholders (e.g. local population and businesses, politicians, foreign owned tourism companies .) involved in positioning a destination brand; clearly then, the complexity involved in brand positioning is to some extent dependent upon the context in which it occurs.

Ultimately, the success of positioning activity is determined by the results of market segmentation and target marketing. Further, positioning activity should be commensurate with an organisations wider promotional objectives.

■ How it works

There is no generalizable, tick-box approach to successfully positioning a brand, nevertheless, as well as the experience and knowledge of the strategists involved, there are several considerations as well as useful tools that could be used to inform brand positioning decisions.

Marketers must evaluate the positioning undertaken by the competition, possibly necessitating consumer research. Based on this evaluation, marketers must next develop an actionable and realistic plan to position their brand. Finally, marketers must implement a positioning plan, before committing to on-going monitoring of consumer perceptions (Fill, 2013). A foundation stage of the process is evaluating competition, and creating a perceptual map represents a useful way to achieve this. A perceptual map conveys how consumers view the attributes of a brand in relation to its competition (Kim & Agrusa, 2005). For example, Figure 6.4 below illustrates possible perceptual map attributes in the squash racket market.

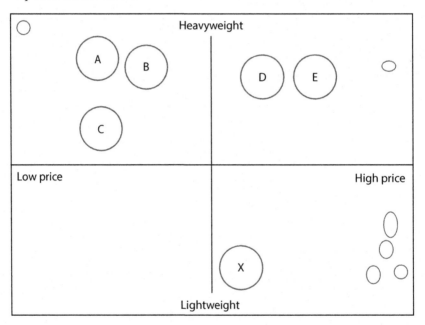

Figure 6.4: Perceptual map for a squash racket

The perceptual map above positions various products (in this case squash rackets) based upon consumer perceptions of selected attributes (in this case the weight and price of the racket). Based on Figure 6.4, we can see that products A, B and C are all positioned in the heavyweight, low price quadrant of the map. These three products are clustered in quite a crowded quadrant, thus, we can see that there is quite strong competition in this area. The high price, lightweight area is also quite crowded, consequently, marketers could consider that product X is located in an area of potential success. Note that product E is in a risky position, it offers a similar weight racket for a higher price than product

D, consequently, it may be a likely candidate for repositioning. Creating perceptual maps provides marketers with valuable insight into the minds of their prospective consumers, allowing them to adjust aspects of brands to enhance perceptions as necessary. Furthermore, mapping allows marketers to distinguish unique and shared attributes of their brand with the competition. Finally, it can inform marketers of the most suitable positioning strategy to employ (Fill, 2013).

■ Positioning strategies

Positioning a brand in an optimum location within the consumer's mind, or perceptual map, is ultimately a reflection of the brand itself, its core values, and its core meaning. In order to utilise brand positioning, marketers must select and deploy the most appropriate strategy, conscious of the influence marketing strategy holds over consumer perceptions, for example, emphasising low price will affect consumer perceptions related to price. Table 6.5 offers description of some brand positioning strategies.

Strategy	Description	Example
Price	Easily influenced by marketers. A low pricing strategy ensures customers are likely to perceive brands as lower quality, higher price generally leads to high quality perceptions. Price is not always appropriate where quality is not accurately reflected.	Aldi and Lidl position themselves as low-cost alternatives to established supermarkets. Waitrose and Marks & Spencer Food use price to indicate perceived quality. Morrison's attribute recent poor performance to holding neither a low nor high price position.
Product	Commonly used approach whereby marketers exert complete control. Product/service benefits are emphasised in relation to competitors' offerings.	The automotive industry uses this strategy, Alfa-Romeo emphasise their Italian roots, and the design and style of their cars; Volvo emphasise safety benefits.
Use	Marketers indicate to consumers when to use a brand, consumers then associate the brand with particular activities, times, events, etc.	Lucozade attempt to position their brand through use, striving to make their drink synonymous with sport and fitness.
Class dissociation	Used in crowded markets, brands position themselves by proclaiming to be different from competitors, establishing distinction messages.	In Japan, Happoshu is a variety of low-malt, low-priced beer. Consequently, brewers of high malt, traditional beer emphasise this purported authenticity, and superiority to dissociate themselves from lower malt content varieties.

6

User	Through communicating the 'typical' users of a brand, marketers can create a brand consumers aspire to associate with.	Popular perfume adverts generally include attractive models of an age similar to the target market and convey ideals of elegance, class and sophistication that consumers will be sympathetic to.
Competitor	Considered high risk, directly positioning a brand against a competitor is a combative strategy.	Rarely used, political parties frequently challenge competitor parties openly and publicly.
Heritage	Imbuing brands with heritage can have powerful results. It can enhance trust and contribute prestige to a brand, it is also difficult to imitate.	Charity brands such as the Scouts or Marie Curie possess a strong heritage, which can increase donor trust and enhance volunteer satisfaction (Curran et al., 2016).
Benefit	Marketers communicate the main advantages of their brand over competitors.	Washing powder brands frequently use benefit branding, emphasising how much whiter their product makes clothes compared to others.

Table 6.5: Brand positioning strategies

The strategies presented in Table 6.5, represent merely a sample of approaches marketers can use to position a brand. Inevitably, marketers will use aspects of some strategies, combined with elements of others, resulting in the application of complex strategies, targeting nuanced segments of the market. Finally, Keller (2014) suggests four ways of identifying and establishing brand positioning:

1 Basic concepts (who the target is; who the main competitors are; how the brand is similar to these competitors; how the brand is different from them),

2 Target market (i.e., market segmentation),

3 Nature of competition (i.e., competitive analysis)

4 Points-of-parity (PoP) (i.e., attributes or benefits that consumers strongly associate with a brand, positively evaluate, and believe) and points-of-difference (PoD) (i.e., attributes shared with other brands; what are the conditions your brand must have?).

■   Repositioning

Critical to maintaining the long-term success of a brand, and ensuring it remains relevant to constantly changing consumer tastes, attitudes, and concerns, while continuing to be superior in some sense to competition, is the process of repositioning (Simms & Trott, 2007). In many cases, through constantly reinforcing images and brand benefits, repositioning can be unnecessary. Nevertheless, more so than ever before, technology is rendering markets increasingly fluid and dynamic, often necessitating repositioning to maintain strong market positions. However the process is often expensive and fraught with danger. For example, UK postal service Royal Mail was facing increasing competition from private delivery firms, and offering services considered to be much extended and removed from the organisation's original offerings. Consequently, to maintain a strong position in the market, Royal Mail was rebranded and positioned as 'Consignia', a supposedly more modern, dynamic, efficient organisation. The repositioning, despite being subjected to substantial prior market research, was a costly failure, and ultimately the name reverted back to Royal Mail. Repositioning can also apply to destination brands, for example the area of Govan in Glasgow has a reputation of social deprivation, however, through the costly and time-consuming process of establishing several cultural tourist offerings in tandem with development of the area's reputation and economy, there are increasing numbers of visitors (Butler et al., 2013). Ultimately, repositioning is vital to maintain market dominance, yet fraught with danger. Even armed with sophisticated market research analysis, repositioning often ends badly, it is costly, time-consuming, and high risk.

Exercise

Create perceptual brand maps for the following markets: Toothpaste, supermarkets, and laptop computers.

Conclusions

Now, more than ever before, marketing is complex, sophisticated, and nuanced. Through rapid developments in technology, marketers can gather information and target segments of markets that were previously undistinguished. Furthermore, globalisation and logistical interconnectedness have increased overall market size. To realise the opportunities this presents, developing the correct brand, delivered using appropriate and effective strategies is increasingly important. This evolution has not been one sided however; consumers too, are increasingly benefitting from the technology, and the information revolution to inform their consumption decisions within ever more crowded markets. As an outcome of these developments, brand equity has risen to prominence in determining the overall value and success of organisations. Building it is an immense challenge, but truly successful organisations understand the importance of maintaining it through constant evaluation.

Who to read

The field of marketing boasts a sophisticated and well-established literature. De-Chernatony and Dall'Olmo Riley (1998) offer excellent insight of the evolution of brands in their paper, while the work of Kevin Lane Keller (2002) offers readers a complex understanding of a wealth of marketing issues.

Exemplar paper

Dobni, D., & Zinkhan, G. M. (1990). In search of brand image: A foundation analysis. *Advances in consumer research*, **17**(1), 110-119.

> This paper explores the concept of brand image. Through analysis of a wealth of prior, conflicting brand image research, the authors hightlight the complexity, and malleability of the concept and attempt to provide clarity. As an outcome, the paper presents what its authors see as the main elements of brand image.

References

Aaker, D. (2000) *Building Strong Brands,* New York: Simon and Schuster.

Aaker, D. A. (1996) Measuring brand equity across products and markets, *California Management Review,* **38**(3), 103.

Aaker, J. L. (1997) Dimensions of brand personality, *Journal of Marketing Research*, **34**(3), 347-356.

ANA (2015) ANA Unveils Star Wars R2-D2 Livery for the 787-9 Dreamliner Aircrast The First and Only Passenger Aircraft to Feature a Star Wars Character, http://www.ana.co.jp/eng/aboutana/press/2015/150416.html [Accessed 30/04 2015].

American Marketing Association (AMA). (1960) *Marketing Definitions: A glossary of marketing terms,* Chicago IL: AMA.

Aurand, T. W., Gorchels, L. & Bishop, T. R. (2005) Human resource management's role in internal branding: an opportunity for cross-functional brand message synergy, *Journal of Product & Brand Management,* **14**(3), 163-169.

Barwise, P. (1993) Brand equity: snark or boojum?, *International Journal of Research in Marketing,* **10**(1), 93-104.

Bharadwaj, S. G., Varadarajan, P. R. & Fahy, J. (1993) Sustainable competitive advantage in service industries: a conceptual model and research propositions, *The Journal of Marketing,* **57**, 83-99.

Butler, R., Curran, R. & O'Gorman, K. D. (2013) Pro-poor tourism in a First World urban setting: Case study of Glasgow Govan, *International Journal of Tourism Research,* **15**(5), 443-457.

Curran, R., Taheri, B., MacIntosh, R. & O'Gorman, K. (2016) Nonprofit brand heritage its ability to influence volunteer retention, engagement, and satisfaction. *Nonprofit and Voluntary Sector Quarterly*, **45**(6), 1234 –1257, doi:10.1177/0899764016633532.

De-Chernatony, L. & Dall'Olmo Riley, F. (1998) Defining a 'brand': Beyond the literature with experts' interpretations, *Journal of Marketing Management*, **14**(5), 417-443.

Desai, K. K. & Keller, K. L. (2002) The effects of ingredient branding strategies on host brand extendibility, *Journal of Marketing*, **66**(1), 73-93.

Dolich, I. J. (1969) Congruence relationships between self images and product brands, *Journal of Marketing Research*, **6**(1), 80-84.

DuBois Gelb, B. & Rangarajan, D. (2014) Employee contributions to brand equity, *California Management Review*, **56**(2), 95-112.

Farquhar, P. H. (1989) Managing brand equity, *Marketing Research*, **1**(3), 24-33.

Feldwick, P. (1996) What is brand equity anyway, and how do you measure it?, *Journal of the Market Research Society*, **38**(2), 85-104.

Fill, C. (2013) *Marketing Communications: Brands, experiences and participation*, Pearson Higher Ed.

Forbes (2015) The World's Most Valuable Brands, available: https://www.forbes.com/sites/kurtbadenhausen/2015/05/13/the-worlds-most-valuable-brands-2015-behind-the-numbers/#5090dbbc5106 [Accessed 2 May 2015].

Gardner, B. B. & Levy, S. J. (1955) The product and the brand, *Harvard Business Review*, **33**(2), 33-39.

Grabner-Kraeuter, S. (2002) The role of consumers' trust in online-shopping, *Journal of Business Ethics*, **39**(1-2), 43-50.

Hassan, S. S. & Craft, S. (2012) Examining world market segmentation and brand positioning strategies, *Journal of Consumer Marketing*, **29**(5), 344-356.

Hsieh, M.-H. (2002) Identifying brand image dimensionality and measuring the degree of brand globalization: a cross-national study, *Journal of International Marketing*, **10**(2), 46-67.

Hsieh, M.-H., Pan, S.-L. & Setiono, R. (2004) Product-, corporate-, and country-image dimensions and purchase behavior: a multicountry analysis, *Journal of the Academy of Marketing Science*, **32**(3), 251-270.

Keller, K. L. (1993) Conceptualizing, measuring, and managing customer-based brand equity, *The Journal of Marketing*, **57** (1), 1-22.

Keller, K. L. (2002) Branding and brand equity, In: Weitz, B. and Wensley, R. ed. *Handbook of Marketing*, Sage, pp. 151-178.

Keller, K.L. (2014). *Strategic Brand Management: Building, measuring, and managing brand equity*, 4th ed., London: Pearson

Kim, S. S. & Agrusa, J. (2005) The positioning of overseas honeymoon destinations, *Annals of Tourism Research,* **32**(4), 887-904.

Knox, S. & Bickerton, D. (2003) The six conventions of corporate branding, *European Journal of Marketing,* **37**(7/8), 998-1016.

Levy, S. J. (1959) Symbols for sale, *Harvard Business Review,* **37**(4), 117-124.

O'Cass, A. & Grace, D. (2004) Exploring consumer experiences with a service brand, *Journal of Product & Brand Management,* **13**(4), 257-268.

Pappu, R., Quester, P. G. & Cooksey, R. W. (2005) Consumer-based brand equity: improving the measurement – empirical evidence, *Journal of Product & Brand Management,* **14**(3), 143-154.

Reddy, S. K., Holak, S. L. & Bhat, S. (1994) To extend or not to extend: Success determinants of line extensions, *Journal of Marketing Research,* **31**, 243-262.

Saunders, J. & Guoqun, F. (1997) Dual branding: how corporate names add value, *Journal of Product & Brand Management,* **6**(1), 40-48.

Schlager, T., Bodderas, M., Maas, P. & Cachelin, J. L. (2011) The influence of the employer brand on employee attitudes relevant for service branding: an empirical investigation, *Journal of Services Marketing,* **25**(7), 497-508.

Simms, C. & Trott, P. (2007) An analysis of the repositioning of the "BMW Mini" brand, *Journal of Product & Brand Management,* **16**(5), 297-309.

Simon, C. J. & Sullivan, M. W. (1993) The measurement and determinants of brand equity: a financial approach, *Marketing Science,* **12**(1), 28-52.

Srivastava, R. K. & Shocker, A. D. (1991) *Brand Equity: A perspective on its meaning and measurement,* Marketing Science Institute.

Swait, J., Erdem, T., Louviere, J. & Dubelaar, C. (1993) The equalization price: A measure of consumer-perceived brand equity, *International Journal of Research in Marketing,* **10**(1), 23-45.

Washburn, J. H., Till, B. D. & Priluck, R. (2000) Co-branding: brand equity and trial effects, *Journal of Consumer Marketing,* **17**(7), 591-604.

Yoo, B., Donthu, N. & Lee, S. (2000) An examination of selected marketing mix elements and brand equity, *Journal of the Academy of Marketing Science,* **28**(2), 195-211.

7 Integrated Marketing Communications

Kitty Shaw

If a brand like Apple supported a campaign about the impact on society of people spending too much time on their laptops and phones, or launched a very basic mobile phone would you think this was strange? This is because Apple has a very clear market positioning based on providing cutting edge technology products, which enhance people's lives. This positioning is evident in everything from its sleek product design to all of its marketing and customer communications across multiple channels. All of their communications are integrated to support their market positioning and brand values. This chapter discusses integrated marketing communications, why it is important for businesses and how to go about delivering an integrated approach. The chapter also looks at the challenges of doing so and the future of integration. It links to the case study on Standard Life plc, which is included in Chapter 12.

Integrated Marketing Communications is commonly abbreviated to IMC and this chapter will use this shorthand.

Defining Integrated Marketing Communications

The term 'integrated marketing communications' was first coined in the 1990s and captured the need for marketers to co-ordinate their communications better, both across their different audiences or stakeholder groups, and their communications channels and promotional tools. Organisations may have worked with a number of specialist creative agencies or intermediaries for different elements of their promotional mix, including advertising, direct mailings, public relations and sponsorship, while customer service communications were handled by another part of the organisation. IMC is about ensuring that all of these elements are joined up and present a unified positioning and image across all communications – both internal and external.

However, IMC is about more than the tactical alignment of messages and colour schemes across different communications channels, media and audiences. It is a strategic management process, driven by corporate and marketing strategy. IMC involves all of the organisation's communications being driven by and supporting corporate and marketing objectives. Kotler (2000: 542) defines IMC as "*the concept under which a company carefully integrates and co-ordinates its many communications channels to deliver a clear, consistent and compelling message about the organization and its products.*" Kotler's definition highlights the objective of IMC – to deliver clear and compelling messages, through whichever communications channels and media the organisation uses, across its multiple audiences.

IMC does not mean that exactly the same messages, images and so on have to be used across all audiences, channel and media, but that all communications support and reinforce the same messages about the organisation, its products and services. From a customer perspective this means that the organisation needs to consider all of the touch-points a customer might have with the organisation and its products and services, and ensure that it delivers consistent positioning through all of these. Figure 7.1 illustrates the broad range of touch-points a consumer might have with an organisation such as Standard Life, and the multiple opportunities or threats that these present to the organisations planned messaging and positioning. IMC is about ensuring that the organisation does everything it can to ensure that each of these touch-points is an opportunity rather than a threat to the organisation.

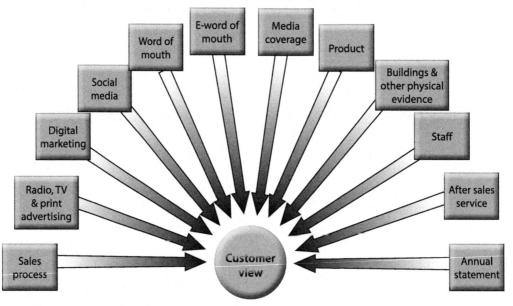

Figure 7.1: Customer touch-points

An important skill in managing IMC, is understanding the needs of each of the organisation's multiple key audiences and being able to translate the positioning and messaging derived from marketing strategy into communications, which are meaningful for each audience. In this way, the IMC approach is linked to the extent to which organisations are market-driven, as those organisations which are most focused on responding to the needs and developments of the outside world and their external stakeholders are best able to produce IMC (Reid, 2005). For any communications initiative, the company must determine which are its key audiences and develop messaging relevant to them through the channels and media which are appropriate and effective for reaching that particular group.

The following definition from the Chartered Institute of Marketing (CIM) emphasises the role of IMC in building relationships with the organisations various audiences.

"IMC can represent both a strategic and tactical approach to the planned management of an organisation's communications. IMC requires that organisations coordinate their various strategies, resources and messages in order that they enable meaningful engagement with target audiences. The main purposes are to develop a clear positioning and encourage stakeholder relationships that are of mutual value." (CIM, 2015)

This definition stresses the role of IMC in providing a clear positioning for the organisation to help customers to understand what the business stands for.

IMC involves managing the organisation's communications across all of its communications tools. These might include some of those shown in Table 7.1.

Table 7.1: The tools of IMC. Adapted from Keller, 2001:820

Advertising	Print, TV, radio, cinema, outdoor
Direct marketing	Hardcopy, email and social media
Sales promotions	Email, in store,
Public relations	Communications with media, regulators and other stakeholders
Point of sale	Livery, staff appearance, look and feel
Sponsorship & event marketing	Celebrities, sports, arts and cause related
Personal selling	Face to face, telephone, email
Customer communications	Post sale servicing and information
Web presence	Website, social media activity, content marketing

Table 7.1 illustrates that there are several tools that marketers can use and that need to be considered in evaluating an IMC approach. Everything from advertising to sponsorship and the look and feel of an organisation can be used to support an IMC approach. At the same time, any of these elements can undermine an IMC approach if they are not aligned to support the organisation's core positioning and values.

To summarise, the key features of IMC are that it:

- is an audience driven approach to communications;
- is a strategic process;
- encompasses all touch-points for customers and other stakeholders;
- presents a single voice for an organisation's positioning and values; and
- aids relationship building by helping customers to understand what the organisation stands for.

The IMC planning process

The integrated marketing planning process needs to be driven by the organisation's strategic marketing plan and brand strategy, which in turn are driven by the overall strategic priorities of the organisation. If for example the high level strategy is for growth, then this will influence the communications objectives, positioning and messaging used. Figure 7.2 illustrates the IMC planning process.

In Chapter 5 we discussed the marketing communications strategy as part of the strategic marketing plan, which in turn is driven by corporate level strategy. Figure 5.2 illustrates that the elements of a marketing communications strategy are positioning, audience(s), creative and media. Delivering IMC means ensuring that all communications and customer touch-points support and reinforce the positioning determined in the strategic marketing plan; that they are in line with the needs of target audiences in terms of messaging; and that channels and media used are in line with audience needs and preferences. Figure 7.2 illustrates how this marketing planning process discussed in Chapter 5 flows through to deliver integrated communications programs, which support high level corporate and marketing strategy.

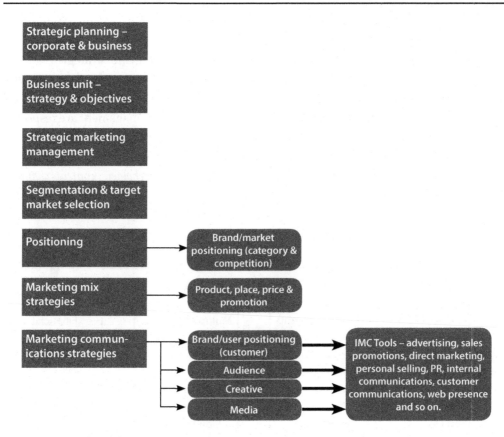

Figure 7.2: Integrated marketing communications as a strategic process

In the case study on Standard Life Plc. in Chapter 12 a clear link can be seen between the corporate objectives, the communications objectives and how these are then worked through to key messages and propositions for key stakeholder groups. In Standard Life's case a broad range of stakeholders are identified as is illustrated by Table 7.2.

Table 7.2: The multiple stakeholders of Standard Life plc.

Customers /clients	Segmented by product and distribution channel
Distributors	Independent financial advisers , workplace consultants
Prospective customers	Segments targeted for growth
Shareholders	Institutional and individual
Employees	Segmented by location, function and level
Media	National press, trade press, online news channels (trade and consumer), radio & TV
Other	Joint venture & strategic partners , UK Government & regulators, overseas governments & regulators

A model for planning and evaluating an IMC approach is provided by Kliatchko (2008). Reflecting recent thinking, Kliatchko's model stresses that the foundation of IMC is an approach to business planning and strategic management which is driven by a deep understanding of the needs of the organisation's multiple stakeholders. Where an organisation is focused from the top on the needs of its customers and other stakeholders, senior management are responsible for promoting a corporate vision and ensuring that the business is organised to deliver this vision. Kliatchko identifies '4 Pillars' of communication that need to be managed to produce effective IMC These are *stakeholders, content, channels* and *results*. The model, which is illustrated in Figure 7.3, is a useful framework to help guide and assess communications integration.

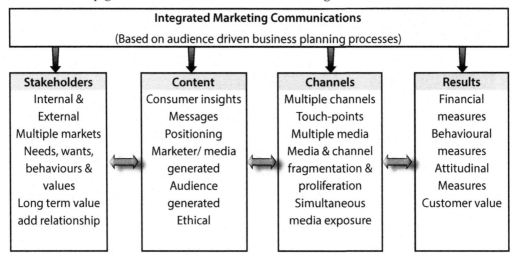

Figure 7.3: Kliatchko's 4 Pillars of Integrated Marketing Communications, Adapted from Kliatchko (2008)

Stakeholders

The Stakeholder pillar encompasses all of the organisation's multiple audiences, from customers to staff and shareholders amongst others, and requires the organisation to build a detailed understanding of their needs, behaviours, values and attitudes. This will range from understanding the targeted customer segments, in terms of their media habits and preferences, to knowing which trade press or social media sites are most likely to influence their opinions and behaviours. The Standard Life case study helps to illustrate this. Within the communications strategy, the overall communication purpose is defined as: *"To enhance Standard Life's brand and corporate reputation through stakeholder engagement and advocacy"*. This stresses the importance to Standard Life of engaging with a number of stakeholders in order that they might become advocates, but also the need to integrate communications across stakeholders. The communications strategy then goes on to show how the group's positioning translates into a proposition for each of its key stakeholders, but all of these individual stakeholder propositions link back to and support the company's communications objectives. Similarly in planning communications for a specific event, such as the acquisition discussed, a key element of the communications plan is identifying all of the relevant stakeholders and their communications needs.

Content

The Content pillar encompasses all communications about the organisation, including messages produced by the company, as well as what others write about the company in the media, and customer views of the company posted on social media. Thus the integrated approach needs to take account of an *Interaction Model of Communications* (Baines and Fill, 2014: 355), where consumers themselves integrate messages from multiple sources, including the media and their interactions with other consumers, in forming their opinions of a company. An example of this is the retailer Marks and Spencer's 'Plan A', which is a strategic focus on sustainability across the business, defined as *"our way to help protect the planet – by sourcing responsibly, reducing waste and helping communities"* (Marks and Spencer, 2016). Plan A is central to the company's strategy and is evidenced and supported across several of company's communications, from in-store displays promoting Plan A, charging for plastic bags to discourage their use, and its "Schwopping" campaign in partnership with the charity Oxfam, which encourages customers to donate unwanted clothes, so that they can be re-used, sold or recycled. Plan A is a consistent theme, which flows through and underscores much of the content of the company's communications. In the same way, the key messages in the Standard Life communications strategy such as *"helping customers plan for the future"* underpin much of its content.

Channels

Kliatchko's third pillar, Channels covers all of the company's communications tools, such as TV, radio, social media, but also includes all other touch-points for the company's multiple stakeholders. Figure 7.1 illustrates the extent of possible touch-points for a company, and in planning an integrated approach to communications the company needs to consider all of these as channels. Again this fits the Interaction Model of Communications (Baines and Fill, 2014: 355) and the need to understand the audience perspective, their multiple touch-points, sources of information and influences, in order to establish the channels, in the broad sense defined above, which will be most effective in influencing each stakeholder. In some instances this may mean building support among, or addressing the concerns of one stakeholder audience in order to influence another audience. For example when Standard Life went through major structural change in 2006, an extensive campaign was undertaken to convince voting policyholders that this was the best direction for the company. An online blog, run by a small group of policyholders with industry experience, was identified as an important influence as *thought leaders* (Baines and Fill, 2014) on policyholders to vote against the proposed change. Significant effort was then invested in understanding the concerns of the group behind the blog and trying to address these concerns both directly and in the press, targeting business and personal finance journalists. This approach was more effective than trying to persuade policyholders directly, when some of them were heavily influenced by the blog run by a group that they could identify with.

Results

The fourth pillar of Kliatchko's model is Results. Businesses need to take an integrated approach to measuring the effectiveness of their communications by looking at their outcomes in terms of behavioural or attitudinal changes among target stakeholders. As IMC is driven by a strategic focus on stakeholder needs, accountability has to be a central feature of its implementation. A number of financial measures can also be used to measure the effectiveness of IMC, including *customer value*, which looks at the value of individual customers, or *return on customer investment* (ROCI), which compares the spend on a specific target customers with their predicted value in terms of sales.

Kliatchko's model is intended to operate both at a higher strategic level and at a more operational level as an integrated approach to communications. In the Standard Life case study we can see how the high-level strategic communications framework applies both at the strategic level and in a more operational level, managing communications exercises around specific events, such as the example given for a business acquisition. In the example of the acquisition, identification of key stakeholders and their communication needs are central to the communications plan which then integrates activity to address these across both content and channels. Finally, the plan has a set of objectives against which results can be measured.

Another example of the IMC approach in action can be seen in the international retailer Marks and Spencer Group plc. The following mini-case sets out how the group's corporate purpose drives communications strategy and then feeds through to tactical campaign activity, which is integrated across several markets and media.

Mini case: Marks and Spencer Campaign – "The Art of "

The company's 2015 Strategic Report defines the group's core purpose as *"Enhancing Lives Every Day"* through the high quality of its own brand food, clothing and home products. The report identifies the quality and provenance of its products as the group's main source of competitive advantage and therefore central to its brand. The brand is supported by four core values: inspiration, innovation, in-touch and integrity.

The report goes on to identify revenue growth as the overarching strategic objective, but building the group brand is seen as an essential part of this growth strategy. The brand and core values are woven in throughout the report contents, supporting strategy in product and channel development, human resource management, and building and managing relationships with customers, shareholders and other stakeholders.

This strategic focus on quality and provenance flows through the organisation from group strategy to marketing strategy and individual campaign level. In September 2015 the group launched a campaign entitled *"The Art of"*, described as *"a new campaign across TV, print and digital platforms designed to put a spotlight on the unique quality and style of M&S products. The new campaign uses a stylish and cutting edge format to celebrate the craftsmanship and fashion credentials across M&S."* Elements of the campaign were used across 50 different global markets.

The following quote from Patrick Bousquet-Chavanne, Executive Director, Marketing and International, highlights the integrated nature of the communications approach. *"To find a distinctive and consistent voice for Marks and Spencer that creates a more joined up journey and ways of talking about the unique qualities of Marks and Spencer."*

By talking about creating "a more joined up journey", Bousquet-Chavanne focuses on the needs of customers and the importance of making it easy for them to know what the business stands for.

Source: Marks and Spencer (2015a) , Marks and Spencer (2015b)

7

The Marks and Spencer mini case highlights an important aspect of integrated marketing communications, which is the need to find the right balance between central control and flexibility for different parts of the business, to respond to the needs of their customers and other stakeholders or local market conditions. This campaign can be traced right back to the group's core purpose and strategic business plan, but is also able to be implemented across 50 different markets. Striking the right balance between centrally determined frameworks and flexibility for subsidiary business units or geographically diverse operations is a critical skill in designing and implementing an IMC approach. While some companies have very uniform approaches to positioning, messaging, tone of voice and look and feel others such as Standard Life and Marks and Spencer have greater flexibility, but all operations will follow some centrally determined brand or messaging guidelines. Lack of integration is more prevalent with social media campaigns, where many of the social media channels are used but only one particular channel is used more than most, for example, Twitter. In addition, there is the issue of detractors, as McDonald's found out, and which has proved to be a lesson to all managers in managing corporate social media consultants. (Hill, 2012). The agents launched a Twitter campaign but lost control of the overall picture, and did not realise the volume of detractors. The launch was an invitation to share stories and experiences of McDonald's at #McDStories (via Twitter). Unfortunately, control was lost when detractors turned the campaign into a #bashtag to share their #McDHorrerStories. Thus, the degree of control versus flexibility that is best for any company will depend on a number of factors, including the organisation's history and culture and the sectors and markets in which it operates.

Why IMC is important

Having an integrated approach to communications is increasingly important for organisations because:

- It makes it easy for customers to know what the organisation stands for
- Consistent positioning and messaging is needed across multiple media
- Cross media effects and synergies generated by IMC can impact both brand equity and sales.
- Once established, IMC infrastructure helps to manage and control unplanned communications, such as responding to negative media coverage.

Producing IMC strategies has become increasingly critical for modern organisations for several reasons. In an increasingly global marketplace for most products and services, consumers face greater choice than ever and look for cues to determine which of the available options best meet their needs. In doing so they will consider information from multiple sources including the media, social media and word of mouth. This makes it vital for brands to have a clear positioning, which allows consumers to understand what they stand for, and that this positioning is consistent across multiple touch-points through which a customer might receive information about them. While companies cannot control word-of-mouth and online chat about themselves, they can work to have a consistent messaging which engages with the relevant audiences in the communications that they do control, such as advertising, and thus influence the way the company is portrayed in the media it does not control, such as word of mouth. Finne and Grönroos (2009) found that consumers also develop their views of brands over time, which means that an integrated approach and consistency of core messaging needs to be sustained over time rather than as a quick fix. As marketing has shifted from a transactional focus to that of customer relationship management (CRM), companies need to be consistent in their positioning and proposition to customers and other stakeholders who are less likely to engage with a company that seems to change its values or market positioning from one month to the next or across different media. It is also important for companies to be consistent in their core positioning and values across different audiences, as many individual customers may also experience the company in other capacities, such as shareholders, employees, suppliers or neighbours. Consistency is therefore important at a number of levels.

The proliferation of media and fragmentation of consumer markets also makes integration vital for many companies. Social and technological advances have led to increasingly fragmented consumer markets, making it more challenging to identify and target sizable customer segments through specific media. At the same time the proliferation of television, radio and other channels, as well as digital media, has resulted in significant fragmentation in media channels. This means that campaigns generally have to be executed across multiple channels to reach their target audiences. Furthermore the value of cross media effects in driving campaign results has been shown in studies such as that of Voorweld et al. (2011), who found that cross media campaigns triggered two positive responses in consumers. First, *multiple source perception* was triggered, where respondents built their perception of a brand from multiple media sources. The second response was *forward encoding*, where consumers' interest is raised in an advertisement where they have previously experienced other related communications. This may mean that a deeper level of processing is applied to the second material encountered. Operating in a multi-media environment requires careful management to ensure an integrated approach and avoid sending mixed messages through the multiple media involved.

Furthermore, an integrated approach to communications can be invaluable for organisations in dealing with any adverse circumstances, as it means that the organisation already has established processes in place to manage communications across all of its channels and audiences. As well as being important in managing day-to-day communications and campaigns, this control is invaluable in the event of a crisis or any event that could potentially be damaging to the organisation. For example, VisitScotland's new 'Autumn Gold' £1.6m campaign was launched to a London audience two days before the death of Diana, Princess of Wales in August, 1997 and was cancelled as it was felt that even having spent up to £250k on media space, the London audience was not in a favourable frame-of-mind to receive promotional messages and appeals of taking an autumn break in Scotland (Bell, 1997). Thus, having integrated processes in place allows an organisation to respond in a more co-ordinated and controlled way to any unforeseen circumstances. For a large company such as Standard Life, having an integrated communications framework in place is essential in being able to respond to any news or developments either from within the company or in the broader market. In planning any communications project, from responding to media criticism or announcing annual results, having an integrated framework in place gives the organisation much better control over messaging across a broad range of stakeholders, channels and geographic areas.

Finally, since the financial crisis of 2008, marketing departments have been under increased scrutiny and pressure to show that they add tangible value to their organisations in delivering measurable returns. A number of studies have shown the value of an integrated approach to communications. Madharavam et al. (2005) show that synergies and efficiencies generated by IMC play an important role in building and maintaining brand equity, while Reid (2005) also shows a positive link between IMC and brand outcomes including awareness and sales. Focussing on specific communications channels, Spotts et al. (2014) find that publicity can affect the impacts of advertising on increasing sales in business to consumer markets.

As well as being important, IMC also has a number of benefits for organisations when it is effectively implemented. Pickton and Broderick (2005: 28) identify 4Es and 4Cs of IMC to stress the benefits an organisation can gain from IMC. The 4Es and 4Cs, illustrated in Table 7.3 below provide a useful way of remembering the benefit of IMC and ensuring that a business is maximising these in its approach.

There are therefore significant benefits for organisations that can effectively implement and manage IMC, in terms of relationships with customers and other stakeholders and more efficient and effective use of resources in achieving communications objectives. These benefits also combine to generate competitive advantage for organisations through having a clear and consistent proposition to consumers across all touch-points, which is delivered through the most efficient use of resources, enabling companies to get more from their marketing spend than their competitors.

Table 7.3: Pickton and Broderick's 4 C's and 4E's of integrated marketing communications. Adapted from Pickton and Broderick (2005, p28)

Enhancing	The different elements in the communication mix work together to augment and intensify each other.
Economical	Synergies generated make best use of financial and other resources.
Efficient	Doing things the best way to get desired results through more detailed planning across media and tools
Effective	Doing the right things to produce the desired outcome by ensuring the right tools and media are used.
Coherence	Communications are logically connected for customers and other stakeholders.
Consistency	Communications don't contradict or undermine each other but are in tune with each other across media, channels and stakeholders.
Continuity	Messages are connected over time for audiences, building and reinforcing positioning.
Complementary	Communications items work together to deliver communications objectives

The challenges of IMC

7

Attempts to design and implement an integrated approach to communications may face a number of challenges both from within the organisation and beyond.

Key challenges are:

Within the organisation

- Organisational structures and politics
- Organisational culture and internal communications
- Internal processes

Outside the organisation

- International regulations and cultures
- Agencies
- Distributors and other 3rd parties

One of the biggest challenges is organisational structure, which often mean that the ownership of different communications channels or stakeholders sits with different parts of the organisation and controlled by different managers. For example while all marketing communications tools and channels may be controlled by a central marketing management structure, customer service and sales communications may be the responsibility of other parts of business.

For instance, see the BA *'Tailfins'* debacle where the marketing department launched a £60m global campaign, which included new logos on planes but did not include the 32,000 BA employees in the planning of the campaign. Lack of buy-in by staff and customers resulted in the Union flag being reinstated on the tailfins. (Marston, 2001). This means all parts of the business have to be bought into the need for integration and may require some managers to relinquish some control. Often politics can act as a barriers to this and some functions such public relations may demand more autonomy for their work.

Organisational culture can also be a barrier to IMC, especially where the culture is such that different parts of the organisation are seen as competing with each other, or where internal cultures differ across the organisation. For example, Ots and Nyilasy (2015) report that where there is a tension between head office and branch cultures this can add to structural challenges in implementing IMC. Linked to this, internal processes and communications can either help or hinder IMC. If internal communications do not promote and support the prioritisation of an integrated approach to customers, then it will not be a priority. Similarly if business processes and technology do not facilitate and support integration, then it is too easy for parts of the business to continue to follow their own agendas.

To overcome challenges from internal structures, politics and cultures, IMC needs to be founded on a strategic decision to pursue integration, which is endorsed and led by senior managers as part of corporate strategy and supported across the organisation in its processes, communications and measures of success.

Where an organisation operates internationally, cultural and other market differences can present problems with integration. For example in China, certain colours carry particular significance, and the colour yellow represents a higher social standing and so needs to be used cautiously. This presented a challenge for Standard Life when setting up a joint venture there, as the company's branding at the time involved a bright shade of yellow. Other challenges can come from nuances of particular words or images used in brand slogans or imagery, but which carry particular connotations in some countries. At the same time culture affects how different nationalities respond to marketing messages and the sorts of messaging and advertising that are most successful in different markets. All of this means that companies must consider local cultures and values when developing IMC, and find a suitable balance between centrally driven positioning and messaging and the needs of local markets.

Where a company works with multiple agencies across different media this can present a challenge to integration, as each agency will have its own interpretation of the brief. Furthermore as strong personalities are often involved, strong management is needed to ensure that the integrity of the positioning and messaging is not diluted or undermined by very different interpretations. Managers responsible for commissioning and managing agencies need to have a very clear view of their positioning and messaging and use this to evaluate all proposed materials. Careful diplomacy may be required to bring some agencies in line with the direction being taken.

Standard Life, which features in Case study 4 in Chapter 12, has faced similar challenges with separate business units in the UK and around the world. The approach by Standard Life was to develop a high-level communications strategy and messaging framework, which supported the group's business strategy. This high-level strategy set out communications objectives and key messages that were agreed to by communications teams across the group. This enabled the group to ensure a level of integration and consistency, whilst also allowing individual business units flexibility in their communications activity to take account of local market conditions.

7

The current drivers of IMC

As consumers become increasingly well informed, connected and critical, having an integrated approach that gives a consistent view of what company stands for is more important than ever. Advances in digital media and how consumers interact with media have huge implications for marketing communications, as software such as Google's Adsense enables a more flexible and real time targeting of consumers, with items that are relevant to them there and then and in the right format for whatever device they are using. At the same time consumers themselves have more control over what they see and are able to share or pass judgements on brands through social media. So while digital advances give advertisers the ability to manage their interaction with consumers at a more individual level, they also have to deal with a more vocal and interactive consumers who will comment on, adapt and share their messaging as they see fit, thus reducing control over how their brand and messaging are seen. Mulhearn (2009) identifies a number of ways in which these developments specifically affect the future of IMC.

- First, consumer insight, which drives IMC, is becoming increasingly sophisticated and enables companies to combine data from multiple sources to build detailed pictures of their consumers, allowing more accurate targeting of campaigns.

- Second, digital media are able to provide valuable live data on consumer behaviours and responses to materials online. This creates the opportunity for much more detailed and responsive planning of campaigns, which previously relied on static demographic categories or previous purchases to identify target customers. This also enables much more precise monitoring and measurement of activities, which should feedback into on-going campaign planning to focus resources where there is greatest success or to improve effort where communications are failing to achieve desired responses.

- Third, digital media make it easier for companies to co-ordinate communications with multiple stakeholder groups. At the same time it means that each stakeholder group is able to see the communication directed at other audiences, which raises the importance of consistency. This also presents opportunities for brands to build communities around them, incorporating a variety of stakeholders.

- Finally, as multiple media channels are deployed in marketing and other communications it becomes easier to integrate communications across media and to ensure consistency.

Digital media and an increasingly global marketplace create great opportunities for increasingly sophisticated integrated communications planning. At the same time this leads to higher expectations from consumers who increasingly expect to receive marketing materials relevant to them and their current circumstances. Consumers are also taking more control over which materials reach them and are more likely to share their views on things they don't like. So while the digital era presents opportunities for integrated marketing, it also presents greater risks for those who get it wrong. For companies that are able to exploit the opportunities of IMC in the digital era, this should give them a source of competitive advantage in being able to target more relevant content to more specific groups of clients, thus building stronger relationships and strengthening brand equity.

Further reading

The Institute of Practitioners in Advertising – www.ipa.co.uk

 The Institute of Promotional Marketing – www.theipm.org.uk

The Chartered Institute of Marketing (CIM) - www.cim.co.uk

Kliatchko, J. (2008) Revisiting the IMC Construct: a revised definition and four pillars, *International Journal of Advertising*, **27**(1), 133-160

References

Baines, P. and Fill, C. (2014) *Marketing*. 3rd ed. Oxford University Press.

Bell G (1997) Personal communication by email/telecon. Featherbrooksbank Media Agency, Edinburgh. August/September, 1997.

CIM (2015) Available from http://www.cimmarketingexpert.co.uk/wp/?wpp=the%20 development%20of%20integrated%20marketing%20communications%20 (IMC)&WPID=3277 (Accessed September 2015).

Finne, A. & Grönroos, C. (2009) Rethinking marketing communication: From integrated marketing communication to relationship communication'. *Journal of Marketing Communications*, **15**(203) 179-195.

Hill, K. (2012) #McDStories: when a hashtag becomes a bashtag. *Forbes Magazine*. http://www.forbes.com/sites/kashmirhill/2012/01/24/mcdstories-when-a-hashtag-becomes-a-bashtag/#1e2d2261193f (accessed Sept 2016)

Keller, K.L. (2001) Mastering the marketing communications mix: Micro and macro perspectives on integrated marketing communication programs, *Journal of Marketing Management*, **17**(2), 819-847

Kliatchko, J. (2008) Revisiting the IMC Construct: a revised definition and four pillars, *International Journal of Advertising*, **27**(1), 133-160

Kotler, P. (2000) *Marketing Management*, London, Prentice-Hall.

Marks and Spencer (2015a) Press Release: The Art Of Campaign For Autumn 2015. http://corporate.marksandspencer.com/media/press-releases/2015/the-art-of-campaign-for-autumn-15

Marks and Spencer (2015b) Strategic Report 2015, http://corporate.marksandspencer.com/media/ad70c9716d2041cc89cdd3821f1e53e6

Marks and Spencer (2016) Welcome to Plan A, http://corporate.marksandspencer.com/plan-a

Marston, P. (2001) http://www.telegraph.co.uk/news/uknews/1329843/BA-restores-Union-flag-design-to-all-tailfins.html (accessed Sept 2016)

7

Mulhearn, F. (2009) Integrated Marketing Communications: From media channels to digital connectivity. *Journal of Marketing Communications*, **15**(2-3) 85-101.

Ots, M. & Nyilasy, G. (2015) Integrated Marketing Communications (IMC): Why does it fail?, *Journal of Advertising Research*, **55**(2), 132-45.

Pickton, D. and Broderick, A. (2005). *Integrated Marketing Communications*. Harlow, UK: Pearson Education.

Reid, M. (2005). Performance auditing of Integrated Marketing Communication (IMC) actions and outcomes. *Journal of Advertising,* **34**(4) 41-54.

Spotts, H., Weinberger, M.G. & Weinberger, M.F., (2014) Publicity and advertising:what matter most for sales?, *European Journal of Marketing*, **48**(11/12), 1986-2008

Voorveld, H., Neijens, P. & Smit, E. (2011) Opening the black box: Understanding cross-media effects, *Journal of Marketing Communications*, **17**(2), 69-85

8 Creativity in Advertising and Promotion

Geraldine Bell

This chapter aims to make sense of creativity within the context of marketing management and marketing communications. Moreover, it specifically addresses the topics of advertising and promotion. In the first instance, it takes creativity to mean the 'big idea' in marketing management, then it tackles creativity in the production and translation of images and other creative materials used in advertising. These two interpretations of creativity make up what is referred to as the 'the creative platform' in advertising and promotion, oftentimes known as 'the creative', or simply as 'the creative treatment', especially amongst agents and practitioners designing, developing and producing creative marketing materials.

Why does creativity in advertising matter?

Advertising matters because, according to a recent report by Deloitte (2013), it fuels the UK economy. Annual advertising expenditures of £16 billion, Deloitte says, supports the creative industries and associated employment. For example, there are the TV and cinema screens as well as the pages of newspapers and magazines, and the space on billboards and in social media. Alongside which there is also the presence in web searches. Within the digital economy, advertising funds the majority of content and services, supporting online consumer research and boosting e-commerce. However, the impact, arguably, stretches across the economy, because it also enables markets to be more efficient. For instance, advertising is at the core of the cycle of competition, innovation and businesses. An increase in advertising spend elevates competition, improving quality and pricing for consumers. Thus, Deloitte's evaluation of UK firms spending £16 billion on advertising has resulted in a figure of £100 billion being the contribution to GDP for 2011. Hence 'advertising does pay' (2013).

One of the essential points in how well advertising may or may not work, is the notion of creativity, which according to Smith and Yang (2004) is a key factor on how effective your advertising can be. The authors assert that creativity contributes to the above-effectiveness equation. As well as advertising paying, as outlined above, there are several other variables that are known to drive advertising effectiveness. For instance, we know how persuasive a selling message can be, along with the fact that the larger your market share is the more likely your advertising is going to perform. And we also know that the execution and delivery is important, for example, media choices, timing and resources. And so, the question is, what contribution does creativity make to the advertisement and does creative advertising matter?

Dahlen et al. (2008) carried out an experiment where they exposed over 1000 consumers to a variety of different creative treatments of the same advert. The most creative of these adverts were selected and agreed as best practice exemplars by an expert panel of advertising executives. Results showed that the consumers who had been exposed to these creative exemplars perceived the brand to be of a higher quality, the sender (firm) to be smarter and the proposition to be superior, and that the firm was much more likely to develop more interesting products in the future.

Therefore, creativity can be seen as a further driver of advertising effectiveness. It is a multiplier in its effect. Dahlen et al (2010: 319) quotes the American Association of National Advertisers as saying that the "selling power of a creative idea can exceed that of an ordinary idea by a multiple of 10". And they describe people's reactions to ads as a continuum from a "Ha!", to an 'Aha!' to an 'Ah!'.[1] This expression of evaluating creative advertising is summarised below as:

Table 8.1: Dahlen's Response Continuum

Ha!	Aha!	Ah!
That's original	Aha, so that's what it means	Ah, that's clever

Source: Dahlen et al (2010: 319); and see Lehnert et al (2014: 275)

1 See Kounios, J. and Beeman, M. (2009). The Aha! moment: the cognitive neuroscience of insight. *Current Directions in Psychological Science.* **18** (4) 210-216. The authors underpin the science of the eureka moment which forms the basis of development of Dahlen's approach to evaluating creative advertising using a response continuum.

Defining a creative advertisement

Thus, an effective creative advert is defined as:

> "A creative ad is perceived by its audience to be novel and different, and whose central message is interpreted meaningfully by, and connects with its audience." Ang et al. (2007: 232).

In dictionary terms, to create something implies making something new by way of a form which requires imagination and skill. The ideal is that the onlooker responds to it positively. This is underpinned by two approaches to creativity: one is about newness and imagination and the second is about appropriateness and/or solving an issue.

■ Characteristics which determines advertising effectiveness

Two dimensions are noted: *divergence* (new, novel, unique) and *relevance* (important, of value and appropriate) as being the two main determinants of creativity in advertising (Smith & Yang, 2004). This is interpreted and summarised in Table 8.2:

Table 8.2: Determinants of advertising effectiveness

Divergent - Ad contains 5 elements that have:	**Relevance** - conveys meaningful info:
• **Originality** = novel, unique, surprising • **Flexibility** = able to switch perspectives/ viewpoints easily and quickly • **Synthesis** = able to integrate and blend easily with other ideas/platforms • **Artistic Value** = able to express richness in humour, colour, fantasy and artistic impressions, & aesthetic representations • **Elaboration** = able to extend above & beyond	• **Ad-to-consumer**: stimulus elements of the advert which create a meaningful link, e.g. music, voice-over, touchstone or situation linking to Generation X for instance. • **Brand-to-consumer**: stimulus elements and/ or useful information attained from the ad which creates & reinforces deeper meaningful links, e.g. Twiggy in M&S ads shows Baby Boomers how to wear the garment/what you would look like, or Apple's iPOD showed audience how to dance and have fun with its new music technology.

Thus far, advertising creativity is **different** and **meaningful**. An additional point, which adds some depth to the discussion, is noting that creative ads, along with being novel (divergent), and meaningful (conveying information relevant to the product) must also be able to **connect** with the audience. (Ang et al., 2007: 232; Lehnert et al., 2014: 275). In this context, the authors have added a sub-text to the point of relevance, as illustrated in Table 8.2. What they suggest is that connectedness goes beyond relevance as being meaningful. It does this because relevance implies that ad information is relevant to the product and thus meaningful, whereas connectedness is connecting to the target audience, and also where the audience is connecting to the advert by being the ad co-creator (Thompson & Malaviya, 2013), implying that co-ownership deepens the connection. Hence ad creativity has the three notable dimensions which make up an ad creativity cube:

■ novel (divergent)

■ meaningful (conveying data in relation to product) and

■ connectedness (to, and 'co-owned' by, the target audience).

How the three dimensions work together is complex, but Ang et al's (2007) 'ad creativity cube' suggests that in pursuing creativity, managers should not necessarily emphasize novelty at the expense of meaningfulness and connectedness. Whilst novelty allows ads to cut through clutter, ads need to adhere to relevant product meaningfulness and be connected to the audience to be effective. Thus, novelty, combined with meaningfulness and connectedness, takes account of both the advertiser and the audience perspectives. Moreover, the ad creativity cube proposes that creative ads which exemplify all three dimensions would generate better recall, more positive feelings, and more favourable attitudes than less creative adverts (Ang et al., 2014). In other words, the creativity cube is more likely to get us, the consumer, to better attend to advertisements.

This helps us to understand the effort by managers to include consumers in the creation of advertising or even in the evaluation of ad concepts, such as Samsung, Dove, Converse and so on. (See *Converse 'Brand Democracy' campaign wins award*.) Likewise, it also suggests that advertising which has explicit direction, for instance a strategic goal, and which scores well against the dimensions of creativity, is more likely be to be successful, but this is not necessarily the case. A compelling and creative advertisement may miss its strategic goal, and still score highly as being creative, and vice versa. And an advert which falls short against the creative dimensions may of course fulfil its strategic intent (Lehnert et al., 2014:275). An example would be where the source is judged in a positive or negative manner.

Source Credibility Theory (SCT) tells us that consumers view the integrity of products and services based on source. Any form of communications, whether it be face-to-face, written text or by electronic means, has been found to be highly influenced by the perceived credibility of the source of the communications. This being the case means that we can take it that SCT forms the basis for shaping persuasive marketing communications along with building both reputation and brands.

Converse 'Brand Democracy' campaign wins award.

Converse, the shoe brand, won this award for being innovative with its brand communications in 2006. It set out to develop more collaborative relationships with its consumers by allowing consumers to 'co-own' the brand. It did this by tapping into user-generated content to design and develop its advertising. *The Business Wire* reported that "short films and artwork from *creative originals* were used as the core components of the Brand Democracy advertising, including target media such as television, print and out of home." Interactive forums were particularly encouraged so that "consumers could showcase their own work and inspire others to join the Converse community". In addition, selected artwork was also featured on the Converse Gallery website, www.converse.com/gallery.

Since 2006, there have been many high profile examples of audience collaboration – Dove's Speedy Spa for instance. However, there is an interesting aside to the co-creation of advertisements, and that is how we, as consumers, react to the knowledge that other consumers are being the *creative intermediary*. When on social media, for example, we are more critical of the creation of the advertising, according to Thompson and Malaviya (2013). They point out that widely publicising an advert as being consumer-generated can "undermine message persuasiveness", particularly if they are contest ads, whereby consumers create ads by means of competitions and forums. In the case of a contest advert, consumers are turned off by knowing that it is created by ordinary people, rather than by professional communicators who are deemed to be more competent.

This is more so in situations of high-involvement, such as ads placed online in social media and other online video-sharing websites, where engagement is likely to be more intense and the resultant critique profoundly more negative. In circumstances where the likely receiver is partially distracted by something else, such as passive involvement with traditional TV advertising, they are more likely to view the co-creation of adverts much more positively. Therefore, you may want to make sure that you do not pre-publicise the source and perhaps even "exclude the consumer source" in some instances (2013: 45).

Visit http://www.businesswire.com/news/home/20060628005749/en/Converse-Brand-Democracy-Earns-EFFIE-Ad-Industrys#.VfriyreFPcs for more details of the campaign.

8

Lowry et al. (2008; 2014), for instance, explain how we treat websites as 'surrogates' of the underlying company.

Websites express both visual and nonverbal traits and are an effective exemplar of *surface credibility* (see Table 8.3, based on Fogg, 2003a, as cited in Lowry et al., 2014).

Table 8.3: Type of source credibility

	Meaning	Example
Surface credibility	Our first impressions of external or surface traits; those on the 'face of' something (judging a book by its cover).	Judging someone or something by initial inspection – the way someone looks; what a firm stands for on first sight of its logo/ webpage; product packaging – for me, or not for me.
Presumed credibility	We believe something to be more credible because of all the general assumptions we hold	A known brand is better than an unknown brand; a more organised fashion retail environment is better than a disorganised one
Reputed credibility	Credibility that comes from a third party reference point	A recommendation from a friend, family member, colleague to buy/not to buy
Earned credibility	Derived from past experience with this entity – person or object	Colleague has positive past experience so this particular music festival is credible

Credibility can be broken down into three sub-dimensions each with several traits, according to Lowry et al. (2013) and these are:

- **trustworthiness** – safety, fair, honest and just
- **expertise** – trained, experienced, skilled and authoritative
- **dynamism** – energetic, fast, colourful, bold, consistent and interactive.

In advertising contexts, especially online, marketing and sales information is framed using these credibility traits in presenting data. But contemporary communications is challenging the status quo. Take for example crowdsourcing – the making of information for the people by the people – which is becoming increasingly important in an advertiser's toolkit. According to Aquino (2013: 31) crowdsourcing is advertising which is commissioned by companies and supplied by the public. Crowdsourcing hooks into the creativity of the masses as a means of increasing engagement and getting fresh content. Intel, for example, invited Millennials to enter into a contest to design a 60 second TV/viral advert around the question "What does Intel mean to you?" and the result was a large volume of submissions. The key for Intel is to show how vital their feedback is, and they do this by connecting more deeply with their millions of Facebook "fans". The advantage for firms is that they are initiating a conversation on the one hand, and accruing much needed branded artwork on the other. Fans of this method of creating advertising say that it is about good storytelling, because the stories have an authenticity about them, whereas critics point out that it is speculative and lowers the value of design services. Whatever your view, curating crowdsourcing does require someone to sift through a pile of submissions and take an impression of the creative treatment and make a judgement.

The creative platform: a framework for understanding creativity in advertising

This discussion centres on the creative product, as per Sasser and Koslow's creativity framework (2008), which specifically defines the creative product as that which relates to creativity within the marketing materials in applied contexts. It does not include either media channels (place) or a focus on addressing how consumers think (process) and consume, and thus respond, to advertising (people). Within the creativity framework, the creative product is taken to mean the creative product/deliverables or creative materials which are subject to content analysis (e.g. pictures, print and billboard ads, video recordings, movies, pictures, radio ads, and so on)

However, it is important to note that what shapes and drives creativity is the both the product and other deliverables; and a good starting point is creating a 'frame of reference' (Kotler et al., 2016; Keller, 2013).

■ Creative platform: shaped by positioning

A frame of reference is shaped by identifying not only the target market but also the competition. This is where an understanding of consumer behaviour is vital, for example, the factors that consumers consider in making choices. In addition, the likely intentions of other brands needs to be considered. Where the product sits by way of category is important here. Consumers process data to help them compare products and also they seek out the criteria which they will use to like one product over another. A competitive frame of reference draws on consumer behaviour, marketing management and competitive strategy and this is what underscores the positioning, customer-value proposition or promise and the brand associations which are translated into creative executions containing the message and appeal – this is then what drives and shapes creativity in advertising. This includes creativity in the form of a 'big idea', which is used as the creative platform, positioning and anchoring the advertising across all elements of the communications mix, and also enabling the development of an 'image' in the minds of the audience. It does this by using creative devices such as humour, music, fun, art, adventure and so on, which makes the message more compelling and appealing and makes us sit up and attend to the communications. A deeper discussion on the positioning concept can be found in Chapters 1, 5 and 6.

■   The creative platform: translating the creative idea

Once the strategic and tactical positioning has been agreed, the message design has to be developed and created. The creative treatment, the translation of the creative idea into creative materials, signals an assurance about the brand so creativity needs to be aligned to the promise (customer-focused proposition). This forms the basis of the marketing communications 'creative brief'. The brand positioning has not yet formed in consumer's minds – the actual communications do this, and do it by projecting a coherent, single voice which reflects and reinforces an ongoing storyline to which the target audience can engage and connect and even help to co-create. The clearer the proposition, the easier it is to execute. In summary, the best propositions are the ones that are the most easily understood, because this makes it possible to communicate a brand's position in an original, attention-getting, but easy-to-catch way – and that is fundamentally the essence of the creative idea (De Pelsmacker et al., 2013).

Strategies for making creative advertising generate increased attention

The 'creative' interpretation of marketing communications strategy involves a creative idea which acts as a conduit for orchestrating communications across different types of platforms such as advertising, brand-led communications or participatory interactions (this is discussed in detail in Chapter 5).

We know that creative adverts are those that are viewed as being divergent, containing elements of novelty, aesthetic expression and which are different and new, and that they make a strong connection. That being said, how do you actually make what you want to say more appealing? In other words, what strategies can you draw on to design, develop and produce advertising that is deemed to be highly creative? Creative strategies are the way marketers translate their messages into a specific communication.

■   Informational and transformational appeals

Creative strategies can be classified into two general strategies: *informational* and *transformational* appeals (Kotler et al., 2016; Fill & Turnbull, 2016). Within the process of designing advertising communication, the two creative motivations – informational and transformational appeals, have several different creative approaches which can be specifically applied to this general categorisation of creative strategy. These creative approaches are discussed and laid out below.

Informational: rational processing

Informational appeals are motivations that appeal to those consumers who have a need for information to help them solve a problem by alleviating negative concerns. A general 'rule of thumb' here is that the market offering tends to be around pricing and quality.

Table 8.4: Informational: problem-solving through logic and reason

Creative appeal	Typical sponsor	For example
Source of problem	Healthcare and detergents – solves a problem	Nurofen "fast targeted relief from pain" or 'kills 99.9% of household germs'
Clear benefit	Household cleaners	"Cillit Bang and the dirt is gone" or a hand wash that "…kills 99.9% of bacteria.."
Product comparison	Best deals such as comparison websites/best service/quality	"Sky TV offers the best satellite programmes", or "To be the best" in the British Army, or Sony Bravia's "Like no other colour"
Testimonial	Celebrity endorser/ influencer	The celebrity/actress, Joanna Lumley endorses Sky TV, whilst Brian Cox (physicist) is used as an expert (influencer) for UK T&I in "Exporting is Great" Britain.

Informational appeals tend to be directed at motivations which are negatively charged, where the feelings of concerns can be reduced by acquiring the relevant information/direction to the product or service.

8

Transformational: emotional feelings

This is where the proposition or promise, relates to consumer feelings. The appeal is designed to 'transform' behaviour in that the intention is to change the end-user's emotional state in order to effect a change of behaviour.

Table 8.5a: Transformational: negative appeals

Creative appeal	Typical sponsor	Source/example
Fear, anxiety, distress, guilt, shame.	Charities, and government, and also trade associations. For instance, fundraising, social care, animal protection, adult/child social issues	Cancer UK "loss" of a loved-one, Save the Children, RSPCA, Alcohol abuse "Drink Responsibly", and personal care such as 'Brush your teeth'!
Stop (what you're doing) – dread, alarm, worry, surprise	Government – Public Liability/ duty of care to public eg health departments, safe transport,	Stop smoking, Drive safely, Safe sex/sexual disease.

Table 8.5b: Transformational: positive appeals

Creative appeal: Humour, love, pride, joy, happiness, laughter – uses borrowed-interest devices, e.g.	Typical sponsor	Source/example
Babies, children	Family health sector, food/drink, outdoor activity	Education sector, Nestle, Kraft, Cadbury, Unilever and P&G
Animals/puppies	Low-involvement goods/services. Animation technique becoming increasingly popular especially in new media.	Andrex toilet paper puppy; Dulux dog; McVitie's biscuits; Meerkats in www.gocompare.com; Cadbury's chocolate
Popular music	Lifestyle -fashion, motor, food/drink, entertainment.	See Insight re: *Paloma Faith*, p. 162
Provocative sex	As above, especially textiles/fashion, beauty.	Calvin Klein, and perfume ads, e.g. DVB
Surprise/astonishment, awesome/'wow'	As above, especially, drinks, entertainment, sport, leisure	Schweppes''sizzle'; Coca Cola's 'Taste'

Borrowed-interest devices are a means of providing a 'hook' to wrap-up your creative treatment. They attract attention and raise the consumer's involvement in the advertising, which in turn increases persuasion and intention. Most brands capitalise on using this technique as a means of cutting through the 'clutter' of today's modern communications environment. Animation in particular is becoming a short-cut to making advertisements more creative in terms of costs of production, and more appealing in terms of attention.

■ Forcing and subversion

Whilst the informational and transformational appeals provide a classification as to motivation, Fill and Turbull (2016) cite the methods of forcing and subversion as being the two key creative tactics of note as a means of getting people to sit-up and take note, that is, attend to your advertising.

- **Forcing** is where the advert forces you to attention through surprise, or shock tactics or through being irreverent in 'far-fetched way'. Examples include Apple's famous "1984" advert shown during the Super-Bowl of 1984, but where Apple mocked IBM, leading the George Orwell estate to regard it as an infringement of copyright. This advert was subsequently hailed as a masterpiece in advertising and garnered a lot of 'hype' around Apple in terms of how dare it take on the might of IBM. Other examples might be AIDS[2] 'tombstone' which forced us to talk about sexual health in

---

2   See www.bbc.co.uk/news/magazine-15886670 for more information on this campaign.

the 1980s, and Australia's "Where the bloody hell are you?" for cultural offence, and more recently Honda's 'car crash' which negatively correlated with the idea of driving freely and safely.

- **Subversion** on the other hand, is where the advert seduces you into a world which is mellow, comfortable, blissful – almost divine! M&S used this strategy with its ads featuring the seductive voice-over of Irish actress, Dervla Kirwan. These ads have not been shown in the UK for the last 10 years but are still memorable – who can forget the 2005 chocolate pudding advert with a sultry female voice telling us that "this is not just any chocolate pudding, but a Marks and Spencer chocolate pudding!" Consequently, sales increased ten-fold around the time it was aired and for some considerable time after. See the case study in Chapter 12, where Marks and Spencer once again tries to seduce us with its food advertising.

Creative content: framing creative appeals

The content of creative advertising is structured around positive and negative appeals underpinned by sociology and psychology (Tsai, 2002) and are based on the hedonic principles of approach to happiness and our avoidance of pain.

- **Positive framing** is where we pursue a positive outcome – such as psychological or monetary advantage, and is supported by the **approach** principle, which is to maximise our happiness, e.g. subverting you to eat chocolate.

- **Negative framing**, in contrast, centres on negative outcomes (psychological or monetary loss) and is based on the **avoidance** principle to minimise pain/loss, e.g. the forcing you to attend to an anti-smoking advert.

The choice appeal is dependent on whether your advertising has a motivation to inform, or one to transform behaviour through emotional appeal. Either way, both use aesthetic appeals by way of creative techniques such as storytelling, music, animation, fear/shock, fantasy and surrealism and humour. There is room here to explore storytelling, and humour and music in more detail.

■ Storytelling

Stories and storytelling, because of their ability to influence and persuade us, has long been a tradition in our way of life. We tend to think naturally in a story-like form and this form is organised in such a way that stories help us to make sense of our world – explaining things, making decisions, creating identities and trying to motivate others with our storytelling abilities. Stories, be they scripts,

8

maps, metaphors or models, are narratives that help us organise our experiences in such a way as to give structure. Moreover, they are easily absorbed. Stories are a type of discourse that draws on poetic and literary genres, and which adhere to dramaturgical styles, most of which is delivered with plenty of ceremony in mind (Whittle et al, 2009: 426). The more exciting the story, the more tension is built and disequilibrium is created relative to our balanced state (Söderlund & Dahlén, 2010).

Therefore, it is every advertiser's intent to exploit the mediated environment available, e.g. advert, TV programme, film, novel, package and event, and create a narrative which typically embeds a story in the form of entertainment, emotion and heightened spectacle. While the story is more likely to be fictional, it can still be personally relevant and provoke authentic reactions - who didn't cry when Elsa the lioness died during *Born Free*? Pop a box of cereal in the film-footage and we'll gladly eat "Simba's best breakfast flakes"!). Soderlund and Dahlen note that some authors have tried to explain the paradox whereby we experience "emotions from stimuli that are obviously not real by stressing that our thoughts (i.e. our imagination) can elicit emotions if we are willing to inactivate our beliefs that the story is not real. We appear to be willing to do so" (2010: 1815). Once we are immersed, we then cluster our further thoughts which are inferred by the story.

A computer vision technology company in the UK, called GumGum, has developed a b2b marketing campaign by asking creative agencies to 'reimagine' seminal campaigns. The Reimaging Advertising campaign asks industry creative chiefs what they would do, given the new media environment, with seminal television campaigns. One of the campaigns they've had to look at is the seminal Nescafe Gold campaign which ran from 1987 to 1993 (https://www. youtube.com/watch?v=RyLHK77YhGQ). Nescafe, and McCann Erickson, all but invented the art of storytelling with the love story of two opposites (actors Tony Head and Sharon Maughan) who slowly attract over a cup of Gold Blend coffee. The adverts themselves became the focus of PR attention with news of a new advert featuring an update of the love story eagerly awaited. In reimagining the campaign, none of the industry stalwarts wanted to deviate from the story, given the new media environments. Of note is that the story still holds sway and new media is used to enhance and extend the reach across the variety of platforms that are now available. As expected, technology plays a bigger part in the story-lines, e.g. kettles and coffee machines, but so does the end-user in co-creating the next phase of the storyline. One idea is to co-create the storylines into valid scripts in order to increase the depth of tension and excitement in waiting for the next instalment, and then for the client/agency to release the TV commercial and develop competitions to see whose draft story was closest to the paid-scriptwriters. The story has been changed to reflect current lifestyles – still the 'boy-girl' romance but with surprise. Meanwhile, Nescafe Gold Blend is the number one coffee brand in the UK (The Independent, 1998; The Drum, 2016) and stories are underpinning digital media as being a key feature of user generated content (UGC). Fill et al. (2013: 752) organises storytelling around two key points of themes and plot. Within these two points are clustered several elements of storytelling. Themes, for instance, include hardship, reciprocity, anticipation and defining moments, and for plot there are the likely elements of help along the way, crises and goal achievement. Again, this outline applies to digital media and creating short films for viral use. The idea here, in terms of co-creation, is to get the consumer to become part of the story themselves, and for the story to underpin word-of-mouth (WOM) which is a key means of communicating and advertising.

Arkwright (2014) suggests that we follow five key questions in developing strategies for good storytelling for advertising:

Table 8.6: Arkwright's key questions in developing strategies for storytelling

Strategy	Question	Creative idea/example
Ideological connection	What is the connection with the brand's past?	Snickers – 'Diva' or 'Warrior' knows how to satisfy hunger (see Mr Bean below)
Deeper connections – level of purpose & emotion	Why (not what)	Persil (OMO) 'Dirt is Good' where it's OK to be dirty because I'm a kid and it's good for me.
Find the brand's resolution	What is the deep desire the brand realises, or what is the deep problem in resolves	BMWs 'MINI UK' which is a great ride! Apple iPOD gives me music on the move.
Experiential (rituals)	Can the story be told by experience (and not just words)	Exhilaration (MINI UK); Attraction (Nescafe Gold); Heritage (Hovis); Togetherness (Harley Davidson)
Innovate (reimagine the brand in the future)	Can the brand's story (central idea) be extended across multi-platforms, and can you create a new chapter in the brand story?	Aesthetic (Apple)

Source: www.marketingmagazine.co.uk and see Arkwright (2014) .

Exercise

Collect a couple of adverts from both online and a magazine collection that are deemed to be revealing, interesting and different. Discuss and evaluate them using Arkwright's strategy for storytelling in creative advertising.

Mr Bean sells Snickers

Rowan Atkinson returns to advertising Snickers for Mars Chocolate UK. The British comedian, Rowan Atkinson, has returned to advertising and is reprising his Mr Bean character in a martial arts spoof. He stars as a Kung Fu master who is not quite feeling himself until he eats a Snickers bar with the proposition being "You're not you when you're hungry". The promise is that because you are very hungry, you turn into something else, for example in a previous execution the celebrity actress Joan Collins was featured behaving like a 'diva' whose behaviour was somewhat questionable. You then have a Snickers bar and your behaviour returns to normal. In the current commercial, Rowan Atkinson plays his iconic character Mr Bean – a character who is comically absurd, awkward, foolish, and yet hilariously funny and beloved by us all. The opening depicts a rooftop scene which reminds us of martial art epics such as 'Crouching Tiger, Hidden Dragon' where one of the group of warriors turns into Mr Bean making the group realise that they have a hopeless warrior in their midst and they don't like this because they want someone who can show what he's made of. He eats his Snickers and returns to being an adventurous and courageous warrior with intent. The commercial has been made in Mandarin with English subtitles reflecting the global target audience as well as the heritage of the ad. This humourous episode has translated well into an extended campaign which features TV, cinema, trade, social media, events and sponsorship. Several other executions are in the pipeline and still featuring Mr Bean in his typically calamitous scenarios.

Sources: Campaign (2014) and Adweek (2014)

■   Humour

No discussion on creating appeals in advertising would be complete without mention of the use of humour. Humour crosses all boundaries – both country, culture and peoples. Mr Bean was successful in every country not only because of humour (he is depicted in funny, wacky, haphazard situations) and British irony, but because of the technique of mime where the character Mr Bean expresses himself visually through storytelling in an entertaining and humorous way – there is no text – no voice-over to reinforce meaning and support the content. Critics often refer to Mr Bean as being the ultimate situation comedy. In the case of Mr Bean, visual rhetoric predominates where the consideration is in how images work alone or in partnership with other elements (such as humour and music) to create a line of reasoning to connect to an audience to get them to attend to it and provoke a reaction – drama, entertainment, advertising (Borghini et al., 2010). Rhetorical communication includes both verbal and visual, for example in animation and storytelling, and can also be used in isolation, such as the visual rhetoric in Mr Bean, which has been reconfigured creatively in pastiche and parody, or the verbal rhetoric in an advert with just large text such as the *The Economist's* "Trump Donald" or "To Be" posters. All of which are humourist depictions of advertising reflecting popular culture and art. In fact, on occasion, the advertising does become art (e.g. Nescafe Gold Blend, product placement in James Bond's Skyfall, and Guinness 'surfer') whereby the advert becomes the focus of the media itself.

Rhetorical convention in advertising uses both visual and verbal creative codes captured from material culture such as irony, playfulness, exaggeration, paradox, metaphor, pastiche (imitation) and parody (satire) and as such are used in-the-moment to reflect current cultural contexts. These codes drive persuasion and are therefore part of the rhetoric and creativity in advertising.

■ Music

A popular means of connecting your brand with consumers is through music. Brands increasingly recognise the value of music in dramatizing their adverts to enhance engagement and boost brand awareness and appeal. There is no doubt that the 1985 Levi commercial called 'launderette' which featured a rendition of the classic Motown track *I Heard It Through the Grapevine* awakened both the advertising and pop music industry to the potential of working together. Fast forward to 2015, and the two sectors are 'locked in an ever more mutually-reliant relationship' (Burgoyne, 2015) so much so, that the music embedded in the John Lewis seasonal advertisement adds to its 'sonic identity', meaning that music may not just be a short term tactical measure but a more strategic long term asset.

According to the British Phonographic Industry (BPI, 2016), the top three industries making the most of music in adverts in 2015 were motoring (Ford, Honda and Volkswagen), food (Sainsbury's, Waitrose and Tesco) and fashion (H&M, JD Williams and House of Fraser), while the brands that turned to music most often for their ads were Apple, who topped the chart with 23 tracks synched to adverts, followed by Tesco with 17 and MacDonald's with 10. It also reveals that pop music which is 5 years old or less, is the number one choice for brands reaching out to younger consumers accounting for nearly a quarter (24.%) of music used in ads, as opposed to heritage recordings that are 20 years or older. BRIT awards CEO, Geoff Taylor, strongly supports an increased collaboration between the advertising and music industry by reinforcing that music plays a vital role in strengthening the appeal of the narrative, making the broadcast, be it a TV drama or an advert, more memorable and giving it stand-out, thus forging a deeper emotional engagement between the viewer and the content.

Insight: Having Faith on your side could guarantee a hit product!

The British Phonographic Industry (BPI) has recently published research (June, 2016) which confirms advertisements as being a key channel for British popular tunes. Music recordings or 'syncs' (synchronisation – the use of music in an ad, film or video game) from British acts accounted for 41% of the tracks used by brands and creative agencies to promote products and services to the public. Leading the way was premier British female artist Paloma Faith, whose music was synced by four major brands (Calvin Klein, Dixons, Simply Be and Eastern Western) in 2015. Faith's hit song *Ready for the Good Life* also lays claim to being the 'most synced' song of 2015 which she shares with Motown classic *Sunny*. Relative newcomers Jess Glynne, Ella Eyre, Charlie XCX and Foxes also led the way with their sounds accompanying adverts for well-known brands such as Emporio Armani, Coca-Cola, O2 and H&M as well as campaigns by Oxfam, National Citizen Service and the United Nations.

Ian Neil of Sony Music UK pays testament to Faith's appeal saying that her principal draw to advertisers is that of a talented artist. *Upside Down* has been a popular track for several years but her breakthrough came with her "astonishing" take on the INXS classic *Never Tear Us Apart* for John Lewis, which has also been licensed by Calvin Klein. And of course, *Ready for the Good Life* conveys the "perfect message for advertisers".

Historically, artists have always been reluctant to allow their music to be used in advertising writes Fildes in *The Times* (10.06.2016), mainly because of artistic control, but the downturn in record sales and smaller deals from record labels have made synchronisation much more appealing to artists to generate more income.

In fact, sync remains an important revenue stream for the whole of the UK music business. Income from music synchronisation to adverts, video games, TV programmes, films and trailers totalled £22.68 million in 2015, up 13.5% on the previous year. TV advertising does best, followed by video games. However, at a global level, the sector is dominated by the USA with 57% of all synch revenues generated – out of a total global revenue estimated to be valued at $335m - with the UK capturing only 9% of worldwide income.

Adapted by G Bell from *The Times* 10/06/2016, UK Trade & Investment and see BPI, https://www.bpi.co.uk/media for more details.

An area that is becoming more important is in the trade of *synchronisation* or sync. (See the *Insight* into Paloma Faith's success.) This is an industry term where the holder to the rights to a piece of music licenses a song or piece of music to a third party who will place the music into audio visual content such as advertisements, trailers, video games, films and TV programmes (BPI, 2016;

Burgoyne, 2015). This collaboration requires all partners to work together, for example, the artist, the artist's management, the music publisher, the record label and the creative agency syncing the new production. The British government agency, United Kingdom Trade and Investment (UKTI) supports an annual trade mission to the USA which enables networking amongst the UK delegation of creative industries in an effort to expand and build future relationships in this sector. This just shows how important this sector is in terms of export of services especially within the area of TV drama.

There is no doubt then, that for brands, a popular and successful music track (and even artist) can be a short cut to the emotional connection that is agreed to be so important in contemporary marketing communications. John Lewis has built a musical world around its brand. It does this by treating music as a core element in its mix, linking the music into its tone of voice (slow and measured) which further illustrates what John Lewis stands for – its values, beliefs, trust. Arguably, it is using music not only to achieve short term objectives, but to also tap into the consumer's deep subconscious, thus creating emotive reactions around its brand values in order to achieve long lasting equity. Sonic branding, as a dimension in both marketing management and marketing communications adds to creative strategy by creating brand expression in sound and providing consistency across all touch points. A brand's armoury would be weakened if it did not have sonic branding to express emotion – as long as it is part of a coherent approach and not bolted-on as an afterthought.

8

Summary

Advertising is often referred to as the "last remaining unfair competitive advantage" (IPA, 2007) and this is because it is one of the key variables that can make "all other things unequal". Thus it is key, because advertising has considerable power and influence in conveying a good idea. This influence is underpinned by the view that creative advertising is perceived as being "more favourable, more likeable and more able to bestow value on brands" (West et al., 2008: 35). Creativity in advertising allows brands to stand out and to influence customer decision making.

This chapter acknowledges that marketing communications draws on consumption, but its emphasis here is on how marketers and 'creatives' develop, design and produce creative advertisements and other marketing materials – hence it takes an organisational point of view in the managing and supply of creative advertising.

Recommended reading

Ang, S.H., Lee, Y.H. & Leong, S.M. (2007) The Ad Creativity Cube: conceptualisation and initial validation. *Journal of the Academy of Marketing Science*. **35**, 220-232.

> This paper explains the ad creativity cube in more detail.

Bernardin, T., Kemp-Robertson, P., Stewart, D.W., Cheng, Y., Wan, H., Rossiter, J.R., et al. (2008) Envisioning the future of advertising creativity research: Alternative perspectives, *Journal of Advertising*, **37** (4), 139-144).

> This will be useful to those looking to carry out further research into this topic.

Reinartz, W. & Saffert, P. (2013) Creativity in advertising: when it works and when it doesn't. *Harvard Business Review*. June. 107-112.

> The authors carry out research into the dimensions of creativity. They then divide the dimensions into 'pairings' to assess the least and most likely pairings to affect creativity in advertising.

References

Adweek (2014) Mr Bean is a hopeless Kung Fu warrior. www.adweek.com/adfreak/mr-bean

Arkwright, D. (2014) Dirt is good: how storytelling gave Persil a boost. *Marketing*. www.marketingmagazine.co.uk

Ang, S.H., Lee, Y.H. & Leong, S.M. (2007) The ad creativity cube: conceptualisation and initial validation. *Journal of the Academy of Marketing Science*, **35**, 220-232.

Ang, S.H., Leong, S.M., Lee, Y.H. & Lou, S.L. (2014) Necessary but not sufficient: Beyond novelty in advertising creativity. *Journal of Marketing Communications*, **20**(3) 214-230.

Aquino, J. (2013) The pros and cons of crowdsourcing. *Customer Relationship Management*. **17**(2) 31-34.

Borghini, S., Visconti, L., Anderson, L. and Sherry, J.F. Jnr (2010) Symbiotic postures of commercial advertising and street art. *Journal of Advertising*, **39**(3) 113-126.

British Phonographic Industry (BPI) (2016) British Female Artists are spot on for music 'synch' TV ads https://www.bpi.co.uk/media-centre/British_female_artists_spot_on_for-music_sync.aspx (accessed 23/06/2016)

Burgoyne, P (2015) The Creative Review Report: Music. *The Creative Review*. **35** (1). Centaur Communications.

Campaign (2014) Rowan Atkinson returns to ads after an 18 year break. www.campaignlive.co.uk/article/

Dahlen, M., Lange, F. & Smith, T. (2010) *Marketing Communications: a brand narrative approach*. UK: J. Wiley & Sons.

Dahlen, M., Rosengren, S. & Torn, F. (2008) The waste in advertising creativity is the part that matters. *Journal of Advertising Research*, **48** (3) 392-403

Deloitte LLP (2013) *Advertising Pays: How advertising fuels the UK economy*. An AA/ WARC Report.

De Pelsmacker, P., Geuens, M. & Van Den Bergh, J. (2013) *Marketing Communications: a European Perspective*, UK: Pearson

Drum (2016) Nescafe's Golden Blend couple: how would today's marketers reimagine this classic ad campaign www.thedrum.com (accessed 05/04/2016)

Fill, C. & Turnbull, S. (2016) *Marketing Communications*. 7th ed. Pearson.

Fill, C., Hughes, G. & de Francesco, S. (2013) *Advertising: Strategy, creativity and media*. Pearson.

Independent (1998) TV Ad: Gold Blend – Another saga in the ultimate coffee break. http://www.independent.co.uk/life-style/tv-ad-gold-blend--another-saga-in-the-ultimate-coffee-break-1145610.html# (accessed 19/02/1998)

IPA (2007) Judging Creative Ideas. Institute of Practitioners in Advertising. www.ipa. co.uk

Keller, K.L. 2013. *Strategic Brand Management: Building, measuring and managing brand equity*. 4th ed. Pearson.

Kotler, P., Keller, K.L., Brady, M., Goodman, M. & Hansen, T. (2016) *Marketing Management*, 3rd ed. Pearson.

Koslow, S. (2015) I love creative advertising: what it is, when to call for it, and how to achieve it. *Journal of Advertising Research*. **55**(1) 5-8.

Lehnert, K., Till, B. D. & Ospina, J. M. (2014) Advertising creativity: the role of divergence versus meaningfulness. *Journal of Advertising*, **43**, (3), 274-285.

Lowry, P.B., Vance, A., Moody, G., Beckman, B. & Read, A. (2008). Explaining and predicting the impact of branding alliances and web site quality on initial consumer trust of e-commerce web sites. *Journal of Management Information Systems*, **24**, 199-224.

Lowry, P.B., Wilson, D.W. & Haig, W.L. (2014) A picture is worth a thousand words: Source Credibility Theory applied to logo & website design for heightened credibility and consumer trust. *International Journal of Human-Computer Interaction*, **30**, 63-93.

Sasser, S.L. & Koslow, S. (2008) Desperately seeking advertising creativity. *Journal of Advertising*. **37** (4) 5-19.

Söderlund, M. & Dahlén, M. (2010) The "killer" ad: an assessment of advertising violence. *European Journal of Marketing*, **44**(11/12) 1811 - 1838

Smith, R. & Yang,. X (2004). Toward a general theory of creativity in advertising: Examining the role of divergence. *Marketing Theory,* **4**(1/2), 31-58.

Thompson, D. V. & Malaviya, P. (2013) Consumer-generated ads: Does awareness of advertising co-creation help or hurt persuasion. *Journal of Marketing,* **44**, 33-47.

Tsai, S. (2002) Message framing strategy for brand communications, *Journal of Advertising Research,* **47**(3), 364-380

West, D. C., Kover, A. J. & Caruana, A. (2008) Practitioner and customer views of advertising creativity: same concept, different meaning? *Journal of Advertising,* **37**(4), 35-45.

Whittle, A., Mueller, F. & Mangan, A. (2009) 'Storytelling and 'Character': Victims, villains and heroes in a case of technological change. *Organization,* **16**(3) 425-442.

9 Digital Media and Marketing Interactivity

Kathryn Waite and Rodrigo Perez-Vega

Do you receive marketing communications using digital technology such as a smart phone, a tablet, a computer? Then you are a consumer of digital media. Digital media is an example of a *disruptive technology* (Bower & Christensen, 1995). A disruptive technology transforms the way that business is conducted within a sector, and digital media have transformed communication industries such as television broadcasting, film, journalism, publishing and music. For example, the digitisation of music has reduced the demand for records, cassettes and CDs, and has resulted in music sales taking place online rather than through physical stores. One of the most urgent questions that organisations are asking themselves today is: "How do we make sure that we are using digital media to the best effect within our marketing communications?" What follows is an overview of the core knowledge areas that will help you navigate this exciting new communications landscape.

Defining digital media

Digital media can be audio, video, written or image-based material that has been digitally compressed (encoded), transmitted and then decoded (activated) upon a digital device. Analogue or 'traditional' media such as print and broadcast media differs from digital media in terms the ease and the degree to which it can be accessed, shared, modified and stored. Analogue media is 'push media', where communications are broadcast to a passive audience of viewers, readers or listeners (Chaffey & Ellis-Chadwick, 2012). Digital media is 'pull media', or a form of 'inbound marketing', where the individual actively seeks information and interacts with brands (Chaffey & Ellis-Chadwick, 2012). Push media" places an advertising message within a marketplace; in contrast pull-media facilitates and stimulates interactions (Mollen & Wilson, 2010).

A key factor determining the choice of digital channel within integrated campaigns is the degree of interactivity.

Interactivity

An interaction occurs when an object has an intended effect upon the other, for example during the process of communication. The addition of "ivity" signifies that interact*ivity* refers to the quality and process of interaction taking place. Consumers like interactivity and this leads to a positive attitude towards the digital communication (Kirk et al., 2015). According to Liu and Shrum (2002) there are three dimensions of interactivity: active control, two-way communication and synchronicity (Table 9.1).

Table 9.1: Three dimensions of interactivity. Adapted from Liu and Shrum, 2002

Dimension of interactivity	Definition	Digital communications example
Active control	Voluntary and instrumental action that directly influences the controller's experience	Banner advertisements that allow you to click through.
Two-way communication	Implicit or explicit reciprocal communication	Changing the digital ads that you see based on previous search tracking (implicit) Online chat with a organisation representative (explicit)
Synchronicity	The delay between sending a message and receiving a reply. Digital media provide an almost instant response.	Entering a search term and getting an immediate response. Customisation of page content

A communications strategy of maximum interactivity would be challenging and expensive. Consumers differ in terms of how much interactivity they want, and some do not value interactivity as highly as others, which means that an increase of interactivity might result in a reduction of message effectiveness (Kim et al., 2011). For example, *digital immigrants* (consumers born before 1980) do not value two-way communication as much as *digital natives* (consumers born after 1980) (Prensky, 2001; Kirk et al., 2015). This means that managers should critically evaluate the degree of each dimension of interactivity for the characteristics of their target audience.

Exercise

Select three digital marketing communications that you saw today, one from e-mail, one from social media and one from a webpage. For each digital marketing communication identify the extent to which you had active control, two-way communication and the degree of synchronicity. Assess whether an increase in interactivity would have increased or reduced the effectiveness of the advertisement for you.

Evolution of communication models

In response to digital disruption, marketing communication models have evolved to account for one-to-many to a many-to-many interactivity (Table 9.1). The one-to-many model represents a one-way communication process where a message is formulated, sent, received and decoded. This does not account for the interactivity that characterises digital media. The one-to-one model reflects developments in digital communications that enable consumers to engage not only in communication with a brand but also with each other in a dialogue. A many-to-many model is where customers can interact with other customers and with the brand (Hoffman & Novak, 1996). This is called a "trialogue" (Chaffey & Ellis-Chadwick, 2012).

Table 9.2: Differences between communications models

Communication model	Description	Example
One-to-many model	One source contacts many receivers with one message, the medium does not allow the customers to respond to the brand	Television advert
One-to-one model	One source contacts each recipient with a different personalised message and the customers can each respond to the source through the same medium	E-mail advertisement
Many-to-many model	One source sends a different message to each participant , customers can each send a message to each other, response to each sender- receiver can be made through the same medium	Social media post

9

Selecting digital platforms

Digital media provides choice in where, how and when communications are accessed, and this causes two types of fragmentation: *audience* and *digital*.

- **Audience** fragmentation refers to a situation whereby individuals make significantly different communication choices that result in a loss of a common understanding and a reduction in social cohesion (Sunstein, 2009). Audience fragmentation means a reduction in the effectiveness of mass communications strategies that are associated with analogue media, for example booking advertising slots at peak viewing times or placing advertisements on the back page of a popular magazine (Chafee & Metzger, 2000). Hence audience fragmentation means that the "reach" (or viewing figures) of analogue communication is reduced.

- **Digital** fragmentation refers to the proliferation in the number and form of devices and platforms upon which the individual accesses digital content. Consumers are moving from device to device and even use devices and platforms simultaneously. This activity means consumer decision-making involves overlapping and multiple sources of information (Powers et al., 2012). Digital fragmentation increases the need for integrated campaign strategies that work together across a range of digital channels and which avoid wasted expenditure and audience attention fatigue, whilst being sensitive to the needs of different consumer groups. Selecting the appropriate platforms for a marketing communication campaign is key to achieving strategic objectives.

Digital channels are selected according to *reach, impact* and *control*.

- **Reach** is measured as the number of times content is accessed, the number of page visits and the time spent on a particular page. A visit, or session, is a "single set of continuous activity attributable to a cookied browser or user which results in one or more pulled text and/or graphics downloads from a site" (Capacity Grid, 2015). Cookies, which are a small data packets placed on the browser, distinguish individual browsers (Google, 2015). However, a cookie does not measure the use of more than one browser (PC + table + smartphone) or the sharing of a browser (two or more people sharing the same computer).

- Digital channel impact is measured using online customer engagement (OCE). OCE can be active or passive and is a key digital communication success measure (Morgan-Thomas & Veloutsou, 2013). Active OCE includes: message creation, content sharing and commenting on the content provided by others, whilst passive OCE includes liking a fan page and viewing content (Mollen & Wilson, 2010). OCE can be evaluated using either quantity or quality measures. Quantity measures count the actions of consumers in response to a digital campaign such as the likes given to a brand, the number of brand followers and the number of times a piece of digital content is shared. Quality measures categorise the nature of the action taken, such as whether a positive or negative comment is made about a brand, satisfaction ratings, whether comments were made on shared content and the length of posts given and whether these are made over a period of time.

- Digital channels differ in the level of marketer **control** (Fill, 2009). Social media facilitates communication among consumers and empowers consumers to actively seek and share information (Rezabakhsh et al., 2006; Harrison & Waite, 2015). It is usual to classify digital media into owned, paid and earned media (Table 9.3).

Table 9.3: Media types and digital platforms. Adapted from: Corcoran, 2009

Media type	Definition	Examples
Owned media	Digital platforms owned by or managed by the organisation	Organisation website Organisation blog Facebook Fan page Organisation's Twitter account
Paid media	Where the organisation is paying for content to be placed on a digital platform	Display ads (banners) in third party websites Sponsored posts in third party blogs
Earned media	Where the organisation "earns" mentions on digital media	Non-paid mentions in third party websites Mentions in social media (Facebook, Twitter, blogs) User reviews

Each media type has strengths and weaknesses.

- **Owned** media gives the maximum level of organisational control but can be considered as less credible as it can be biased towards the organisation (Chu and Kim, 2011). The reach and frequency of owned media is many times lower than with other types, unless the owned media has a high volume of organic traffic already visiting the sites. In addition, owned media in Web 2.0 platforms such as blogs or Facebook fan pages are susceptible to the effects of highly engaged consumers who can express their views and affect both positively and negatively the organisation's image.

- **Paid** media allows for very specific segmentation of viewers in terms of geographic and psychographic variables. In paid media the organisation has control over what is being said, as well as the frequency of message display.

9

However, consumers can have "advertising blindness" which means they ignore paid media on digital platforms (Margarida Barreto, 2013).

■ **Earned** media is a form of word-of-mouth (see next section). Earned media is perceived as being the most credible and unbiased. However, organisations have limited control over message content, which can be not only positive but also negative. There is also no organisational control over reach. Positive messages on earned media can have a lesser reach if not complemented by other paid marketing efforts (such as paid posts), however negative messages can become viral and out of control.

The concept of eWOM

Marketing messages that use the opinion of other consumers are very powerful. Word-of-mouth (WOM) influences consumer choice, consumer expectations and attitudes, before and after purchase (De Bruyn & Lilien, 2008; Bone, 1995). Electronic word of mouth or eWOM is "any positive and negative statements made by potential, actual, or former customers about a product or organisation, which is made available to a multitude of people and institutions via the Internet"(Hennig-Thurau et al., 2003: 39). The difference between WOM and eWOM is that eWOM is accessible online. eWOM is considered to be commercially unbiased, and is usually supported by the degree of trustworthiness that the source has, whether that source is a friend or someone who is respected such as an expert or a celebrity.

Exercise

Organisations are trying to promote the generation of positive eWOM from their customers. Identify three organisations from different industries and list the activities that they are doing in order to achieve this goal.

■ eWOM characteristics

There are five main characteristics of eWOM communication according to literature (Table 9.4): valence, focus, timing, solicitation and intervention (Christodoulides et al., 2012; Yang et al., 2012).

Table 9.4: Five eWOM Characteristics

Characteristic	Definition
Valence	How positive or negative the message that is transmitted by the sender is.
Timing	When the message is received, i.e. pre- or post-purchase
Focus	The audience(s) of the communication and the outcome desired from that audience
Solicitation	Whether the message was sought by the users, of if the user had access to that experience without asking for it.
Intervention	The efforts that organisations make to promote the interaction between consumers within their own controlled platform

- **Valence** can be complex. Positive messages help to sell a product, but negative valence can also positively affect awareness of certain products and increase purchase likelihood if the receiver does not identify with the sender, i.e. you might like restaurants your parents do not like.

- The **timing** of eWOM can have a significant effect on product evaluation (Arndt, 1967; Herr et al., 1991; De Bruyn and Lilien, 2008; Bone, 1995; Lim & Chung, 2011). eWOM from other consumers prior, during and after their purchase can influence not only purchase but also post-purchase satisfaction.

- **Focus** means not only targeting prospective customers of a product but also a wider audience who might be linked to the brand, for example employees, suppliers, job-seekers for recruitment, as well as decision influencers and referrers. For example, recruitment eWOM is found on websites such as Glassdoor, where current employees share their work satisfaction rankings, their salary and the questions they were asked at interview.

- **Solicited** eWOM is more influential than unsolicited; since the receiver is actively seeking information. However, unsolicited eWOM is most common and passes as informal conversation between friends. As Table 9.5 shows consumers might share eWOM for reasons such as self-involvement or to find relief for the tensions that the purchase originated. Certain social media websites (e.g. Facebook Check-ins, Linked-In Sponsored Stories, Instagram picture postings) push unsolicited eWOM messages to their users. Indeed, additional exposure to brand names and logos increases the probability of product purchase through creating familiarity and awareness (Mitchell & Valenzuela, 2005).

- Organisations might promote and reward eWOM. This is called **intervention**. For example, organisations might allow their consumers to review their products or send direct emails in order to entice customers to generate reviews based on their experience.

9

■   Motivations behind eWOM communication

Understanding the motives that consumers have to generate eWOM is important as it can help organisations develop activities to harness this type of marketing communication. One of the most prominent studies in this subject is Dichter's work (1966) that identifies four main motivations: product-involvement, self-involvement, other-involvement, and message-involvement. However, the study only considered traditional WOM and did not account for the possibility of positive and negative valence of this type of communication. A later study by Sundaram et al. (1998) takes into consideration the valence of WOM communication and identifies four motivations for positive WOM and four for negative WOM (Table 9.5).

Table 9.5: Motivations for the generation of positive and negative eWOM. Adapted from: Sundaram et al. (1998)

eWOM valence	Motivation	Description
Positive eWOM	Altruism	Consumers want to help other consumers to make satisfying purchase decisions.
	Product-involvement	Consumers' use of the product/service is highly important that speaking about it helps vent those positive feelings.
	Self-enhancement	Consumers share their experiences to enhance their image among other by projecting themselves as intelligent shoppers.
	Helping the organisation	Similar to altruism, only that in this case the consumer wants to help the organisation because of the positive experience that they had with it.
Negative eWOM	Altruism	Consumers want to help other consumers by preventing other consumers experiencing the same problems that they had encountered.
	Anxiety reduction	Consumers want to share their negative experience with others in order to reduce their own anger, anxiety and frustration.
	Vengeance	Consumers express their negative experiences publicly to retaliate against the organisation associated to that experience.
	Advice seeking	Consumers share their negative experience with the intention to get advice on how to resolve their problems.

Organisations looking to generate positive eWOM among consumers should take into account the different motivations behind the generation of it. Organisations taking a passive approach to eWOM would not try to facilitate the generation of this valuable type of marketing communication, and would let consumers express themselves in online media without enticing and monitoring the generation of this type of messages. An organisation taking an active approach would generate the platforms where consumers can express themselves, and set in place mechanisms that would entice consumers to express their views. For example, several mobile applications introduced pop-up messages for their users to share their views on the app via online reviews. These pop-up messages appear a few days after the consumers has been using the app (Figure 9.1). Consumers agreeing to share their views of the app may do so from a desire to be altruistic for other prospective users and spare them the bad experience of downloading the app if it crashes and has many bugs, or to download it if its performance is considered beneficial or enjoyable.

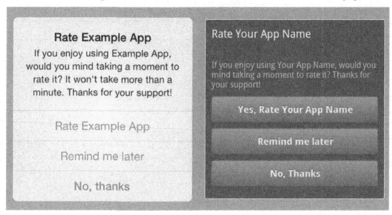

Figure 9.1: Example of online mechanisms to encourage eWOM in mobile applications. Source: Kissmetrics, N.D.

Viral marketing

9

Viral marketing is when consumers mutually share and spread marketing information, initially sent out by marketers to stimulate and capitalise on word of mouth (WOM) behaviours (Hinz et al., 2011). There are several advantages to viral campaigns. The content is a form of e-WOM which gives the message credibility (Dobele et al., 2007: 292). Viral campaigns can be cost-effective and able to reach niche consumer groups, which solves the problem of audience fragmentation (Dobele et al., 2005). However, viral campaigns offer limited control over the message reach, the speed of spread and message content. Viral campaigns can be a stimulus for user generated content or UGC and the original message can be reformulated either positively or negatively.

■ Planning a viral campaign

The key elements of planning a viral marketing campaign are shown in Figure 9.2.

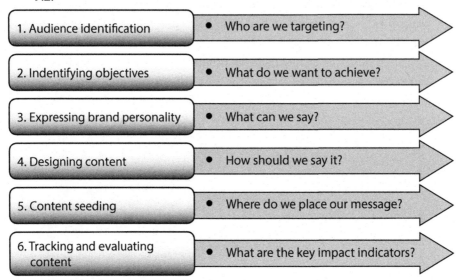

Figure 9.2: Planning a viral campaign

■ Viral audience identification? Who are we targeting?

Consumers generally dismiss digital mass messaging, which is often called 'spam'. This means it is important to use segmentation to define the target audience and fine tune the message in terms of content and placement. In addition to using behavioural, psychological and demographic profile variables, we can also use digital technology to define the target audience. For example, a leisure organisation found that the majority of the women between the ages of 18-34 years within its target audience used Facebook and tended to access this platform through smart phones when commuting. It is important not confuse the terms *target audience* and *target market*.

■ A **target market** comprises the people we wish to buy and use the product or service.

■ A **target audience** includes not only potential consumers but also influencers, who shape the opinions and behaviours of the target market (Pickton & Broderick, 2005). Influencers might be the consumer's social circle, celebrities or experts, such as bloggers, tweeters or vloggers (video bloggers).

Organisations can use a range of online monitoring tools to identify influencers such as: Hootsuite, Synthesio, Radian6, Brandwatch, Lithium and Socialradar.

For example, Facebook uses an algorithm called EdgeRank to decide who will see a Facebook Fan page post depending on the type of message, how the user has interacted before with that message and the temporal immediacy of the message itself (Edgerank, 2015). In choosing which tool to use, it is important to check that it meets the criteria listed in Table 9.6.

Table 9.6: Criteria for selecting an online monitoring tool

Criteria	Key criteria	Key questions
Platform coverage	Does the tool pull data from platforms that are of importance for the brand?	Is there coverage of both social and mainstream media? Can this tool be used for a range of languages and countries? How long does an enquiry take?
Data presentation	Is the data presented in a way that is informative, engaging and interactive?	Are real-time dashboards available? Can the dashboard be customised? Can data be exported and stored?
Data analysis	Can we apply the appropriate filters to group data in a way that is meaningful for our brand?	Can we analyse responses but age, gender, country, interests, influence etc? Is trend analysis available?
Data drill down	Is it possible to move from headline results to finer levels of detail?	Can we see how the follower base breaks down across social networks? Can we measure positive and negative sentiment?

Exercise

Visit the website of one or more organisations that provide online monitoring tools to learn about what the range of services they offer; focus if you can on the client case studies. Use Table 9.6 to differentiate the organisations.

9

■ Viral campaign objectives: What do we want to achieve?

Viral campaign objectives will link to the overall marketing communications objectives and strategic plan (see Chapter 5). Table 9.7 summarises objectives for a viral campaign. I is common to have several objectives but all viral campaigns need the message to be shared (a conative marketing objective). For example, a car manufacturer combined multiple objectives to gain insight into the barriers to adoption of one of its brands. A viral campaign used a short video clip of a car being parked into a particularly tight parking space. An analysis of shares and likes showed that female drivers tended to forward the clip with supportive and positive comments, whilst male drivers tended to forward the clip with negative comments. Based on this insight the organisation designed a follow-up marketing campaign using the positive sentiments and targeted female drivers.

Table 9.7: Viral communication objectives

Objective	Definition	Example
Conative	Aiming to result in a particular form of behaviour	Purchase or product through accessing voucher User engagement such sharing content
Affective	Seeking to change or reinforce attitudes	Liking a particular post Communicating humour
Cognitive	Aiming to create knowledge and awareness	Communicating a particular idea about an issue

■ Brand personality: What can we say?

A brand personality is "the set of human characteristics associated with a brand" (Aaker, 1997: 347). Brand personalities differ along key dimensions such as sincerity, excitement, competence and sophistication (Ivens & Valta, 2012). Brand personality can be expressed in social media through the brand's "tone of voice", which covers vocabulary, grammar and register (mood). Several organisations issue tone of voice documents, which outline whether the brand would write posts that were, for example, formal or chatty, detached or warm, professional or wacky, serious or humorous, relaxed or lively. The brand personality guidelines may cover not only how the brand communicates proactively but also how it responds to customers.

■ Viral content design: How should we say it?

Viral content should make a connection with the consumer (Dobele et al., 2007). In Chapter 8 you read how advertising appeals can be divided into rational and emotional appeals. Viral campaigns are successful if they make an emotional connection (Eckler & Bolls, 2011). Surprise, joy, sadness, anger, fear and disgust all result in message forwarding behaviour, and messages that combine humour and surprise are more likely to be shared (Dobele et al., 2007). In addition, campaigns which are high in uniqueness create a 'buzz' which results in more sharing (Dobele et al., 2007: 292).

■ Viral content seeding: Where do we place our message?

Content seeding is the planned release of content within digital channels and involves not only channel selection but the order of use. Simple seeding is where the content is initiated within owned media, and advanced seeding is where content is placed within earned or paid media. Advance seeding involves more effort, cost and planning, however if the appropriate influencers are selected then the campaign may spread faster and further than only using owned media. The aim of content seeding is to get content read, noticed and spread, and it is possible to use advertising consultants who specialise in content seeding.

■ Evaluating viral campaign impact: What are the key performance indicators?

Each person who shares a viral campaign validates its content and increases its reach. Barker et al. (2012) identify three forms of sharing:

- **Primary** sharing, when the creator posts content online,
- **Secondary** sharing, when fans, friends and customers spread the video within their social circles and
- **Tertiary** sharing, when content is shared by individuals who have no connection with the original video's creator i.e. non-customers.

Other forms of OCE are adapting and mimicking of the original content as discussed in *Old Spice* Case study in Chapter 12. A very successful viral campaign might become an internet meme, which is when a message stimulates UGC that spreads rapidly. An example meme is the 'Ice bucket challenge' (IBC), which involved each person being filmed having a bucket of water with ice cubes in it poured over their head, and sharing this on social media to raise money for the charity, Amyotrophic Lateral Sclerosis association (Motor Neurone Disease Association in the UK). As of 2014, there had been 2.4 million videos placed on Facebook and 28 million people had made IBC related posts.

9

Summary

Digital marketing communication channels offer a distinct combination of performance attributes that are not always fully captured within analogue communication models. It is important to recognise the interactive and pull characteristics of digital media and also the reduction in the degree of control that an organisation has over message content and reach. Digital channels enable an organisation to leverage the benefits of positive electronic word of mouth. This chapter has provided a range of motives that consumers have to generate eWOM, which can help organisations develop activities to harness this type of marketing communication. It also introduces the concept of viral marketing and provides a six-stage process by which marketers might stimulate and capitalise on word of mouth (WOM) behaviours.

Further reading

Kietzmann, J. H., Hermkens, K., McCarthy, I. P. & Silvestre, B. S. (2011). Social media? Get serious! Understanding the functional building blocks of social media. *Business Horizons*, **54**(3), 241-251.

Beverland, M., Dobele, A. & Farrelly, F. (2015). The viral marketing metaphor explored through vegemite. *Marketing Intelligence & Planning*, **33**(5).

Exemplar paper

Perez-Vega, R., Waite, K. and O'Gorman, K. (2016). Social Impact Theory: an examination of how immediacy operates as an influence upon social media interaction in Facebook Fan pages. *The Marketing Review*, **16**, 4.

A conceptual paper that reviews the literature on social influence and presents Social Impact Theory as an appropriate theory to explain consumer engagement behaviour on Facebook fan pages. The paper looks at the types of interactions that occur with Facebook fan pages and the associated meaning of these interactions. The paper argues for a need to develop the concept of immediacy in online contexts and proposes that physical, social and temporal immediacy can have different effect on engagement behaviours in social media settings. The paper presents a framework to be tested empirically.

References

Aaker, J. L. (1997). Dimensions of brand personality. *Journal of Marketing Research*, **34**, 347-356.

Arndt, J. (1967). Role of product-related conversations in the diffusion of a new product. *Journal of Marketing Research*, **4**, 291-295.

Barker, M., Barker, D. I., Bormann, N. & Neher, K. (2012). *Social Media Marketing: A Strategic Approach*. Cengage Learning.

Bone, P. F. (1995). Word-of-mouth effects on short-term and long-term product judgments. *Journal of Business Research*, **32**(3), 213-223.

Bower, J. And Christenson, C. (1995). Disruptive technologies: Catching the wave *Harvard Business Review*, **73**(1), 43-53

Chaffee, S.H. and Metzger, M.J. (2001), The end of mass communication?, *Mass Communications and Society*, **4**(4), 365-379

Chaffey, D., & Ellis-Chadwick, F. (2012). *Digital Marketing*. Pearson Higher Ed.

Christodoulides, G., Michaelidou, N. & Argyriou, E. (2012). Cross-national differences in e-WOM influence. *European Journal of Marketing*, **46**(11/12), 1689-1707.

Chu, S. C., & Kim, Y. (2011). Determinants of consumer engagement in electronic word-of-mouth (eWOM) in social networking sites. *International Journal of Advertising*, **30**(1), 47-75.

Corcoran, S. (2009). Defining earned, owned and paid media. Available from: http://blogs.forrester.com/interactive_marketing/2009/12/defining-earned-owned-and-paid-media.html (Accessed 12-07-2015).

Capacity Grid (2015), *Internet Advertising Glossary,* Available at http://www.capacitygrid.com/wp-content/uploads/2015/03/Advertising-Glossary1.pdf (Accessed 5th August 2016)

De Bruyn, A. & Lilien, G.L. (2008). A multi-stage model of word-of-mouth influence through viral marketing. *International Journal of Research in Marketing*, **25**, 151–163.

Dichter, E., (1966). How word-of-mouth advertising works. *Harvard business review, 44*(6), pp.147-160.

Dobele, A., Toleman, D. & Beverland, M. (2005). Controlled infection! Spreading the brand message through viral marketing. *Business Horizons*, **48**(2), 143-149.

Dobele, A., Lindgreen, A., Beverland, M., Vanhamme, J. & Van Wijk, R. (2007). Why pass on viral messages? Because they connect emotionally. *Business Horizons*, **50**(4), 291-304.

Eckler, P. & Bolls, P. (2011). Spreading the virus: Emotional tone of viral advertising and its effect on forwarding intentions and attitudes. *Journal of Interactive Advertising*, **11**(2), 1-11.

Edgerank (2015). What is edgerank? http://edgerank.net/ (Accessed 12-07-2015).

Fill, C. (2009). *Marketing Communications: Interactivity, communities and content.* Pearson Education

Google (2015). Measuring reach and frequency. Available from: https://support.google.com/adwords/answer/2472714?hl=en (Accessed on: 19-07-2015).

Harrison, T., & Waite, K. (2015). Impact of co-production on consumer perception of empowerment. *The Service Industries Journal*, (ahead-of-print), 1-19.

Hennig-Thurau, T., Walsh, G. & Walsh, G. (2003). Electronic word-of-mouth: Motives for and consequences of reading customer articulations on the Internet. *International Journal of Electronic Commerce*, **8**(2), 51-74.

Herr, P. M., Kardes, F. R., & Kim, J. (1991). Effects of word-of-mouth and product-attribute information on persuasion: An accessibility-diagnosticity perspective. *Journal of Consumer Research*, **17**, 454-462.

Hinz, O., Skiera, B., Barrot, C., & Becker, J. U. (2011). Seeding strategies for viral marketing: An empirical comparison. *Journal of Marketing*, **75**(6), 55-71.

Hoffman, D. L., & Novak, T. P. (1996). Marketing in hypermedia computer-mediated environments: conceptual foundations. *The Journal of Marketing*, **60**, 50-68.

Ivens, B., & Valta, K. S. (2012). Customer brand personality perception: A taxonomic analysis. *Journal of Marketing Management*, **28**(9-10), 1062-1093.

Kim, J., Spielmann, N. and Mcmillan. S. J. (2012) Experience effects on interactivity: functions,processes, and perceptions. *Journal of Business Research* **65**, 1543-1550.

Kirk, C. P., Chiagouris, L., Lala, V. & Thomas, J. D. (2015). How do digital natives and digital immigrants respond differently to interactivity online? a model for predicting consumer attitudes and intentions to use digital information products. *Journal of Advertising Research*, **55**(1), 81-94.

Kissmetrics (N.D.). 5 clever ways to increase mobile apps reviews. Available from: https://blog.kissmetrics.com/increase-mobile-app-reviews/ (Accessed 14-07-2015).

Lim, B. C. & Chung, C. M. (2011). The impact of word-of-mouth communication on attribute evaluation. *Journal of Business Research*, **64**(1), 18-23.

Liu, Y. & Shrum, L. J. (2002). What is interactivity and is it always such a good thing? Implications of definition, person, and situation for the influence of interactivity on advertising effectiveness. *Journal of Advertising*, **31**(4), 53-64.

Margarida Barreto, A. (2013). Do users look at banner ads on Facebook? *Journal of Research in Interactive Marketing*, **7**(2), 119-139.

Mitchell, A. & Valenzuela, A. (2005). How banner ads affect brand choice without click-through. In Haugtvedt, C.P., Machleit, K.A. & Yalch, R. (eds.) *Online Consumer Psychology: Understanding and influencing consumer behavior in the virtual world*, pp 125-142, Mahwah, N.J. : Lawrence Erlbaum Associates.

Mollen, A. & Wilson, H. (2010). Engagement, telepresence and interactivity in online consumer experience: Reconciling scholastic and managerial perspectives. *Journal of Business Research*, **63**(9), 919-925.

Morgan-Thomas, A. & Veloutsou, C. (2013). Beyond technology acceptance: Brand relationships and online brand experience. *Journal of Business Research*, **66**(1), 21-27.

Pickton, D. & Broderick, A. (2005). *Integrated Marketing Communications*. Financial Times Prentice Hall.

Powers, T., Advincula, D., Austin, M. S., Graiko, S. & Snyder, J. (2012). Digital and social media in the purchase decision process: a special report from the Advertising Research Foundation. *Journal of Advertising Research*, **52**(4), 479-489.

Prensky, M. (2001). Digital natives, digital immigrants, 1. *On the Horizon*, **9**(5), 1-6.

Rezabakhsh, B., Bornemann, D., Hansen, U. & Schrader, U. (2006). Consumer power: a comparison of the old economy and the Internet economy.*Journal of Consumer Policy*, **29**(1), 3-36.

Sundaram, D. S., Mitra, K., & Webster, C. (1998). Word-of-mouth communications: A motivational analysis. *Advances in Consumer Research*, **25**(1), 527-531.

Sunstein, C. R. (2009). *Republic.com 2.0*. Princeton University Press.

Yang, J., Kim, W., Amblee, N., & Jeong, J. (2012). The heterogeneous effect of WOM on product sales: why the effect of WOM valence is mixed? *European Journal of Marketing*, **46**(11/12), 1523-1538.

10 International Advertising and Communications

Babak Taheri and Sean Lochrie

The internationalisation of marketing communications

International advertising can be defined as a "phenomenon that involves the transfer of advertising appeals, messages, art, copy, photographs, stores, and video and film segments (or spots) from one country to another" (American Marketing Association, 2015). International advertising encompasses areas such as planning, budgeting, resource allocation issues, message strategy, media decisions, local regulations, advertising agency selection, coordination of multi-country communication efforts, and regional and global campaigns (Percy & Rosenbaum-Elliott, 2012; Solomon, 2013).

It is suggested that advances in communication technologies have led to consumers around the world increasingly desiring the same products (Levitt, 1983). As Levitt (1983: 93) highlights, "the world's needs and desires have been irrevocably homogenised. This makes the multinational corporation obsolete and the global corporation absolute". Therefore, Levitt (1983) argues that international firms should stop acting like 'multinationals' which tailor their products to fit local markets, instead, they should become global through standardising the manufacturing, distribution and advertising of their goods across all nations. In other words, organisations should follow an internationalisation strategy, which can be described as an approach to designing, producing, distributing and advertising products and services that are easily adaptable to different countries, cultures and languages (Turnbull & Doherty-Wilson, 1990).

Despite this focus on standardization, the need for organisations to embrace local needs and tastes is of great significance (Kanso & Kitchen, 2004; Melewar & Saunders, 1999). For example, American fast food restaurant KFC, originally branded Kentucky Fried Chicken, successfully penetrated the Chinese market by balancing the fundamental core of their brand, fried chicken and fast service, with offering China-specific food to supplement its standard Western cuisine. This exemplifies the argument made by Quelch and Hoff (1986, p. 59) that the pertinent question in international marketing "is not whether to go global but how to tailor the global marketing concept to fit each business".

Internationalisation in advertising can be traced back to the start of the early twentieth century, but the importance of this phenomena was given credence when in 1899 American marketing communications agency, J. Walter Thompson, opened its first office in London. The internationalisation of advertising has been studied from several perspectives. For example, Levitt (1983) argues that a common advertising campaign with some minor adjustments can help to promote the same service or product across borders. However, it requires separate messages for consumers in different markets, as there are some incompatible differences (e.g., cultural, economic and media elements) between countries or even between regions in the same country. Additionally, Pappavassilliou and Stathakopoulos (1997) argue that adaptation of advertising decisions is not a dichotomous one and such decisions can be viewed on the continuum, as there normally exist degrees of international advertising adaptation. Moreover, geographers and economists examine a variety of issues with regards to the international evaluation of ad agencies and the international regulatory implications on the companies as a result of liberalisation of advertising services (Roberts, 1998). Turnbull and Doherty-Wilson (1990: 12) note that "the internationalisation of the advertising agency business has made it necessary for multinational as well as national agencies to direct more attention to corporate strategy and policy decisions. While agencies generally see internationalisation as a natural business progression, whether they choose to exist as a multinational or a national agency, they must position the agency properly within that environment to ensure their survival and prosperity". They also argue that ad agencies sometimes utilise employee-related and non-related diversification strategies in both domestic and international levels.

International marketing communications is a challenging phenomenon. According to Monye (2000: 4) an important element in the planning of marketing communications is how different organisations can communicate with "a range of messages about value, quality, reliability and brand image to a whole variety of global audiences". Pivotal to successful marking communications is the organisation's ability to develop a brand that means something to its target audience. In today's world, geographic and cultural borders are *permeable* because of the internet, cable and satellite television. Globalisation and increased geographical mobility mean that even regional advertising has to attend to the different cultural frames of reference of non-indigenous populations. This in return can create potential foreign markets for domestic producers and increases competition in the market (Hackley, 2012; Percy & Rosenbaum-Elliott, 2012). For instance, in Europe there are stereotypical beliefs that the best policemen are British, the best chefs French, the best mechanics German, the best lovers Italian and the best organisers the Swiss. As the old joke goes, "Hell is where the police are German, the chefs are British, the mechanics are French, the lovers Swiss and it is all organised by the Italians" (Hackley, 2010: 196).

As another example, popular Scottish clothing brands such as Harris Tweed and Pringle have been able to penetrate global markets, taking once domestic and local brands to the world stage. If a fashion brand A is successful and active in the foreign market, then fashion brand B also would like to play active role in this particular foreign market and remain competitive in the domestic market. However, international and cross-cultural communication remains an area of tension between local cultural norms of meaning systems and global (often Western) brand ideologies. For example, even within one country a given advert can be exposed to heterogeneous consumers whose interpretive frame of reference is informed by specific cultural norms which reflect ethnic, religion, family, sub-culture, peer-group and other values and presuppositions and advertising regulation (Hackley, 2012; Percy & Rosenbaum-Elliott, 2012). Furthermore, the differences in international advertising regulation and the different interpretation of frame of references in dissimilar cultures can influence the standardisation and advertising campaigns. Therefore, a particular advertising campaign might be acceptable in a country (e.g., portraying nudity) but not be acceptable in another country.

10

Exercise

Consider a popular brand – for example, a sports clothing brand, a car manufacturer, or a restaurant chain. Can you identify elements of their marketing communications which are distinguishable and can be seen to exemplify an internationalisation approach to advertising? You may want to consider things such as logo, colours, and slogans.

Standardisation and localisation of international marketing communications

Grein and Gould (1996: 143) define the globally integrated marketing communications as "a system of active promotional management which strategically coordinates global communications in all of its component parts both horizontally in terms of countries and organizations and vertically in terms of promotion disciplines. It contingently takes into account the full range of standardized versus adaptive market options, synergies, variations among target populations and other market-place and business conditions". Here, globalisation is a process leading to greater interdependence and mutual awareness among economic, political and social units in the world, and among actors in general (Kitchen and Schultz, 1999). Ultimately, when operating in different countries managers must determine how to market and communicate their products and services in each country (Solomon et al., 2009). Therefore, in international marketing, managers must consider a number of key questions. For example:

1 To what degree will the organisation have to adjust their marketing communications to the tastes and needs of the local market?

2 Will the same products and services be attractive to the local market?

3 Will the price of the offering need to be altered?

Much of this debate concerns itself with the different perspectives related to standardisation and localisation of international marketing communications (Terpstra et al., 2012). Standardisation is the process of extending and effectively applying domestic target-market-dictated product standards, tangible and/or intangible attributes, to markets in a foreign environment (Szymanski et al., 1993). For example, in 2013, NIVEA launched a global campaign using the slogan 'It starts with you' to promote the launch of its new men's Active Age Range. Running across various communicative channels, the campaign was first launched in the UK and Germany, before being rolling out globally. The global template used by NIVEA highlights the approach of a company using the same marketing mix to penetrate multiple markets – in other words, standardisation.

The standardise-or-localise question arose partly because communications infrastructure has evolved to make standardised global advertising possible (e.g., DVD technology, satellite TV, the internet and international travel). Creating standardised ads that translate to differing cultures requires a common denominator of meaning for the brand, product or service which allows them to 'travel well' worldwide. In some cases, standardisation is possible because the commodity being promoted has the same meaning to consumers in different cultures. Localisation can facilitate global marketing strategy by placing global brands in a local cultural context (Ramarapu et al., 1999). This can also facilitate localised positioning and segmentation approaches. For example, local agencies often employ a culturally-specific interpretation of the brand values, which may not always be the interpretation that the organisation conceived in its strategic planning. Interestingly, some international brands have found that neither localisation nor standardisation serves their purpose. In response the term 'glocalisation' has been coined and refers to the local adaptation of globally oriented marketing themes and products (Koekemoer & Bird, 2004). Global brand organisations seek to control the presentation of their brand at a certain level, allowing local ad agencies some licence to portray the brand in ways that will correspond with local cultural meaning systems (Hackley, 2012; Lee & Carter, 2012).

There are also differences between the standardised and adapted marketing mix. The standardised marketing mix involves selling the same products and using the same marketing approaches worldwide, whereas the adapted marketing mix involves adjusting its elements in each target market, which incurs more costs but holds the hope of a larger market share (Egan, 2015; Lee & Carter, 2012). Table 10.1 shows three main questions (when? why? and how?) with regards to standardisation.

Table 10.1: The three questions of standardisation

Question	Explanation
When?	Commonalities in customers' needs across countries
	"Made in" image is important to a product's perceived value - for example, France for perfumes, Sheffield for stainless steel, Scottish salmon, and Aberdeen Angus beef.
	Homogeneity of markets, i. e. markets available without adaptation - e.g., denim jeans, NIVEA for Men, David Beckham aftershave, and Beats by Dr. Dre headphones.
	Cultural insensitivity – e.g., this would be of little problem to products such as Apple iPhones, but is important to fast food providers such as McDonalds and Pizza Hut who operate in Muslim countries where Halal products are a necessity.
Why?	Economies of scale in production, marketing/communications, research & development
	Minimizing costs
	Easier management and control
How?	Usually considered in the context of product, pricing, marketing communications; particularly advertising, branding, packaging

10

However, sometimes marketers don't understand foreign culture, and thus they fail to adapt properly. There are factors that force marketers to focus outside globally consistent marketing communications (Vrontis et al., 2009). Lee & Carter (2012) highlight two main factors preventing standardisation of marketing communications, both are exhibited in Figure 10.1.

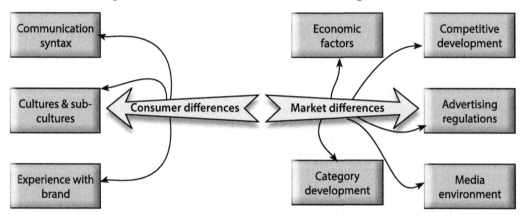

Figure 10.1: Factors preventing standardisation of marketing communications. Adapted from Lee & Carter (2012)

As Figure 10.1 highlights, Lee & Carter (2012) indicate that market and consumer difference are the two main factors which prevent the standardisation of marketing communications.

- First, **market differences** can vary depending on the brand, sector and country. This includes: economic factors (e.g., consumers level of affordability across different countries); media environment (e.g., consumers consume media differently); advertising regulations (e.g., restriction in advertising with regards to certain age groups or vulnerable people); category development (e.g., segmenting markets into different groups or sub-groups); and competitive development (e.g., how to enter into the particular competitive market) (Busch et al., 2006; Martenson, 1987).

- On the other hand, **consumer differences** play an important role, and refer to the disparities between individuals which have the ability to influence the way in which marketing communications are understood and processed. This includes issues relating to: cultural differences (e.g., attitude towards the consumption of particular product in a specific culture); communication syntax (e.g., understanding social habits and values of different countries); and experience with the brand (e.g., understanding how consumers use or engage with a brand).

Advantages and disadvantages of global marketing

Keller (2011) explains the advantages (Figure 10.2) and disadvantages (Figure 10.3) of global marketing with regards to branding and marketing communications.

Advantages of global marketing programs

Uniformity of marketing practices	Economies of scale in production and distribution	Lower marketing costs
Ability to leverage good ideas quickly and efficiently	Consistency in brand image	Power and scope

Figure 10.2: Advantages of global marketing programmes (Keller, 2011)

- **Uniformity of marketing practices** occurs by keeping the core of the marketing program constant, allowing marketers to pay greater attention to making refinements across markets and to improve effectiveness over time.

- **Economies of scale in production and distribution** can be seen as manufacturing efficiencies and lower costs that derive from higher volumes in production and distribution.

- **Lower marketing costs** can arise from uniformity in packaging, advertising, promotion, and other marketing communication activities.

- **Power and scope** refers to the ability of a global brand's profile to communicate credibility. For example, the American car rental company, Avis assures its customers that they can receive the same high-quality car rental service anywhere in the world, further reinforcing a key benefit promise embodied in its slogan 'We Try Harder'.

- **Consistency in brand image** is about an organisation maintaining a common marketing platform all over the world with the intention of nurturing a consistent brand and company image. For example, American Express communicates the prestige and utility of its credit card worldwide.

- The **ability to leverage good ideas quickly and efficiently** takes place when marketers can leverage effective ideas across markets as long as the right knowledge transfer systems are put into place. For instance, IBM has a web-

10

based communications tool that provides instant multimedia interaction to connect marketers. (Keller, 2011).

Despite these benefits, there are disadvantages of global marketing programs.

Figure 10.3: Advantages of global marketing programmes (Keller, 2011)

- **Differences in consumer needs, wants, and usage patterns for products** lead customers to behave very differently. Therefore, product strategies that work in one country may not work in another. For example, in France, more expensive cookware products sell much better than in the USA, where customers buy more plastic containers.

- **Differences in consumer response to branding elements** is problematic and normally occurs when linguistic differences across countries can change the meaning of a brand name.

- **Differences in consumer responses to marketing mix elements** relate to the differences in price sensitivity, promotion responsiveness, sponsorship support, and other activities that can occur across countries.

- **Differences in brand and product development and the competitive environment** arise because products may be at different stages of their life cycle in different countries. The nature of competition also differs.

- **Differences in the legal environment** can also be challenging, for example, Venezuela, Canada, and Australia stipulated that commercials had to be physically produced in the native country.

- **Differences in marketing institutions** is an issue that makes implementation of the same marketing strategy difficult. For example, the penetration of cable television, cell phones, supermarkets, may vary considerably, especially in developing countries.

- **Differences in administrative procedures** is a problem and aries when it may be difficult to achieve the control necessary to implement a standardised global marketing program. (Keller, 2011)

Exercise

Consider the advantages of a global marketing strategy. Search a popular brand of your choice and identify how they have benefited from such an approach. Don't only consider what they have done well, but reflect on what they haven't. What recommendations would you give them?

Country of origin effects

Country of origin effects can bestow a halo of prestige on brands emanating from particular countries (Pappu et al., 2006). For example, UK and German motor-car design and engineering, Japanese technology, Swiss watches, French food and wine, Italian fashion, Colombian coffee, Indian tea, Belgian beer, and Thai food (Hackley, 2012; Yoo et al., 2000). Country of origin is also a powerful image variable that could be used to achieve competitive advantage in international marketing (Chao, 1993). That images have the power to stimulate and thus affect a consumers' choice process is widely documented. Normally, during the development of a company's marketing communication mix, the marketing or advertising manager is often vigorously involved in creating, adapting, monitoring, maintaining and managing images (Bertoli, 2013).

Additionally, brand equity may not be wholly understood without examining its sources, which are the contributing elements to the formation of brand equity in the consumer's mind. The majority of brand equity studies concentrate on the marketing mix variables such as advertising, distribution, price and product quality as the contributing drivers (Yoo et al., 2000). In the buying process, consumers are not just concerned about the quality and price of a product, but also other factors such as the brand's country of origin. One of the most effective conceptual frameworks of brand equity is presented by Yoo et al. (2000) who incorporated country of origin image as an antecedent of brand equity. In this framework, individual dimensions of brand equity are linked to the outcome, and the antecedent of brand equity is linked to the dimensions

10

of brand equity. Thus, to manage brand equity, the relationships between the antecedents and brand equity dimensions and between the dimensions of brand equity and brand equity outcome, should be determined.

Exercise

Identify a number of the brands which you think have gained a competitive advantage in international marketing through the country of origin effect. What did these brands specifically do which contributed to their success? Can you think of any brands which have been damaged through their association with their country of origin? Can you think of alternative strategies which these brands could have employed?

Advertising translation

The reason why this chapter centres its attention on standardisation and international marketing is because its effectiveness has been questioned in cross-cultural communications. Research in translation studies suggests that layout does not normally carry any cultural meaning, which implies that text and images are utterly independent. Here, it is important to highlight the implications of the terms 'translator' and 'translation'. There is a general belief that translators go beyond their traditional role as experts on linguistic transfer (i.e., cultural mediation, adaptation and creativeness), and therefore these two terms seem to be insufficient to express the multiple dimensions in global communications. Some of the names suggested to replace the term 'translator' include: 'transcreator', 'copywriter' and 'adaptor'. In advertising, the terms 'translation' is normally avoided and replaced by terms such as 'copy adaptation' and 'localisation'. In recent years, there has been a growing amount of literature on global marketing communications with regards to advertising translation. For example, some studies discussed assisting translators with concepts within the decision-making process; some explored the role of translation from a multidisciplinary view; and others researched the effect of globalisation on the media, which is a common channel of distribution for commercial advertising. The main concern here is the fact that globalisation can lead to homogenisation as well as the dominance of the Anglo-Saxon culture and language from world power countries resulting in irregularities and an 'unequal cultural exchange' (Hackley, 2012; Keller, 2011).

As a result, researchers should pay attention to whether the powerful standard commercial messages distributed through global media convey the same meaning to consumers from different cultural backgrounds. Marketing scholars can use cultural-dimension frameworks. For example, Edward Said's Orientalism focuses on the interplay between the 'Occident' and the 'Orient'. The Occident is his term for the West (e.g., Britain, France, and the United States), and the Orient is the term for the romantic and misunderstood Middle East and Far East. Michel Foucault concentrates on social power, cultural imperialism and feminism. Greet Hofstede's six dimensions of national cultures including *power distance, individualism, uncertainty avoidance, masculinity, long term orientation*, and *indulgence vs. restraint*. However, one should give extra attention to selecting the most suitable framework in different research settings in global marketing communications and advertising studies.

Conclusions

Today's marketplace is truly global in nature and offers organisations the opportunity to enter various countries and target different consumer groups across the world. However, for organisations and their brands to flourish successfully, marketing managers must learn to tackle the intricacies of the global marketplace. This chapter has highlighted that there are advantages for an organisation that can successfully standardise the marketing communication process and find a common denominator of meaning that transcends cultures. Despite this, the attractions of international markets and the appeal of brands that cross national boundaries have to be understood in terms of local cultural meaning systems. All communications are very sensitive to local culture and conditions and, without due attention, can be problematic for marketers. This chapter has also emphasised the importance for marketing managers to consider the advantages and disadvantages of global marketing programs, as well as the issues surrounding country of origin effects. All forms of international marketing communications have a central purpose: to ensure that the intended messages are communicated accurately between the transmitter and the recipient. However, as this chapter has highlighted, the choices which encompass international advertising and marketing are complex and require carefully planning and strategic thinking.

10

Recommended reading

Hackley, C. (2012). *Advertising and Promotion: An Integrated Marketing Communications Approach* (2nd ed.). London.

Levitt, T. (1983). The Globalisation of Markets. *Harvard Business Review, 61*, 92-102.

Pappavassilliou, N., & Stathakopoulos, V. (1997). Standardisation versus Adaptation of International Advertising Strategies: Towards a Framework. *European Journal of Marketing, 31*, 504-527

References

American Marketing Association (2015) American Marketing Association Dictionary, available at: https://www.ama.org/resources/Pages/Dictionary.aspx

Bertoli, G. (2013). *International Marketing and the Country of Origin Effect: the global impact of 'made in Italy'*. Cheltenham: Edward Elgar Publishing.

Busch, R., Seidenspinner, M. & Unger, F. (2006). *Marketing Communication Policies*. Berlin: Springer Science & Business Media.

Chao, P. (1993). Partitioning country of origin effects: consumer evaluations of a hybrid product. *Journal of International Business Studies*, **24**(2), 291-306.

Egan, J. (2015). *Marketing Communications*. London: Sage Publications Limited.

Grein, A. F. & Gould, S. J. (1996). Globally integrated marketing communications. *Journal of Marketing Communications, 2*, 141-158.

Hackley, C. (2012). *Advertising and Promotion: An Integrated Marketing Communications Approach,* 2nd ed. London.

Kanso, A. & Kitchen, P. J. (2004). Marketing consumer services internationally: Localisation and standardisation revisited. *Marketing Intelligence & Planning*, **22**(2), 201-215.

Keller, K. L. (2011). *Strategic Brand Management: Building, measuring, and managing brand equity,* 4th ed. UK: Pearson.

Kitchen, P. J. & Schultz, D. E. (1999). A multi-country comparison of the drive for IMC. *Journal of Advertising Research*, **39**(1), 21-21.

Koekemoer, L. & Bird, S. (2004). *Marketing Communications*. South Africa: Juta and Company Limited.

Lee, K. & Carter, S. (2012). *Global Marketing Management,* 3rd ed. London: Oxford University Press.

Levitt, T. (1983). The globalisation of markets. *Harvard Business Review*, **61**, 92-102.

Martenson, R. (1987). Is standardisation of marketing feasible in culture-bound industries? A European case study. *International Marketing Review*, **4**(3), 7-17.

Melewar, T. C. & Saunders, J. (1999). International corporate visual identity: standardization or localization? *Journal of International Business Studies*, **30**(3), 583-598.

Monye, S. O. (2000). *The Handbook of International Marketing* Oxford: Blackwell

Pappavassilliou, N. & Stathakopoulos, V. (1997). Standardisation versus adaptation of international advertising strategies: Towards a framework. *European Journal of Marketing*, **31**, 504-527.

Pappu, R., Quester, P. G. & Cooksey, R. W. (2006). Consumer-based brand equity and country-of-origin relationships: Some empirical evidence. *European Journal of marketing*, **40**(5/6), 696-717.

Percy, L. & Rosenbaum-Elliott, R. (2012). *Strategic Advertising Management*, 4th ed. London: Oxford.

Quelch, J. A., & Hoff, E. J. (1986) Customizing global marketing. *Harvard Business Review*, **64**(3), 59-68

Ramarapu, S., Timmerman, J. E. & Ramarapu, N. (1999). Choosing between globalization and localization as a strategic thrust for your international marketing effort. *Journal of Marketing Theory and Practice*, **7**(2), 97-105.

Roberts, J. (1998). *Multinational Business Service Firms: The development of multinational organisation structures in UK business services sector*, Aldershot: Ashgate Publishing.

Solomon, M. R., Marshall, G. W., & Stuart, E. W. (2009). *Marketing: Real people, real decisions*. Harlow: Pearson Education.

Solomon, M. (2013). *Consumer Behavior: Buying, having and being*. Harlow: Pearson.

Szymanski, D. M., Bharadwaj, S. G., & Varadarajan, P. R. (1993). Standardization versus adaptation of international marketing strategy: an empirical investigation. *The Journal of Marketing*, **57**(4) 1-17.

Terpstra, V., Foley, J. & Sarathy, R. (2012). *International Marketing*. US: Naper Press.

Turnbull, P. W. & Doherty-Wilson, L. (1990). The internationalisation of the advertising industry. *European Journal of Marketing*, **24**, 7-16.

Vrontis, D., Thrassou, A. & Lamprianou, I. (2009). International marketing adaptation versus standardisation of multinational companies. *International Marketing Review*, **26**(4/5), 477-500.

Yoo, B., Donthu, N., & Lee, S. (2000). An examination of selected marketing mix elements and brand equity. *Journal of the Academy of Marketing Science*, **28**(2), 195-211.

10

11 Marketing Communications Research and Evaluation

Geraldine McKay and Graham Pogson

"I know that half the money I spend on advertising is wasted; the trouble is I don't know which half." This 19th century quote attributed to retailer and US postmaster John Wanamaker (Compaine & Cunningham, 2010) continues to resonate for today's marketers as they try to account for the effectiveness and efficiency of their promotional and communications activity. Measuring the effectiveness of marketing communications is a challenge amplified by the plethora of new media opportunities, communications tools and also the increasing numbers of stakeholders influencing organisational goals. Moreover, target audiences are increasingly fragmented and global, further increasing complexity for those wishing to research and evaluate communications activity. This chapter will discuss the research commonly undertaken by marketers whilst planning, developing, implementing and analysing communications tactics. It also considers how the strategic and integrated marketing communications efforts are evaluated in the longer term.

Starting out – communication planning

Advertising spend in the UK in 2015 was etimated at over £18 billion (AA/WARC, 2014). This is significant for both the economy and any organisation be it a small business, global firm or non-commercial organisation. Many organisations spend large amounts of money but are unsure of the short and long term consequences of their investment, and whether results can be fully attributed to their communications campaign. Alongside effectiveness there is the need to measure efficiency and to question whether fewer resources might have been employed with similar outcomes. However, an efficient campaign that is not effective is not worthwhile. Research during the planning stages will help the marketing team forecast possible campaign outcomes, timeframes and costs.

One of the first tasks for the planning team is to consider the campaign objectives, i.e. what the campaign is expected to achieve. The objectives of communication effort influences both the strategy employed and how ultimately to measure the success or otherwise of the campaign. Sales metrics may be appropriate where the objective is to build market share, but if the aim is to achieve shifts in brand positioning then prior and post campaign attitude measures will be needed. A highly integrated campaign requires intricate research to provide an understanding of the contribution of each tool, employed alongside an evaluation to show how the methods worked holistically.

Table11.1: Secondary research sources for objective setting.

Research type and source	Sample data	Rationale
Academic research: Journals Conferences	How communication works- theoretical and empirical data Consumer behaviour theory Case studies of communications practice	Broad guidelines for objective setting, creative treatments and potential methods
Industry data: Trade and consumer press Trade association reports Commercially produced market research Government reports	**Customer:** Market size and share Demographic and other segmentation data Competitor insight Industry reports **Other stakeholders:** Share price movement Average salaries Top employers lists	Realistic and quantified objectives. Target audiences Industry benchmarks. Customer insight and behaviour
In house (internal) data: Accounting information Previous customer research HR databases CRM systems Historical communication activity results.	**Customer:** Number of current and lapsed customers Sales channels Profitability by customer/ acquisition point Sales trends Acquisition and retention data Customer satisfaction data **Other stakeholders:** Staff turnover figures Historical campaign results	Determining what needs to be achieved Setting baselines

Secondary research data generated from both internal and external sources should be the first port of call for an organisation to set objectives that are realistic and achievable.

Once objectives have been agreed then the research required to help campaign development comes into focus.

Campaign development

This section will consider the research and testing required throughout the campaign development process, from initial idea generation to campaign development (including media and tool choice) as shown below.

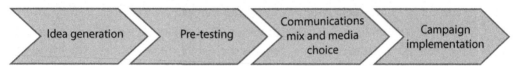

Figure 11.1: Campaign development process

■ Idea generation

Secondary research provides competitor and sector insight; audience profiles and media usage research provide consumer knowledge to spark creativity. Consumer and employee based primary research methods are also used to generate and develop promotional campaigns.

User studies and other qualitative techniques such as brainstorming, group discussions, in-depth interviews and projective techniques will generate and filter creative ideas. Ethnographic methods have been used by consumer goods manufacturers such as Proctor and Gamble (Zaltman, 2003) to provide insight into how consumers use products in everyday life. Such data is structured around incidents to reveal the "dramatic heart" (Cayla & Arnould, 2013: 8) of the narrative and insight to emotions. Crowdsourcing of ideas and user generated content from customers is seen as useful for idea generation and iterative testing (see Petavy, 2014; Dickinson-Delaporte & Kerr, 2015).

Typically both qualitative and quantitative research methods are used to generate two or three approaches for more detailed concept or pre-testing.

11

Insight: Search optimisation to guide creativity

Within the fashion industry, knowledge of search words provides insight to customer segments. Data shows that the peak period for searching for party wear is pre-Christmas, with traffic coming primarily from search engines, then shopping sites and finally lifestyle blogs. Further investigation showed that the word "dress" was commonly searched in conjunction with "black", "Christmas", "cocktail" and "designer." It is easy to understand how insight into popular terms can help content design and copy. (Experien, 2015)

■ Pre-testing

Marketing communications ideas are pre-tested amongst target audiences using a number of available methods to ensure that planned creative treatments are relevant and understood. Copy testing is often undertaken within focus groups or through consumer panels. Proposed creative treatments are shown to the participants and their reactions noted. Ideas can be presented as storyboards outlining the draft design and text of a commercial as a "rough" or more fully developed into finished advertisements. Testing continues until the final creative solutions are agreed. The benefits of group methods are:

- Instantaneous feedback.
- Ability to probe for more in depth understanding.
- Expense and time constraints.
- Specialised knowledge and equipment not always required.

Although popular, group discussions face criticism, not least because they consider the views of relatively small numbers of people who can be influenced by the dynamics within the particular group.

Fully developed advertisements are tested in naturalistic settings whereas possible. Print advertisements are inserted into realistic "dummy" publications and participants will either be observed whilst looking through the publication or questioned at some later stage about whether the advertisement has caught their attention, how much interest they had, how likeable it was and what they remembered. Brand preference, awareness, choice and purchase likelihood will be ascertained before and after the test to evaluate whether exposure had impact (Change et al., 2010: 3, cited in Fill, 2013). TV, video and film testing may take place in a theatre setting or distributed digitally to panels of research participants who feed back responses throughout the viewing. Consumers feedback emotive reactions (often real time, on line) to creative treatments such as voice overs, music choice, actors and message.

Physiological responses can also be monitored, where eye tracking, pupil dilation and changes in skin temperature (using galvanometers, similar to lie detectors) assess heightened excitement or arousal. Brain scans indicate neurological reactions to stimuli and indicate brain activity during exposure. However the link between changes in physiology and future action is not predictable, and analysis of biological responses in isolation ignores social and other influences that might affect response. Considered as reductionist by some, intrusive research techniques offer perceived potential for manipulating customers and raise ethical concerns. Interest in neuroscience is growing but techniques are not widely used as they are specialist, expensive and currently unscaleable.

Pre-testing unveils initial customer reactions to creative treatments which counter any (potentially biased) enthusiasm from the creative team. However criticisms of pre-testing are widespread.

- Pre-testing includes relatively small numbers of participants
- Results not generalisable
- Pre-tests commonly consider a single exposure to an advertisement.
- Unfinished animatics or mock ups fail to replicate "real life" conditions, although multidimensional CAD technology may alleviate this to some extent.
- Immediate post-exposure tests favour short term memory of rational facts; emotional brand effects typically build over time (Binet & Field, 2013).

Commercial research suggests that in the long term, emotional appeals outperform both rational messages and campaigns employing both emotional and rational methods (Binet & Field, 2013). The relative effectiveness of emotional appeals is supported by a meta-analysis of 30 years of advertising data (op. cit.) and accounts for the increasing popularity of highly emotional advertisements aired during the Superbowl - the most expensive advertising slot in the world (Vranica, 2015).

Direct response campaigns are able to use experimental approaches and split tests of different creative treatments being run with directly compared results. Testing digital creative assets is more sophisticated, takes place in real time and provides dynamic feedback, allowing appropriate changes to be made (and retested) almost immediately.

Once the creative treatment has been assured through pre-testing, research continues to select the most appropriate communications mix and media for the message to reach target audiences.

11

Mix and media choice

The communications mix decision will be guided by the campaign objectives, consumer habits, past experience and both academic and industrial secondary data. Monitoring competitor activity (their tools and expenditure) will help determine the appropriate mix and set goals for 'share of voice'. This section will discuss some of the research available used to guide media choice

Advertising space is the most expensive component of communications activity, and media decisions warrant considerable research effort. In many countries, but not all, vast amounts of published data is available to steer the advertiser toward the best media and target audience fit and it is important to consider what is available. Mis-targeted media spend will result in low message exposure amongst the intended audience(s).

■ Audience research

Audience research is carried out by independent commercial research agencies or consortia of media with those wishing to sell advertising space paying to have their media included in the research. Much of the data provided is independently verified (audited) by industry bodies and typically more trustworthy than unaudited research. In the UK, India, New Zealand and South Africa this is carried out by the Audit Bureau of Circulations (www.abc.org); in North America, the Alliance for Audited Media undertakes this research. The terminology used varies across the different media but measures generally consider the reach (or the number of people who access the media), penetration (the percentage of the target population who are reached by the media) and the average number of times that the audience has an opportunities to see (OTS) an advertisement over a prescribed timescale. Measurement can be detailed, even down to the time of day.

Table 11.2: Media research terminology.

Media	Metric	Expressed as	Note
Print	Circulation	No of copies distributed or sold.	Consider readership split by platform - print, online or mobile.
	Readership	Numbers seeing an average issue - higher than circulation, e.g. airline magazines gain eight readers per copy.	
TV/ Radio	TV ratings (TVRs) Radio ratings	Percentage of market likely to be viewing/ listening in defined period, summed throughout campaign.	25 TVRs = 25% seen advert once. 500 TVRs= 50% seen it 10 times or 100% seen it 5 times.
Digital	Reach	No of unique visitors to the site	Cookies used but can over estimate

■   Audience research methodology

The methodology used by research groups to estimate potential reach of traditional media is worthy of discussion. Traditional media still accounts for more than half of advertising spend worldwide, although this dominance is losing ground to digital advertising (McKinsey, 2015). Research uses a representative sample of the population to estimate potential audiences.

- **Print**: The National Readership Survey (NRS) is a longitudinal study of readership habits. Respondents are classified as readers if they have 'seen' or 'read' the publication for at least two minutes in the past 12 months. Additional questions pinpoint the recency, frequency and length of time spent with the publication and access through traditional, digital or mobile platforms (nrs.co.uk)

- **Television:** The Broadcaster's Advertising Research Board (BARB) provide minute-by minute viewing figures using set meters installed in a panel of 5,100 UK homes. Household members record their presence and complete a viewing diary. The growth of digital and smart TV sales will impact the methods used to provide this data in future (www.barb.co.uk).

- **Cinema**: A fortnightly omnibus survey (FAME) captures the behaviour of 24,000 adults and 3,000 children annually by interviewing 1,000 respondents each month. (http://business.pearlanddean.com/audience_research_fame)

- **Radio**: A listening diary (RAJAR) is completed by 110,000 respondents each year to show the weekly reach and listening hours for national and local radio stations (www.rajar.co.uk).

- **Outdoor**: ROUTE estimates the likelihood of a piece of outdoor advertising being seen. It combines eye tracking data and traffic intensity models, obtained from the results of 30,000 people using a GPS monitor for 9 days. Results for sites which are dynamic or illuminated will be subject to a multiplier as they are more likely to be noticed (www.route.org.uk)

Paid for print readership is in decline in the UK, although digital access (often free) has risen significantly, but in Malaysia press readership figures show that both Bahasa Malaysia titles and Chinese language papers are still growing. The *Harion Metro* newspaper has an average circulation of over 300,000 copies and a readership of 3.8 million people. (AdQrate, 2015).

Precise media choice requires a breakdown of the reach or penetration amongst the target demographic (such as higher income females) and not just the total population. Delivering large numbers from the wrong demographic is wasted money and high penetration of the whole market is only required

11

where market dominance is the main objective and mass communications methods such as TV advertising would then be appropriate. The CPM (Cost per thousand) metric allows direct comparisons between (intra) media (e.g. radio versus TV) and within (inter) media (choice of programme or location). CPM is the amount spent on advertising to reach 1000 people in the target audience. It is found by dividing the cost of space/ airtime by the circulation (or reach) and multiplying by 1000.

Insight: Combining data from different sources

In the UK, consumer lifestyle data from the Target Group Index report, cross-referenced with readership and viewing data from Nielson, the NRS and BARB gives insight into consumer media habits. Qualitative research will also be used to provide in-depth understanding of the quantitative data.

Every time an advertisement appears there is the chance to increase the reach. Extra insertions or an increase in frequency provides those who have already seen the advertisement additional opportunities to see (OTS) it. Established brands tend to require less frequent exposure and in these circumstances brand choice is more affected by reach. Advertising planners need to balance budgets with desired reach and frequency goals in order for their creative efforts to be seen and acted upon.

For all media it should be noted that the figures used for media planning are projected estimates and may not be realised. The reach achieved will not be known until the campaign has run its course (post-campaign) and the research undertaken at the end of the campaign or part of regular monitoring during implementation will now be discussed.

Campaign implementation

Communications activity is dynamic and continuously monitored (often in real time), throughout the campaign, with research used to fine tune and adjust tactics as required. This section will consider the monitoring and measurement that takes place during implementation. Promotional effort does not maintain the same level of effect throughout a campaign. Some campaigns take time to wear in, especially those with complex, emotional or ambiguous content, whereas others decline or wear out more quickly.

Direct measurement considers the actions taken in response to the promotion such as making a sale, using a coupon, requesting information or taking part in a competition. **Indirect measurement** monitors the antecedent effects to action, such as awareness or attitude change or whether the promotion was likeable. Much activity is evaluated using both approaches.

■ Advertising

Many of the metrics initially used to assess advertising are quantitative and about volume, although these may be followed up with qualitative research to give more depth. They have been derived from the premise that advertising works by taking the customer from total unawareness through to action, which might be measured as a single transaction or as an ongoing customer relationship with the company or brand. Companies will undertake both primary and secondary research to monitor responses, as shown in Table 11.3. They will benchmark against past campaigns/ competing products.

Table 11.3: Hierarchy of communication response

Response	Measure	Metric	Difficulties
Unaware	Single exposure to the advertisement	Reach/ circulation/ readership/ viewing/ listening/ page landings.	Potential reach only. Cross platform duplication possible.
	Multiple exposure to advertisements	Opportunities to see Gross rating points	Good creative may mean fewer exposures.
Aware/ Attention	Spontaneous "top of mind" awareness.	What brands ....have you seen advertised?	First mentioned noted. Results influenced by familiarity.
	Prompted Awareness	Which of the following..... Have you seen?	Respondents may want to please
	Aided recall	Have you seen this… recently?	Exposure but not impact effectiveness
Interest/ Understanding	Strength of recall or vividness. Active involvement	What do you remember…?	Engaged, remembers and links ad to brand.
Conviction	Likeability	What do you like or dislike about this …?	Like to dislike ratio.
	Social engagement	Have you discussed …with friends?	Negative or positive WOM/ e-WOM
Desire	Intention	How likely are you to buy …?	Stated intention ≠ action
Transaction	Action	Purchase data	Not always attributable to respondent.
Relationship	Will recommend to others.	How likely …to recommend ….to others?	Net Promoter Score (see non financial metrics section)

Consumers have significantly changed their viewing habits, with video on demand allowing consumers to 'binge watch' advertisement-free programmes when subscribing to services such as Netflix or Amazon Prime. Attention is divided across many devices and traditional metrics are not currently linking up the data. Much of the research is carried out by the individual media companies promoting their own advertising space. This is a concern for the practitioners and is now being addressed by audience researchers who are working on ways to provide a 360 degree view of consumer media habits.

Contemporary audiences may not be passively attending to advertising and whilst watching may be commenting on what they have seen. For example 115.2 million viewers tuned in for the Superbowl in 2016 and 3.8 million people authored 16.9 million tweets about what they had seen. Surprisingly perhaps, not all tweets were about the game or the teams and players and 4.6 million tweets were sent about the adverts aired (Neilson, 2016).

■ Digital advertising

More sophisticated methods are utilised to judge digital promotional effectiveness. Click-through to web page measures are instantly available but may not predict long term outcomes. Digital methods offer the opportunity to assess the full customer journey from awareness to purchase and beyond.

Many of the effectiveness tests for web-based promotion were developed to replicate testing in the off-line world. Internet intercept studies aim to recruit consumers via pop-ups who have seen the digital asset (for example a banner ad) and test responses against those who have not been exposed. The sample is self-selected, response sizes tend to be small, possibly not representative of all exposed to the digital asset, and sample stratification and response weighting may be needed. For a discussion of these issues and best practice in internet advertising studies see Lavrakas et al. (2010) and Gluck (2011).

Google analytics provide basic measures which, combined with company data give a rich picture of digital presence effectiveness.

Companies are now able to pull together data from numerous sources to create a better understanding of how activity on line results in consumer behaviour in terms of actions such as spend, return sales, loyalty and advocacy. Of course this wealth of information needs to be analysed and made sense of and marketers sometimes feel that they are drowning in data (Steible, 2015).

Table 11.4: Digital metrics - the basics. Adapted from De Mers (2014)

Number of searches	Searches for brand or chosen search word	Avoid double counting
Number of visits	Total website or landing page visits	
Unique visitors or new sessions	Number of new visitors	Identifies need to create awareness.
Attribution/ Source of traffic	Where visitor generated	Direct - external links from other sites Organic - found through search engine Social - from social media activity
Bounce rate	Numbers leaving site without acting or going to another page.	Visit quality.
Stickiness	Time spent on site	
Engagement	Time spent on site and number of pages visited	
Conversions	Numbers who acted in line with campaign objectives.	Requests for further info, purchases, comments, survey completion, location map seen
Return on investment Average order value	Revenue gained for each visit	

Insight: Smart measurement for Smart Energy

Smart Energy is a not for profit organisation whose aim is to convince UK households and small businesses to install smart meters to reduce energy consumption and bills. Research amongst 27,000 consumers and over 100 stakeholder groups led to an animated creative treatment. The objective was to reach 100% of households including hard-to-reach vulnerable groups. Census, attitudinal data and media research combined with econometrics identified segments and optimised media spend. Results included:

- 1.2 million views of YouTube content. 73% of those reported interest in meter installation

- Top 5 search engine listing

- 60% recall of radio advertising campaign (benchmark 40%)

- 75% of those seeing the campaign taking action including website visit.

Source: Woolley (2015)

11

■ Direct response activity

Measurement of direct response promotional activity should be relatively straightforward but sometimes the data required is not directly attributable to the individual promotion, as much activity is supported by additional effort to raise awareness. Quantitative measurements show the effectiveness and efficiency of effort and allow comparisons across media/creative treatment/source of response.

- ■ Direct marketing: email, SMS, mail, direct response adverting (e.g. banner ad), pay per click placements.
- ■ Sales promotion: competition entries, coupon redemption, pricing promotions such as buy one get one free
- ■ Personal selling: face to face or telesales with results compared across representative.

Table 11.5: Direct measurements

Personal Selling:	Sales Promotion &Direct Marketing
Sales volumes or value	Sales volume/ value uplifts over promotion period.
New customers	Number of responses
Cost per lead	Cost to reach 1000 targets (CPM)
Acquisition cost	Cost for each lead becoming a customer for the first time
Cost of each sale	Cost per response
Call frequency	Response rates as a percentage of those reached.
Lead to close ratio	Conversion rates- numbers who purchased as a percentage of those who responded
Customer retention	Frequency, recency and monetary value of retained customers

Comparisons showing the contribution of each direct response activity, treatment and touchpoint require the cost for each lead, conversion rates and value of each customer to be calculated. Marketers need to be numerate to be able to mine the data available and make sense of the results.

■ Public relations

A range of measures are used to assess the effectiveness of all PR activity and the choice of which is guided by intended objectives and tools employed. Public relations monitoring can be undertaken at corporate, brand or product level or of all stakeholders. Evaluation should be regular, and longitudinal to ensure that trends are spotted early enough for positive action. It is important to take a more holistic (quantitative and qualitative) approach to evaluation of public relations activity within the digital environment (MacNamara, 2014)

Table 11.6: Public relations measurement by stakeholder

Stakeholder	Quantitative measures	Qualitative measures
Current/ potential employees	Staff turnover Applicants for each vacant post Staff satisfaction surveys Rankings in best place to work surveys	Employee reviews through social media monitoring e.g. Glass Door reviews
Shareholders	Share price	Press analysis
Customer/ potential customers/ general public	CSR rankings/ brand trust indices/ price elasticity	Social media sentiment

■ Media relations

One of the goals of media relations is to generate positive brand coverage. It is commonly quantified by calculating the equivalent cost to place an advertisement in the space take up by the coverage. Media monitoring services calculate both the AVE (Advertising Value Equivalent) and make a qualitative judgment about whether the coverage is positive, using content analysis and weighing this up according to media credibility.

Writing and distributing news is not restricted to professional journalists. Social media and other digital coverage pick up on public feeling well in advance of traditional methods. Crude quantitative measures, such as the number of 'likes', provides initial influence but not long-term engagement. Starbucks had 3,813,472 Twitter followers in 2013 and 34,547,696 face book fans (Barnes, 2014) but this figure does not indicate popularity or engagement. Media specialists monitor what's being said with relevance to the organisation, using clustering techniques, to score 'sentiment' (the tone), 'brand advocacy' and 'impact' to demonstrate prominence and influence compared to benchmarks. Consolidated engagement results across several platforms (Facebook, Snapchat, YouTube Pinterest, Tumblr and LinkedIn as examples) are available using dashboards such as Hootsuite to track, analyse and help schedule future activity.

11

Post-campaign evaluation

Many of the methods discussed are implemented during and after the campaign. This section will focus on post-campaign evaluation, especially the strategic, long-term effect of integrated communications. Evaluation should consider the following questions:

■ Target audience(s)? Did the campaign speak to current or new customers? Are other stakeholder groups, such as employees, shareholders or public opinion leaders equally important?

- Reactions to be monitored? Overall strategic goals such as customer loyalty will not be realised until sub objectives have been realised.

- Atomistic/Holistic? Evaluation at the tactical, tool or campaign level or overall impact on the corporate brand?

- Term- when to measure and for how long? Longitudinal approaches allow adjustments where required but snapshots before and after the campaign are less resource intensive. Campaign improvements may be unsustainable or lag behind expenditure. The Institute of Practitioners in Advertising (Binet & Field, 2013) suggest that long term effects only become apparent between 6-9 months from the start of the campaign.

- Evaluation method? Qualitative, quantitative or mixed methods most appropriate? Is Return on Investment or the bottom line effect the most meaningful measure?

- Resources- How much should be allocated to evaluation in terms of money and people?

- Specialist-Expertise required.

"Consumers differ in the way their minds and hearts respond to marketing communication" (Pauwels et al., 2013: 57) and this means that the return on investment of marketing communications is not just monetary. Table 11.7 details the factors affecting the measurement of marketing communications:

Table 11.7: Campaign measurement

Factor	Explanation	Notes
Expected/ Unexpected	Campaigns are designed to achieve expected returns but unexpected outcomes do occur.	Setting objectives and attributing success or failure is difficult.
Quantitative/ Qualitative	Revenue is quantitative; brand feeling is qualitative.	Quantitative returns are easier to measure.
Long /short term	A campaign is designed to achieve a return in a few days, weeks, months or years.	Short term returns may mitigate longer term efforts e.g. short term sales effects spill over to devalue brand equity.
Industry/ market	Different industries/markets not expected to produce the same results.	Compare concrete and ice cream expected returns.
Product life cycle	Dynamic across the cycle.	Well established brands show different advertising elasticities due to carryover effects.
Planned/ Unplanned	Returns may not be as planned and further unplanned communications necessary.	Contingency resources required

■ Financial metrics

Monitoring revenue and profit changes is a direct way to evaluate returns from marketing communication strategies. Micro and macro environmental influences affect revenues and therefore changes may not be attributable to communications activity. The worldwide recession of 2007/8 caused a fall in revenue for many organisations, even if their marketing communications would otherwise have been successful. Externally, competitor activity can influence price competitiveness, share of voice achieved and overall impact of campaigns. Graham and Frankenberger (2011) found the link between promotional spend increases and future earnings was stronger during recession, supporting the argument that organisations should spend more during those times.

There are four stages for consideration in the development of marketing communication measures (Schultz et al., 2004). These are:

- **ROI:** return on investment; measurement in general terms, considering the total amounts spent and the associated increase in sales and hence profitability.

- **ROBI:** return on brand investment; viewed as being more sophisticated and moves the emphasis to the customer/brand relationship and all activity that supports the brand.

- **ROCI:** return on customer investment; has value in the measurement of past returns and for forecasting future returns.

- **ROTPI:** return on touch-point investment is the next stage in measuring marketing communications return, where a touch-point "represents a channel through which customers interact with the firm's products, or with the firm itself" (Schultz, 2004: 64).

Studies have shown (Tellis, 2009) that a 1% increase in advertising spend leads to a 0.1% increase in sales, but generalisations do not hold for every brand/category in every region. Attributing sales changes to advertising spend requires all other variables to be controlled and this is rarely possible. Never the less an understanding of past or typical **advertising elasticities** helps set goals and standards to judge future activity. Price sensitivity is an indicative quantitative measure of brand strength, with successful brands able to charge higher amounts whilst maintaining customer loyalty.

Understanding **customer lifetime value** is central to long term measurement as it helps determine objectives, choose appropriate strategies and communications investment across the customer journey. However for many businesses (particularly those which do not have a direct relationship with the

11

buyers) **customer retention** rates are not available through the usual customer databases and additional primary research on either a longitudinal or ad hoc basis is required.

■ Non-financial metrics

Marketing communications activity influences nearly every measure of **brand equity** or strength by contributing to awareness, brand identity, associations and credibility by helping the consumer to form brand feelings and judgements. By influencing brand perceptions, communication takes the lead in making a promise to the customer. When perception exceeds expectation, the customer experiences a positive 'promise' gap and views the quality of the product (hence the brand) as being good. The **Promise Index** devised by Simms (2007) demonstrates that "although 66% of the brands surveyed had positive promise gaps, only 15% had gaps that impacted significantly on business performance" (Fill, 2013: 282). The conclusion here is that a marketing communications campaign can result in delighted customers, but does not necessarily result in higher return to the organisation. Marketing communications may 'over promise and under deliver' resulting in quality perception being lower than expectation (a negative promise gap) and this can damage the brand. A careful balance is needed to ensure that the campaign communicates the true benefits of the brand.

Customers develop cumulative experience through advertising exposure over time. Rosengren and Dahlen (2015:p2) call this "advertising equity" and they propose that this affects the willingness of customers to pay voluntary attention to future brand activity. One recently popular measure, the **net promoter score** (Markey & Reicheld, 2012) computes a score for the number of people who would recommend a brand minus those who would not recommend. It asks a single question, but the answer tends to be based on communications effectiveness, customer experience and the brand relationship. The tool has been criticised for suggesting that all respondents have identical brand attachment or advocacy worth.

Most non-financial measures are qualitative, value-based judgments by the consumer in response to communications activity, initially researched through qualitative methods. Very often they will be assigned a numeric score using quantitative research amongst a wider population. Companies insist on a quantifiable return and marketers have become adept at using the language of the boardroom to demonstrate that their work is achieving results.

■   Qualitative returns

In spite of the array of quantitative measures that are available, campaigns will also be subjectively judged by customers and other stakeholders. One key qualitative measurement is how a campaign is judged by peers within the advertising industry. Industry awards are a way of rewarding 'best practice' or 'creative' campaigns, and are highly sought after by those who work in the industry as they give authority to the work, as the judging panel is made up of very experienced professionals in the industry. Moreover, they often generate wider publicity and increase attention, but some would argue that unless there is a financial improvement it could be argued that they are not worthwhile because there is no direct financial metric.

Example: Customer Engagement Indices- Reddi-Wip

Reddi-Wip was a campaign designed by DDB California. Research showed that consumers were unaware that the product was low calorie. The advertising featured this benefit and showed Reddi-Wip as fresh fruit accompaniment. The objective was to try and establish the product as an everyday product and increase sales by 3.1% outside of the holiday periods of Thanksgiving and Christmas. 59% of consumers were aware of the campaign and 60% of those linked the campaign correctly to the Reddi-Wip brand. A customer engagement index (which includes measures of visibility, branding and persuasion) of 169 was reported by the advertising agency who won an award for their work. (ARF, 2014).

Resources for research

Communications research rarely receives the same level of enthusiasm as other activities. Viewed as a 'necessary evil', it is used to discover why a campaign didn't deliver objectives or to justify a creative treatment or request bigger budgets, and there is a general push to ensure greater accountability, particularly when budgets are being squeezed. Research activity should be planned and adequate resources made available to ensure systematic, valid and reliable data is obtained. Research is an important part of the marketing plan. Decisions are required on when to research and whether it should be continuous or ad hoc. Where the required level of research knowledge, expertise, technologies or data is not available internally, then a company can draw upon a wide number of commercial providers, including the planners within their creative agencies (see Jacoby et al., 2015). Even where the research activity is to be subcontracted, in-house marketers must have the ability to assess the limitations of each service

11

offered and interpret the data, to have sufficient insight into whether campaigns have reached their intended audience(s) and achieved their objectives.

■ And finally

This chapter has considered the role of research throughout the communications process, from idea generation through to both long and short term post-campaign evaluation. Anyone involved in the planning and execution of marketing communications at any level should be familiar with the research available. The power of integrated marketing communications is clear but without due consideration of how to judge communications effort, brands will never be given the appropriate support to meet consumer needs and fully achieve their potential.

Additional reading

Ha, L. (2008) Online advertising research in advertising journals: A review. *Journal of Current Issues and Research in Advertising*, **30**(1), 31-48
A good review of the research completed up till 2008 on advertising

Hatzithomas, L., Boutsouki, C., Pigadas,V. & Zotos, Y. (2016) PEER: Looking into Consumer engagement in e-WOM through social media, in Verlegh et al. (eds.), *Advances in Advertising Research (Vol. VI)*, European Advertising Academy.
Outlines a way of evaluating social media engagement from a cognitive affective and action perspective.

Bearden W.O., Netemeyer R.G. & Haws K.L .(2011). *Handbook of Marketing Scales: Multi-item measures for marketing and consumer behaviour research*. Sage Publications
Detailed discussion of scales used in marketing to research reactions.

References

AA/WARC (2014) UK Expenditure Report 2015/16. http://expenditurereport.warc. com/ (Accessed January 2016)

AdQRATE (2015) AdQRate. http://www.adqrate.com/genre/list?&sort=readership%7 CDESC&tid=1 (Accessed May 2016)

ARF (2014). David Ogilvy Awards. Unleashing the joy of Reddi-Wip and Fruit. http://thearf-org-aux-assets.s3.amazonaws.com/ogilvy/14/reddi-wip.pdf (Accessed May 2016)

Barnes, N.G. (2014). Social commerce emerges as big brands position themselves to turn 'follows', 'likes' and 'pins' into sales *American Journal of Management* **14**(4), 11-18

Binet, L & Field, P (2013). *The Long and Short of It. Balancing the short and long-term effects of marketing.* Institute of Practitioners in Advertising.

Cayla, J. & Arnould, E. (2013). Ethnographic stories for market learning. *Journal of Marketing,* **77**, (July): 1-16.

Compaine, B. & Cunningham, B. (2010). Scholars help answer John Wanamaker's query: Which half of my advertising is wasted? *Journal of Media Economics.* **23**(1), 1-4

De Mers, J. (2014). 10 Online Marketing Metrics You Need To Be Measuring *Forbes* Aug 15. www.forbes.com/sites/jaysondemers/2014/08/15/10-online-marketing-metrics-you-need-to-be-measuring/#10bc3684355f (Accessed April 2015)

Dickinson-Delaporte, S. & Kerr, G. (2015). Agency-generated research of consumer generated content. the risks, best practices and ethics, *Journal of Advertising Research,* **54**(4), 469-478

Experien (2015). Demonstrating ROI with competitive intelligence. www.experian.co.uk/marketingservices (Accessed April 2015).

Fill, C. (2013). *Marketing Communications: Brands, Experiences and Participation,* Harlow: Pearson

Gluck, M. (2011). Best practices for conducting online ad effectiveness research. Internet Advertising Bureau. https://www.iab.com/wp-content/uploads/2015/05/IAB-Whitepaper-Best-Practices-for-Conducting-Online-Ad-Effectiveness-Research.pdf (Accessed February 2016)

Graham, R.C. & Frankenberger, K.D. (2011). The earnings effects of marketing communication expenditures during recessions *Journal of Advertising.* **40**(2), 5-24

Jacoby, E.J., Freund, J. & Araujo, L. (2015). 'Is there a gap in the market, and is there a market in the gap?' How advertising planning performs markets *Journal of Marketing Management* **31** (1-2): 37-61

Lavarakas, P. J., Mane, S. & Laszlo, J (2010). Does anyone really know if online ad campaigns are working? An evaluation of methods used to assess the effectiveness of advertising on the internet. *Journal of Advertising Research,* **50**(4), 354-373

MacNamara, J. (2014). Breaking the PR measurement and evaluation deadlock: A new approach and model. *International Summit on Measurement, Amsterdam AMEC.* http://amecorg.com/downloads/amsterdam2014/Breaking-the-PR-Measurement-Deadlock-A-New-Approach-and-Model-Jim-Macnamara.pdf (Accessed March 2016)

11

Markey, R. & Reicheld, F. (2012). Loyalty insights. Net promoter: Creating a reliable metric. Bain and Company. http://www.bain.com/Images/LOYALTY_ INSIGHTS_2_Creating_a_reliable_metric.pdf (Accessed January 2016)

McKinsey, (2015) *Global Media Report 2015*, McKinsey and Co.

Neilson (2016) Super Bowl 50: Nielsen Twitter TV Ratings Post-Game Report, (9 Feb) http://www.nielsen.com/us/en/insights/news/2016/super-bowl-50-nielsen-twitter-tv-ratings-post-game-report.html (Accessed April 2016)

Pauwels, K., Erguncu, S. & Yildirim, G. (2013) Winning hearts, minds and sales: How marketing communication enters the purchase process in emerging and mature markets, *International Journal of Advertising Research in Marketing*, **30**, 57-68

Petavy, F (2014) Five predictions for crowdsourcing in 2014, crowdsourcingweek. com/blog/five-predictions-for-crowdsourcing-in-2014/ (Accessed May 2016)

Rosengren, S. and Dahlen, M. (2015) Exploring advertising equity: how a brand's past advertising may affect consumer willingness to approach its future ads, *Journal of Advertising*, **44**(1), 1-13

Schultz, D.E, Cole, B. & Bailey, S. (2004) Implementing the 'connect the dots' approach to marketing communication *International Journal of Advertising: The Review of Marketing Communications*, **23**(4), 455-477

Simms, J. (2007). Measuring a brand's image against consumer experience, *Marketing*, (December 13)

Steible, J. (2015). Drowning in big data - finding insight in a digital sea of information. Forbes, (March 25) http://www.forbes.com/sites/joshsteimle/ 2015/03/25/drowning-in-big-data-finding-insight-in-a-digital-sea-of-information/ (Accessed August 2016)

Tellis, G.J. (2009) Generalisations about advertising effectiveness in markets, *Journal of Advertising Research*, **49**(2), 240-245

Vranica, S. (2015) Many Super Bowl commercials were sobering and heartfelt. *Wall Street Journal*. http://www.wsj.com/articles/many-super-bowl-commercials-were-sobering-and-heartfelt-1422847521 (Accessed January 2016).

Woolley, S. (2015) Conducting a smart campaign. *The Marketer*, 12 October. http:// exchange.cim.co.uk/editorial/2015/october/12/conducting-a-smart-campaign/ (Accessed May 2016)

Zaltman, G. (2003) *How Customers Think: Essential insights into the Minds of the Market.* Boston: Harvard Business School Press

12 Case Studies

Geraldine Bell, Kitty Shaw, Elaine Collinson and Kathryn Waite

There are six case studies in this chapter. The case studies have been designed so that deeper insight is gained and developed, and to give an opportunity to evidence critical application of theory. These are mini-cases which give an overview of a marketing management and marketing communication(s) problem which has either been resolved or is being evaluated with several options open to marketing managers. In some cases, it may be that the scenario is a review of a campaign which requires you to evaluate it. You should tackle the case by underpinning the scenario with the theoretical concepts drawn from the relevant chapters in this book, and by answering the questions relative to both theory and the practice illustrated in the scenario, and also critically question the case by looking at alternative exemplars to enrich your answer. Note that most of these cases relate to more than one chapter in this book and therefore the chapter references are for guidance only.

Outline answers are available online at:
   www.goodfellowpublishers.com/marcomms

1: 'Dirt is good' – Planning for marketing communications

Persil's new research says Dirt is good!

"Who would've thought that dirt could be so good", said the researcher on reading the results from the recent consumer feedback. Unilever, which manages Persil/Omo, had just created one of the most noted modern-day brand stories ever developed. The brief had been to not just understand that the brand had a strong connection with the human side of consumers and their relationship with laundry, but to be more meaningful in the space within which the brand existed. Thus, the backbone of being 'humanist and connected' was formed. The value link was between mothers, children and dirt. The creative agency however, made it more value-creating when they pitched it as being not just between mothers, kids and dirt, but also between adventures and experience. This spark of ingenuity came about through research into exploring the link between true emotion and the everyday chore of cleaning laundry. This deep insight was translated from "if you are not free to get dirty, you cannot experience life and grow". The meaning here was that a parent's desire for a 'free' child was relative to the constraints of being clean and not messy. Growing up can be a dirty business indeed! Persil were now able to develop a narrative arc based around the promise that "dirt is good" because without it there would be no experience. On the Persil website they outline the basis of this assurance with the premise that:

"Dirt is the mark of adventure. It's a sign that we're getting stuck in and learning from life. Children don't only learn by being taught. They learn by doing. Hands on experience, discovery, and trial and error are vital to every child's healthy happy development. Laundry might not be fun, but don't worry – Persil will take care of even the toughest of stains, so you can concentrate on the important stuff. Dirt is essential experience of life".

As David Arkwright, the former global brand director for Unilever's laundry business says this is the story "that would shift the banal to the truly meaningful" and live on for a long time. Industry experts view "Dirt is Good" as a best practice illustration in creative development within brand communications, because it resonates by addressing parent's inherent tension between controlling instincts relative to getting too dirty and their desire for a child to grow up through play and being free to do so. Prior to this dirt was seen as the enemy. The big idea here is a game-changer and is disruptive in that it was fairly provocative and generated buzz around the brand. The creative treatment can now be fully developed across multiple media platforms.

Source: Adapted from Hernandez R (2012) www.millwardbrown.co.uk , Arkwright (2014) in www.marketingmagzine.co.uk and www.persil.co.uk.

Review questions

To help you develop and gain insight, you can draw on Chapters 5 *Planning for Marketing Communications*; 6 *Brands and Brand Communications*; 8 *Creativity in Advertising and Promotion* and 11 *Evaluating Marketing Communications*.

1 Discuss what is meant by a creative treatment which is developed to be used across multiple media platforms. What kind of a creative platform is "Dirt is good"?

2 What exactly is a brand's promise and identify the underlining meaning of Persil's promise that "Dirt is good"?

3 How important is the customer value proposition in terms of
    a) Integrated Marketing Communications (managerial perspective)
    b) Consumer (the consumer/end-user perspective)

4 a) Explain how you would use research in developing brand communications? And,

    b) How would you expect to use research in evaluating the outcome?

12

2: 'Cadbury's Taste' – Translating creativity in advertising and promotions

It's all in the words when two global players collide over 'taste'!

Cadbury has replaced its 'Free the joy' tagline with 'Tastes like this feels' and commentators in the trade press have been quick to point out that this proposition is very similar to the mighty Coca Cola's 'Taste the feeling' – in fact, so similar, that they are predicting a 'war on words'!

Cadbury has rolled out a new global brand campaign for its Dairy Milk brand. The tagline 'Taste like this feels' is a departure from the previous one which was all about wanting us to feel free to make more of those 'joyful' moments. (Remember comic actor James Cordon in Cadbury's 2014 'free the joy' campaign which features him lip-synching to an Estelle track. See more at http://www.campaignlive.co.uk/article/james-corden-frees-joy-cadbury-campaign/1281269). The new advertising is centred on the premise of the 'consumption experience', hence the word *'taste'* in 'Taste like this feels'. This is translated into executions which focus on the unique taste sensations that each chocolate bar in the range delivers, leading to that ultimate 'moment of joy'. Cadbury's say that they are moving on now but the aim is still to remind people that joy is never too far away. Taste is a sub-branch of the 'free the joy' idea, according to Cadbury's global brand equity director, Nikhil Rao when questioned recently in marketing week, reinforcing that in going forward "the spotlight was now on taste".

And so for now, Cadbury is saying that this focus is a point of difference from Coke's. Whilst its focus is on the consumption experience, Coke's 'Taste the feeling' is focused on the consequence of when a customer consumes its products. In other words, Cadbury is saying that *taste* comes before *feeling,* that is, the sensation of taste predetermines the way that taste makes you feel, hence, the consequence. In asking several chocoholics and committed coke drinkers for their views, it turns out that the consumption experience includes both taste and the consequence, so the end-user just thinks it's all a bit of a war on words. The point of difference may well be in the execution and the medium, for example, the storyline and social media platform. Cadbury's creative treatment includes animals enjoying a delightful moment set to popular music tracks – Cadbury's Dairy Milk Medley features a cat and a dog relaxing and having an indulgent moment, Cadbury's Dairy Milk Big Taste features a dog having an adventurous experience enjoying a free-ride as a motorbike sidecar passenger, and Cadbury's Dairy Milk classic features a bear getting intense satisfaction by satisfying its itch up against a tree. (You can see the bear enjoy a good scratch to the music of KC & the Sunshine Band's *That's the Way (I Like it)'* at https://www.youtube.com/watch?v=Dd_GSSQQGNY.)

All three creative treatments are using a metaphor to elicit that 'wonderful feeling' which Cadbury's Dairy Milk product variants can give you. The first TV spot was aired during a commercial break in the UK during Saturday night's Ant and Dec show (2 April, 2016). However it is a multi-platform push and will extend to social, experiential, digital and PR. Following its prime spot airing on STV, there was an experiential event at Westfield, one of London's large shopping malls. Shoppers were invited to take their weight off their feet by slipping off their shoes and stepping onto the some bubble wrap and indulge in a chocolate treat having a blissful few moments of fun during their hectic shopping day. (You can see more of this at https://www.youtube.com/watch?v=JFGbizQShPI.)

Meanwhile, Coke's advertising "dramatizes everyday moments in life and how Coke makes you feel as a result of consumption", says Rao of Cadburys. Sound familiar? In this case, forget about the battle of words – what about the visual? The battle here is in the *pencil* as well as the pen.

Adapted from: www.marketingweek.com [accessed 05/04/2016]; www.thedrum.com/news 01/04/2016 [accessed 05/04/2016]; www.campaignlive.co.uk [accessed on04/04/2016] and www.adnews.com [accessed 05/04/2016].

Review question

To help you develop and gain insight, you can draw on Chapters 5 *Planning for Marketing Communications*; 6 *Branding and Brand Communications* and 8 *Creativity in Advertising and Promotion*.

1 Discuss the rationale for a brand proposition.

2 Evaluate the creative strategies that a marketing manager and/or creative agent can draw on, and discuss the tactics applied in this case.

12

3: Creativity in advertising and promotion: 'Seduction'

Marks and Spencer tries to seduce us yet again!

It is almost 10 years since M&S's iconic food advertising put the food department of the lifestyle retail store on the specialist 'foody' map with its "this isn't just…" strapline. In 2010, M&S finally ditched this strapline and moved towards a new proposition "just because …" it's Marks and Spencer. Today, in 2016, it has tinkered with the positioning and now its advertising features "adventures of…" see for example, *Adventures in Fiesta*, summer 2016. (www.marketingweek.com/2016/04/21/how-ms-transformed-its-schizophrenic-food-marketing/)

The new advertising is a far cry from its seductive past, or is it? In 2005 it was sultry, and not that long ago, it was still fairly sensual with some movement with a bit of 'food wobble' to entice a more emotive connection. However, today, it's safe to say that M&S has become much more dynamic and yes, exciting. Not only is there a lot of movement in the ad, but there is also a definite shift to a younger audience. And price isn't mentioned once. There are no promotional or seasonal offers – yet. What there is a very stylish filmic production with lots of creative advertising content. The music is brisk and moves you along; the colour is primary and bright; there are strong cues in food shapes, textures and types; lots of combinations. And it is very dynamic – there are patterns and there are explosions. It dazzles and it's fun. It makes you smile, it makes you happy. And that of course, is what summer and the holiday season is all about.

It is clear that the brand attributes displayed in the advertising, and across all the different creative treatments of the new campaign, are that its food in its food hall is "different, exciting, fresh and new" confirms Ansall, M&S's global customer director. He now takes on the unenviable task of translating this 'adventurous' positioning across the fashion department. Meanwhile, rewiring our brains away from the infamous, and much parodied food pornography of 2005 where the slow and husky voice told us that "this is not just any chocolate pudding, but a Marks and Spencer chocolate pudding!" is going to be hard. But as Scotland's advertising trade magazine points out, the new advertising finishes on a gorgeous-looking shot of a chocolate orange cake being sliced ready for eating. Meanwhile, Ansall defends M&S saying "we're trying to make new neuro connections"! So, food porn isn't quite dead in the water just yet!

Source: Adapted from www.huffingtonpost.com, 02.04.2014; www.marketingweek.com, 24.03.2010, 12.04.2016 & 09.05.2016; and The Drum, 22.04.2016. All sources accessed on 25/07/2016.

Review questions

To help you develop and gain insight, you can draw on Chapter 8 *Creativity in Advertising and Promotion*.

1 Identify which type of motivational appeal Marks and Spencer are using to make its creative advertising generate increased attention. Why?

2 Evaluate the significance of framing creative appeals.

3 Discuss the tactics M&S uses to get you to sit up and attend to its advertising.

4 a) Explain what a borrowed-interest device is and evaluate how M&S uses devices in its advertising.

b) Highlight at least three best practice exemplars that use different borrowed-interest devices to attract attention.

12

4: Integrated marketing communications at Standard Life

The investment company, Standard Life plc., based in the UK, is one of the top 500 companies worldwide by revenue, as listed in the 2015 Fortune Global 500. The business has around 4.5 million customers and clients around the world with operations in the UK, North America, Europe, Asia and Australia, while its joint ventures and partnerships in India and China support a further 25 million customers. Around the world the group employs 6,500 people. Listed on the London Stock exchange, Standard Life has around 1.2 million individual shareholders across 50 countries. It is therefore a very large and complex business with an extensive and diverse range of stakeholders to consider. In short Standard Life has multiple communications sources and many other touch-points for a broad range of stakeholders around the world ranging from customers to shareholders. Therefore an integrated approach to communications is critical.

Communications context

Historically, the Standard Life group has comprised a number of distinct business units which each having their own communications functions, focusing on the needs of their own markets and stakeholders. Recognising the need for greater consistency of communications across the group, the Communications Executive was established in 2014, led by the Group Director of Communications and Brand. The Communications Executive, which included members of each business unit, as well as core group-level communications functions, drew up a group communications strategy to support the group's business strategy. This strategy, which sets out the communications objectives and key messages to support the business strategy, is designed to provide overarching guidance for all communications, both internal and external, while giving individual business units the freedom to respond to the needs of their own markets and stakeholder groups. This integrated marketing communications strategy covers the period 2014-2016. Figure 12.1 illustrates the group's communications strategy and its links to corporate goals.

High level communications strategy

Standard Life's corporate goal in 2014 was to *"Drive shareholder value through being a leading customer–centric business focused on long-term savings and investments propositions."* Figure 12.1 shows how the communications strategy flows from the corporate strategy and is worked all the way through to messaging, and what this should mean for key stakeholder groups. The Communications Purpose, which focuses on enhancing brand and corporate reputation through engagement and advocacy among stakeholders feeds into six communications objectives intended to support the achievement of the business objective. These are then developed into propositions for each of the business's stakeholder groups. Customers for example should be able to look forward to the future with confidence, while the media should see the company as providing thought leadership to the industry, driven by market and customer insight. Key messages are then developed to support the delivery of this strategy and positioning. The group's brand values, shown at the base, support and underpin the whole strategy and framework.

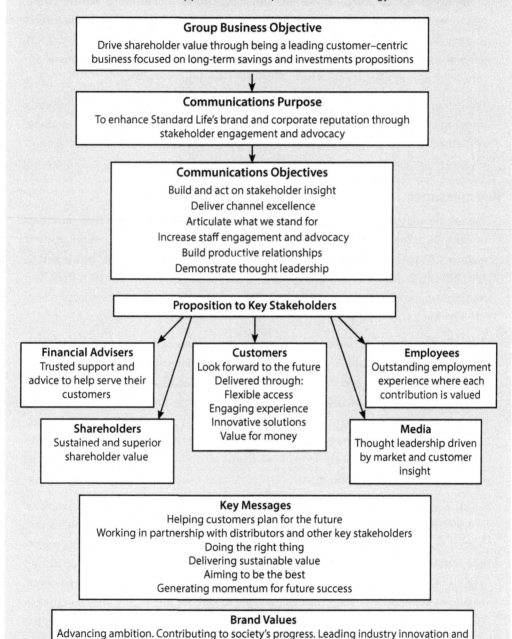

Group Business Objective
Drive shareholder value through being a leading customer–centric business focused on long-term savings and investments propositions

Communications Purpose
To enhance Standard Life's brand and corporate reputation through stakeholder engagement and advocacy

Communications Objectives
Build and act on stakeholder insight
Deliver channel excellence
Articulate what we stand for
Increase staff engagement and advocacy
Build productive relationships
Demonstrate thought leadership

Proposition to Key Stakeholders

Financial Advisers
Trusted support and advice to help serve their customers

Customers
Look forward to the future
Delivered through:
Flexible access
Engaging experience
Innovative solutions
Value for money

Employees
Outstanding employment experience where each contribution is valued

Shareholders
Sustained and superior shareholder value

Media
Thought leadership driven by market and customer insight

Key Messages
Helping customers plan for the future
Working in partnership with distributors and other key stakeholders
Doing the right thing
Delivering sustainable value
Aiming to be the best
Generating momentum for future success

Brand Values
Advancing ambition. Contributing to society's progress. Leading industry innovation and improvement

Figure 12.1: Group communications strategy

12

This is a high-level communications strategy, which is intended to influence and guide all strategic and tactical communications activity across the group whilst still enabling individual business units and geographic operations to have the flexibility to respond to the needs of their particular markets and stakeholders. All individual activities from press releases to social media and sponsorship should have a clear link back to the agreed strategy illustrated in Figure 12.1. As well as ensuring that all communications support this high level framework, it is equally important that there are no communications which contradict the key messages and thus undermine the group's credibility.

This group communication strategy is reviewed annually in line with the wider business planning cycle, to ensure that communications continue to support business strategy. While the high level purpose and brand values remain relevant, individual objectives and key messages may change as business strategy develops.

Key messages

The key messages in the framework underpin all communications activity. They can either be obvious in their expression, or perhaps not explicitly expressed in communications materials. Regardless as to the intensity of expression, they are and should be evident to stakeholders as an expression of the way in which the organisation conducts itself. The messages in the framework articulate what the company and its brand stand for and how the business wants to be seen.

Taking a closer look at how the messaging framework is applied, *'Helping customers plan for their future'* is articulated in a number of ways, including using customer and market insight to drive strategy and thus ensuring that the company's propositions, including its communications, are driven by customer needs, preferences and aspirations. This follows through to shaping the internal culture so that the whole organisation has a customer-centric approach. In this way a core positioning and set of messages is applied across all stakeholder groups and touch-points from media relations to marketing materials and customer servicing communications.

In 2015, at a more tactical level, this resulted in proactive work by UK spokespeople to provide thought leadership pieces on social media, covering pensions and investment related matters. The group has also conducted a number of consumer research projects which have then been released though press releases and social media, and published various research reports which are intended to help customers manage their finances by highlighting important issues, such as the need to plan for retirement, and the possible impacts of changes to legislation for customers, whilst at the same time supporting the group's positioning as a source of thought leadership and influence on issues important to the business.

Evidence of the key messages is one of the ways in which the company measures the success of its communications. Research is conducted on media coverage of the business, which specifically looks for evidence of these messages in how the business is reported in the media. This gives an indication of the success of communications activity in delivering and supporting these key messages.

Stakeholders

There are several different stakeholder groups or audiences to consider in a large and complex business like Standard Life. Table 1 below illustrates some of the key audiences to be considered by Standard Life in planning any communications. Individual business units may also have other audiences to consider and any significant Group communication would also need to take account of the London stock exchange and city analysts.

Table 12.1: The multiple stakeholders of Standard Life group.

Customers /clients	Segmented by product and distribution channel
Distributors	Independent financial advisers , Workplace consultants
Prospective customers	Segments targeted for growth
Shareholders	Institutional and Individual
Employees	Segmented by location, function and level
Media	National press, trade press, online news channels (trade and consumer), radio & TV
Other	Joint venture & strategic partners, UK Government & regulators, Overseas Governments & regulators

In planning for any communications, key audiences have to be identified and the needs and preferences of each audience considered. For example a new product launch in the UK may need to consider only UK stakeholders, while changes to the company structure or operating model may also need to be communicated to overseas partners and regulatory bodies. The international nature of the business and the availability of news 24 hours a day mean that it is critical that any major communications are carefully co-ordinated to reach different time-zones around the world in the right order.

Communications planning for individual projects

An integrated approach is also important for any individual communications project. In any initiative, the company must determine which are the key stakeholder audiences and develop messaging relevant to them through channels and media, which are appropriate and effective for reaching that particular group whilst supporting the business objectives. For example, in communicating the recent acquisition of a distributor in the UK where the overall aim of the communications plan was to co-ordinate and facilitate the successful announcement of the acquisition. This was achieved by delivering the right messages to the right audiences via the most appropriate channels for each. The communications

12

team developed a detailed communications plan and identified the following as key audiences and stakeholders, which had to be considered in the communications plan: employees, clients, intermediaries and media and investment analysts. Having developed the key messages for the project, the specific needs and interests of each of these audiences was considered in developing a detailed communications plan. For example while employees would want to understand the rationale for the acquisition and city analysts would want to understand the fit with broader strategy, intermediaries would need to be reassured that this acquisition would not in any way affect the company's relationship with them, or that it would not bring the business into competition with them. Materials were then prepared for each of these audiences, which would deliver the key messages for the project but also address the needs of each audience in terms of the content, communications tools and channels used.

The overarching objective in developing an integrated communications plan here was to ensure that the delivery of messages to a diverse range of stakeholders was coordinated, supported the core business rationale for the acquisition, and addressed the key concerns of the various audience groups. The communications plan for a project like this would contain the elements shown in Figure 12.2.

Communication objectives
For example to communicate the business drivers and rationale for the acquisition
Communication Principles
To position the acquisition in the wider business context
Key stakeholders and their needs
Employees, Clients, and so on.
Key messages
E.g. How the acquisition strengthens Standard Life's business in the affected areas
Sign-off process
The governance process that underpinned the development, approval and delivery of communication outputs.
List of materials to be produced,
Including the responsible person and the target audience for each
Communications Timeline
 Detailing when each audience should receive communications, with which content and through which channel. For example, employees might receive a face-to-face briefing at the same time as the media are to be briefed by emailing a press release.

Figure 12.2 : Outline communications plan

Summary – striking a balance between global and local

The Group Communications strategy developed by Standard Life strikes a balance between ensuring a consistent positioning and messaging framework which supports the business strategy and giving each part of the group a degree of autonomy over their communications, which need to be tailored for their own market conditions. Some examples of how this works in practice can be seen in the screen shots that follow from websites belonging to different parts of the group. The first one is from the corporate website, www.standardlife.com and is about their sponsorship of the tennis player Andy Murray. This is replicated in style and tone on the company's Hong Kong Website, which follows. The next two shown are from the company's operations in the Republic of Ireland and Germany. Sponsorship of Andy Murray is less relevant to customers in these countries and so does not feature, but there is strong similarity in the style and tone of the websites to the Hong Kong one. So content is adapted for local markets but the look and feel are the same.

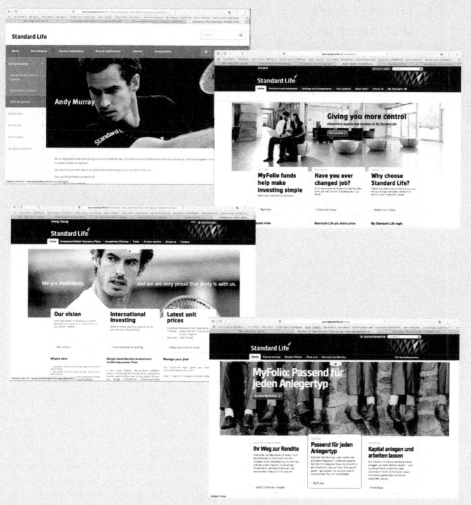

Thus the overarching objective is achieved where the messages and appeals that are directed and delivered to a diverse range of stakeholders are fully co-ordinated and integrated thereby addressing the various target audience groups.

12

Review questions

1 Why is it important to have a goal-directed communications strategy at Standard Life Plc?

2 How does this communications strategy provide direction to all Standard Life's stakeholders?

3 Critically evaluate the role that key messages play in the overall communications strategy.

4 How important is planning when targeting multiple stakeholders?

5 In conclusion, what does integration of communications mean to a company like Standard Life?

5: Old Spice Guy: From traditional to new media

This case study and the next draw on material from all marketing knowledge. However, this case specifically draws on Chapter 9, *Digital Marketing*.

Old Spice Guy

Old Spice is a brand of male grooming products which was created in 1938, and was a very popular mass-market brand. The product had distinct smell of orange, vanilla and nutmeg, and its television campaigns promoted the idea of the "Old Spice Man" as an athletic surfer. However by 2010 the Old Spice brand was perceived to be traditional, boring and no longer relevant for the younger consumer. These attitudes resulted in collapsing sales in a growing marketplace for male toiletries. In 2010, a video was launched on YouTube and Twitter which featured Isaiah Mustafa, an actor who was formerly an American Football athlete, as the "Old Spice Guy". The video begins with Isaiah Mustafa standing in a shower addressing "Ladies" who might be sitting next to a man who might not look like Isaiah but who might smell like Isaiah. The video is extremely humorous and satirises traditional ideas of machismo. The video was primarily shared on Youtube and Twitter. An advertising agency created "response videos", where the "'Old Spice Guy" replies to comments from online influencers and celebrities. The campaign was immediately successful resulting in significant views, an increase in Twitter followers and an increase in traffic to the company website. In terms of share of voice, Old Spice accounted for 75% of the conversations in the male grooming category during 2010 and half of these conversations came from women. As a result of the campaign there were hundreds of parody videos made and posted online. Sales of the product rose by 55% in the three months during the campaign.

Source: Adapted from Barker, M.S., Barker, D.I., Bormann, N.F. & Neher, K.E. (2013) *Social Media Marketing: A Strategic Approach*. Cengage learning

Review questions

1 Discuss the extent to which the many-to-many marketing communication model can be applied to the 2010 "Old Spice Guy" campaign

2 Identify how the 2010 Old Spice Guy Campaign matched the brand's marketing objectives.

3 What might be the risks of this type of viral campaign?

12

6: Losing control at Qantas : Controlling digital marketing/ viral campaigns

Qantas and control over viral campaigns

Qantas Airways Limited is an Australian airline group founded in Queensland in 1920. The company has grown to become Australia's largest domestic and international airline and employs over 30,000 people worldwide (Qantas, 2015). From the marketing and PR perspective, several of the activities organised by the company in the last years are a perfect example of the challenges that organisations are facing when conducting marketing activities in Web 2.0 environments. The airline ran into trouble in October 2011, when more than 68,000 passenger were stranded worldwide due to a labour dispute with three company unions (Rourke, 2011). The Australian government intervened and held emergency court sessions. Qantas aircraft were back in the air after three days, with a ruling from the court to resolve the dispute within 21 days or face a binding arbitration decision (McGuirk, 2011).

With the matter with the unions still unresolved, Qantas launched on November 23rd of the same year another competition to win one of 50 pairs of Qantas first-class pyjamas and a luxury amenity kit (Miller, 2011). The company invited its followers to participate in this contest using the hashtag #QantasLuxury, yet the initiative backfired and the hashtag was used by Qantas' customers to express their frustrations with the airline. The initiative quickly became a mechanism were consumers were complaining for being stranded due to the labour dispute, as well as other unrelated complains such as baggage loss and poor customer service. Within an hour of the hashtag being shared it reached over 500,000 users and resulted in 1.4 million impressions (Social Media News, 2011).

Kennedy (2011), a practitioner in social media monitoring, suggests that Qantas did not pay enough attention to the sentiment of its users prior to launching this initiative. She argues that before launching a social media campaign, companies need to check the temperature of the online channel they are planning to use. Evidence back then suggests that Twitter users had still in their minds the bad experience of the flights that were grounded just a weeks before.

References:

Qantas, (2015). Our Company | Qantas. http://www.qantas.com.au/travel/airlines/company/global/en (accessed 6.14.15).

Rourke, A., (2011). Qantas grounds entire worldwide fleet. *The Guardian*. http://www.theguardian.com/business/2011/oct/29/qantas-grounds-fleet-industrial-action (accessed 6.15.15).

McGuirk, R., (2011). Aussie court ends Qantas strike, fleet grounding. *Yahoo News*. URL http://news.yahoo.com/aussie-court-ends-qantas-strike-fleet-grounding-152252309.html (accessed 6.15.15).

Miller, D., (2011). Qantas Twitter campaign takes nosedive. *ABC News*. http://www.abc.net.au/news/2011-11-22/qantas-twitter-hashtag-backfires/3686940 (accessed 6.15.15).

Social Media News (2011). The #QantasLuxury Fail. http://www.socialmedianews.com.au/the-qantasluxury-fail/ [Accessed on: 22-07-2015].

Kennedy, A., 2011. Qantas makes hash of tweet campaign. *Traveller*. http://www.traveller.com.au/qantas-makes-hash-of-tweet-campaign-1nsa4 (accessed 6.15.15)

Review questions

1   What motivations can you identify behind the generation of negative eWOM in Qantas' promotional activity?

2   Once the campaign went live, was there any way in which Qantas could have minimised the impact of the negative eWOM?

3   According to the steps discussed in this chapter to plan a viral campaign, which ones were overlooked by the Qantas team and resulted in the outcome described in the case study?

12

7: Research and evaluating marketing communications: Aegon and measurement in action

Aegon is an established provider of financial products. Aegon has approximately £542 billion assets under management, with businesses in over 25 countries. In the UK it serves around two million UK customers. The Aegon brand has evolved but stays steadfastly committed to its original purpose - helping people take responsibility for their financial future.

Historically the financial services sector was very fragmented, with products bought through intermediaries with the cost of advice invisible to the customer. In 2012 the regulations changed and this resulted in many "orphaned clients", who typically had a series of individual pensions with previous employers or a self-employed pension, but with limited knowledge of the pension value or how best to invest. The changes led to a seismic shift in the industry requiring the focus on the end customer using direct methods of communication rather than through an agent, broker or advisor.

Aegon used primary research to discover that low numbers were saving towards their retirement and only 32% of working-aged people had a dedicated retirement package. In 2004 they responded to this by launching an innovative on-line product branded as Retiready, which gives all individuals (not just Aegon customers) control of their own financial management via a digital platform. They can use the product to calculate a personal retirement score, work out their readiness for retirement and determine the steps and decisions required to achieve financial security. Retireready proves easy, on-line access to a wide range of products such as savings accounts, pension products and investments from a number of providers, including Aegon. Competing financial service firms usually offer such services to existing customers based around their own products.

Given that this is a digital product the platform was designed to be easy to use and understand and relatively quick to progress through each level. Each stage leads the customer through a series of questions building a picture of their retirement goals, calculating their readiness for retirement, identifying suitable retirement related products and a "shop" facility for additional savings products. Lastly the option of having a financial coach to support the customer is available.

At launch the key objectives of the campaign were to raise visibility, create media awareness and digital chat about the product. Additional support included sponsorship of the 2014 Queens Tennis Tournament, which promoted the Retireready brand alongside the company name. Existing customers were e-mailed to encourage them to transfer their existing products onto Retiready.

Measurement methods included:

- Time taken to transfer existing products
- Unique web visits
- Browsing behaviour
- Uplifts in visits following press campaigns
- Numbers completing Retiready score
- Conversions
- Additional products purchased
- Web fallout point
- Amount of funds under Aegon measurement

In addition to website data, Aegon use Google Analytics with a combination of on-line and manual reports to inform future campaigns. Measures are analysed daily, weekly, monthly and quarterly and refinements made to marketing campaigns where required.

Head of Channel Marketing, Tracy Clifton explains:

"We use the data to refine our targeting, by customer type, those who have upgraded, undertaken score only, or score and email supplied. What all of these refinements have enabled us to do is firstly have much more up to date and comprehensive data on our customers, whilst also integrating our measurement systems……. Our focus now is on retaining a strong customer base, continuing to convert more customers to… Retiready…., whilst up-selling across our products and after sales advice."

The Aegon example shows that measurement is a dynamic process, combining a wide range of measures, both internal and external, but which result in enhanced customer understanding and fine tuning of communications activity. In addition to campaign specific information this business has benefitted from a more integrated approach to customer information management and brand development. For further information, see https://www.aegon.co.uk/index.html.

Review questions

1 Identify the marketing environmental conditions which enabled Aegon to launch this product.

2   What are the key challenges for a company launching a new product through a new channel?

3 When measuring how customers were using the product and its success rate, identify the criteria the company used and explain the importance of up to date data.

12

Index

Printed in the United States
By Bookmasters